GEORGE BEATTIE
of St Cyrus

A Poet Lost in Time

A Story of Love, Betrayal, Conspiracy
and Murder

Barry Dominic Graham

and

John Molloy

George Beattie of St Cyrus: A Poet Lost in Time was first published in 2013.

This complete and definitive third edition
includes additions, revisions and enhancements.

Copyright © Barry Dominic Graham and John Molloy (2013, 2015, 2017)

Excluding certain public domain excerpts, photographs, quotes,
and the works of George Beattie;
the moral right of Barry Dominic Graham and John Molloy to be
identified as the authors of this work has been asserted by
them in accordance with the Copyrights, Designs and Patents Act 1988

Registered with

UK©CS
The UK Copyright Service
Nos. 284672969 - 284703778

All rights reserved

ISBN-13: 978-1542610223
ISBN-10: 1542610222

**THIRD
EDITION**

[COMPLETE AND DEFINITIVE]

Cover art, interior design, text and layout by
Barry Dominic Graham

THE GEORGE BEATTIE PROJECT
www.thegeorgebeattieproject.co.uk

"Mare ditat, Rosa decorat"

(The Sea enriches, the Rose adorns)

"Montrose... a beauty that lies concealed, as it were, in the bosom of Scotland; most delicately dressed up, and adorned with excellent buildings, whose foundations are laid with polished stone, and her ports all washed with silver streams that trickle down from the famous Esk."

Richard Franck

Captain in the parliamentary army and author

1624 – 1708

*This book is profoundly dedicated
to the memory
of
George Beattie, Esquire
and to all those we have loved…
past and present.*

"Mare ditat, Rosa decorat"

(The Sea enriches, the Rose adorns)

"Montrose... a beauty that lies concealed, as it were, in the bosom of Scotland: most delicately dressed up, and adorned with excellent buildings, whose foundations are laid with polished stone, and her ports all washed with silver streams that trickle down from the famous Esk."

Richard Franck

Captain in the parliamentary army and author

1624 – 1708

*This book is profoundly dedicated
to the memory
of
George Beattie, Esquire
and to all those we have loved…
past and present.*

MONTROSE
(High Street)
AROUND THE TIME OF GEORGE BEATTIE

by

**Alexander Mill
(or Milne)**

1820 – 1842

*"That plots were laid by others to oust me
and secure miss Gibson's fortune …
I know well from the inquiries that were made at myself
from a certain quarter.
Those who interfered were far too many for me !"*

George Beattie

1786 - 1823

Contents

Preface..xi
Introduction..xv
Prologue...xvii
Novella :
Chapter One..23
Chapter Two..27
Chapter Three.......................................31
Chapter Four...33
Chapter Five..36
Chapter Six..40
Chapter Seven......................................45
Biographical Research :
Overview...59
The Romance..71
The Maelstrom.....................................75
The Conspiracy....................................91
Caribbean Slave Trade.........................95
Original Memoranda, Statements & Letters :
STATEMENT OF FACTS......................111
SUPPLEMENT TO STATEMENT OF FACTS..............125
ADDITIONS TO SUPPLEMENT.........137
THE LAST...141
Original Poems....................................169
An Original Essay.................................243
Epilogue...253
In Memoriam.......................................255
Bibliography..cclxxiii
Acknowledgements............................cclxxv
Mission Statement..............................cclxxvii
About The Authors..............................cclxxix

Preface

The beach of St Cyrus is embraced by majestic and foreboding cliffs of volcanic rock.

The unspoiled, mournful beauty of this place leaves an indelible impression on the mind of its beholder.

It is here that this story begins… and ends.

The kirkyard, also known as Kirkside Cemetery, rests near the beach and is nestled at the base of the cliffs to the south of St Cyrus (56°.45.9649N, 002°.25.1157W).

Upon beginning our research, it soon became apparent that there were many strange and inexplicable omissions, contradictions and anomalies which would have to be dealt with.

Thanks to the fortuitous acquisition of a unique copy of the 1863, A.S. Mt Cyrus biography, which had been owned, inscribed and enriched in 1874 by a Mr W.J. Melvin (who had been personally acquainted with the author), we were given rare details and a priceless insight into our subject, thereby, a profound impetus and head start with the work which lay ahead.

Mr Melvin of Lauriston, had obviously gone to a great deal of effort with this particular book.
He had laboriously and painstakingly added copious notes of personal knowledge into the margins etc., as well as attaching his own added pages of hand-written information and old newspaper clippings, delicately and precisely within it.

We also acquired various other original publications and documents, which included two of the hand-written copies of George Beattie's 'Statement of Facts', which were being produced during the period of 'information suppression' apparently imposed by Mr William Smart of Cairnbank et al, prior to the printing and publication of the, one and only, 1863 biography.

By discovering a great deal of disinformation and misinformation in the traditionally accepted version of events, we became evermore aware of an apparent past agenda to obfuscate and suppress the real story of George Beattie and to malign his name and memory.
A consequence of this agenda has been the virtual erasure of his literary legacy from general public awareness.

In short, we believe that George Beattie somehow became a threat to certain socially powerful individuals and was ultimately the tragic victim of a cold-blooded conspiracy to 'remove' him… by whatever means necessary.

It is our deep and fervent hope that we can be instrumental in attaining some kind of permanent public memorial to the noble memory and literary legacy of George Beattie.

The following narrative encompasses facts and fictionalised events based on known factors and speculations derived and concluded from extensively researched information.

This book was written in conjunction with public domain material derived from the 1863 work of the late-lamented, Mr Andrew Smith (A.S. Mt Cyrus) of Lauriston Mains. Whilst creative license has been utilised where necessary… the 'novella' is based on recorded facts and educated speculation.

We have also included in this volume our personally transcribed original 'Statements' which were written by George Beattie himself in 1823.

Please kindly note, that we have deliberately opted for the use of open punctuation in the writing of this book.

So, please, now join us on a journey back through the mists of time and experience the life, tragic romance and events which prematurely and cruelly ended George Beattie's happiness… and life.

ST CYRUS
(north)

ST CYRUS
(south)

Introduction

It is perhaps the most sincere privilege of our lives to be instrumental in reintroducing and restoring the life history of the most deserving, noble and true heart that was George Beattie, back into the realm of current public conscience.

May truth, honour, integrity and courage always be the virtues we strive for and be Blessed to leave this world possessing.

Barry Dominic Graham and John Molloy

Prologue

Obituary from the
'MONTROSE REVIEW'
on Thursday, October 9th, 1823

"It is with no ordinary feelings of regret that we have to record the death of Mr George Beattie, writer here, which happened on the 29th ultimo.
In his professional capacity, Mr Beattie was eminent for his integrity, abilities and conciliatory disposition, which made him regard what was just, rather than what was scientific. As a scholar, nay, as a philosopher, his mind was stored with whatever is excellent in literature; and he admired whatever is grand, impressive, and interesting in nature.
He was both a man of observation and reflection; and his remarks were listened to with that degree of attention which a superior judgement always commands. Above all, as a man, as an upright, independent, generous, and sociable man, he was honoured, esteemed, and beloved; nor was this tribute paid to the qualities of his heart in a common or a partial degree, but warmly and generally.
His satirical powers (which, keeping a judicious aim, become an active virtue itself), were elucidated in many instances and thrown with subtle keenness against vice, folly, and corruption. In testimony of this, he has left behind him many admired specimens both in prose and verse. The milder effusions of his genius abound in sentiment and pathos, equal at least to many of the more lauded poetical pieces of the day; and had he prosecuted…

with ardour that gift with which he was favoured, he might have laid claim to a palm which a less qualified muse may now possess.

His humour was unbounded, and was of such a nature that it delighted all who had the honour of his acquaintance, without hurting the feelings of any.

He was a firm patriot, a universal philanthropist, and a warm friend: noble, generous, honest, modest, unassuming, feeling: he was a man who mixed with opposite parties, and was equally beloved by all.

It may be thought by those who shared not the pleasures of his society, that this outline of Mr Beattie's character and qualities is a laboured panegyric; and we confess that, of an individual at a distance, we should have suspected so, but to those who knew him, it will appear only an attempt to draw the contour of a picture which every one admired in its natural perfection.

As public journalists, we have no right to intrude with our own private feelings, in lamenting the death of this worthy and valuable member of society; but it would have been doing injustice to the public, whose concern is deep upon this occasion, to have said less; and we are assured that none will contradict us when we declare, that no man in this town and neighbourhood was ever more generally beloved in his life, or more universally lamented in his death."

MONTROSE

I die, but when the grave shall press
  The heart so long endeared to thee
  When earthy cares no more distress
  And earthy joys are nought to me.

  Weep not, but think that I have past
  Before thee o'er the sea of gloom.
  Have anchored safe and rest at last
Where tears and mourning can not come.

  'Tis I should weep to leave thee here
  On that dark ocean sailing drear
  With storms around and fears before
  And no kind light to point the shore.

  But long or short though life may be
    'Tis nothing to eternity.
  We part below to meet on high
  Where blissful ages never die.

Emily Brontë

1818 – 1848

Novella

Chapter One

It is Christmas Eve, 1798.

Gazing wistfully through the undulant crown glass pane of his shared 'blackhouse' bedroom window at the shimmering crystalline snowflakes as they drifted gently from the heavens, morphing tenderly into the silent glistening white landscape… young George 'Geordie' Beattie was lost in dreamy reflection of his eleventh 'summer' in the idyllic Scottish north-east coastal paradise of St Cyrus.

As he had, in recent years, during the blissful spring, summer and early autumn months, with his pet jackdaw perched precariously on his shoulder, George would delightedly roam and explore his treasured seaside 'Arcadia' with its amazing abundance of flora and fauna.

The mournful, majestic beauty of its volcanic rock cliffs embraced an almost secluded, perfect and seemingly endless tawny-silver sand shoreline.

George detested not being able to wander and play outdoors as he had enjoyed in earlier months. His surviving siblings, Catherine and David, were too young to care, and his elder brother James, having recently turned eighteen, was helping his father, William, work their humble croft which nestled cosily at the base of the 'Hill of Morphie' in an area known as Whitehill on the 'Straton' owned 'Kirkside estate'.

Due to the infamous Highland Clearances enforced by tyrannical and avaricious 'landowners' many people had been evicted and forced to emigrate from their beloved homeland, whilst others, as with the Beattie family, had been pushed to small crofts in marginal areas near the ocean or to highly elevated areas which were less conducive to the extremely lucrative pursuit of sheep farming.

The Beattie family's 'blackhouse' was a long, relatively narrow, single storey building with walls made of rough boulders, filled in with peat and earth for insulation. A large wooden frame of triangular trusses was placed across the top of the walls, and over the top of these was laid a combination of turf, heather, straw, and reeds which were usually replaced annually. The thatch was secured by a fishing net weighed down at the edges with large rocks, with further rocks laid on top of the walls to give the roof extra security.

There was a central hearth and no chimney and the smoke would swirl around the roof-space before escaping out of a small hole.

Because the soot would blacken the inner thatch, over the course of a year, as with the outer, it too was stripped off annually and used as fertiliser.

As the smoke was not as thick near the ground, the family would sit on low wooden chairs (called creepies) around the peat fire, as it gave off a significant degree of light as well as essential warmth.

The fire burned day and night ensuring the family were kept warm.

The blackhouse was unique in that it provided all round shelter for the crofter, his family, his crops, and his livestock.

The animals were housed in an earthen-floored byre at one end of the building with drainage at the centre, whilst a flagged area at the other end of the house provided accommodation for the family.

A part of the house, tucked up into the eaves, was also used for the storage of grain and other food.

The small-scale production of crops and livestock has always been the backbone of a crofter's life.

Barley, potatoes, turnips, and herbs were the most common crops, providing food for the family and winter fodder for their livestock.

William Beattie had to fertilise the land heavily to provide enough soil for crops to grow.

Such as in this case, crofting areas near the sea was achieved by creating small ridges to make the soil deeper and then piling on seaweed as fertiliser. These were called 'lazy beds'.

The number of animals that the family were permitted to keep on their croft was dictated by the amount of rent that they paid to their landlord... Joseph Straton, the 7th Laird of Kirkside.

For every pound paid in rent, the crofter was allowed to keep a cow and 'her followers', along with several sheep.

The Beattie family paid six pounds per annum and thus owned a reasonable degree of livestock.

Cattle were sold each year in order to pay the rent.

Much of the harvest was cut by hand with heavy scythes and stacked into traditional 'stooks' in the fields to dry. Later they would be moved into the storage sections of the croft house.

Afterwards the harvest grain was winnowed and threshed by hand with flails.

Working the farm by hand was hard work, and, due to the harshness of the landscape, output from farming was often not sufficient to support a crofter and his family. Crofters have always had to be prepared to work with the landscape.

For some crofters, where timber was hard to come by, driftwood was one of the main sources, and thus, any that was available was too valuable to burn.

Crofters turned to the landscape to solve this problem and cut peat from the boggy

moorland. The peat was cut into small blocks and then stacked up to dry.
The marine environment of St Cyrus enabled William Beattie to supplement his family's income with seasonal salmon fishing.

The lifestyle of a crofter was basically part farmer, part labourer and part fisherman.

As Elizabeth (Scott) Beattie, George's mother, laboured purposefully in the preparation of the family's traditional Christmas fayre, from a small adjacent dwelling, William Beattie Snr., (the paternal and only surviving grandfather of George and his siblings), surreptitiously hid little gifts he'd made for the children in various nooks and crannies around the Beattie home.

Tragically, infant and child mortality had a devastating impact on the populace in general, and the Beattie family were no strangers to its horrors.
George's siblings: Joseph, Elizabeth and Mary, had been tragically reclaimed from this mortal realm at profoundly tender ages.
Lamentably, Joseph and Elizabeth were very young babies at death; but sweet little Mary, being significantly older when taken, was held dearest of all in the hearts of the family; especially that of George.
For him, in particular, she was, and would always remain, the purest expression of angelic perfection.
The 'lost' Beattie children had been laid to rest at the foot of the St Cyrus cliffs in the south-east corner of the historic and fateful 'Auld Kirkside Graveyaird' (or 'Auld Nether Kirkyard') adorned with a simple white wooden marker which had been lovingly carved by their grandfather William.
The melancholic contentment evoked by the serenity and beauty of this kirkyard made it a site of frequent visitation by George.

The snow continued to descend delicately, but persistently.
Much to his consternation, fearing the possibility of cold induced illness, Elizabeth Beattie stubbornly refused to allow her son to exit the house whilst it continued.

"I promise I won't get cold... please Mama?" he pleaded pathetically.

"Sorry Geordie, it's not worth the risk... you know that!" she answered, with her usual 'end of discussion' tone.

"I'll need your help anyway. Your father and James will be coming in for their dinner shortly!"

"Damn it!" murmured George, quietly under his breath.

"What did you just say young man?" questioned his mother, glowering daringly at him to repeat the phrase.

"Nothing mama", he grudgingly replied, head down, frowning indignantly.

For William Beattie Jnr., and his son James, this would be their final Christmas as crofters, as they both had acquired positions as 'Officers of Excise' in the famous coastal 'Abbey' town of Aberbrothock (Arbroath); primarily thanks to their laird, Joseph Straton, who possessed a great fondness for the family and was aware of their unusual degree of intelligence.

The family would still remain in St Cyrus for a further four years, until the death of William Beattie Senior in 1802.

School holidays had now become a greater pleasure and relief than ever before due to the former parish schoolmaster, Mr Todd, having left and been promptly replaced by Mr Alexander Anderson; a rabid disciplinarian.
Schooldays were far from joyful.
The tall, round-shouldered, irascible Mr Anderson may have been an 'effective' teacher, but his brutish methods were all too often taken to excess.
Apart from the first Monday of the year, known as Handsel-Monday, merely the dropping of one's slate pencil would result in an enthusiastic thrashing by cane, followed by an extensive session of kneeling on the cold stone floor.
A more 'serious' offence, such as talking, would result in a profoundly memorable punishment indeed.

Sadly, it is teachers such as these, who consciously choose to instil fear, and gratuitously inflict humiliation and pain, that engender resentment towards the educational system.

Nevertheless, George gleaned all the necessary information from the process, despite its inhumane delivery.

Offsetting the trials of his life, he adored entertaining his fellow man with verbal humour, mimicry, harmless practical jokes and trickery; all of which, he would continue to indulge throughout his future days.

Chapter Two

It is July 19th, 1802.

The Beattie family now reside five miles to the south of their beloved St Cyrus, in the historically significant seaport town of Montrose, which sits on the north bank of the estuary formed at the mouth of the South Esk by the sea, sweeping round and forming a broad basin inland behind the town.

William Beattie and his eldest son James, having now been assigned to 'Excise' posts in Montrose, were thriving financially.

It was now time for young George to become apprenticed. His father paid the entry fee for him to enter a trade in the mechanical profession; however, a single day was more than enough for George to know that it was not appropriate for him, as he detested every second of it.

Shortly afterwards, providence provided a placement for him in Aberdeen as a clerk in a law office.

Akin to the 'Dickensian' character of 'Mr Fezziwig', George's new employer was an unusually kind, generous, and fun loving gentleman named Jonathan Flyte.

Sadly, after only six weeks, Mr Flyte departed this earthly dimension due to pneumonia. George was devastated.

Mr Flyte had taken a particular shine to him and had actually altered his Will to bequeath to him the substantial sum of fifty pounds.

Now possessing aspirations to pursue a career in the legal profession, young George returned to a newly acquired position in Montrose, as an apprentice in the office of Procurator Fiscal, Mr Colin Alison.

Again, George was treated with profound kindness.

When the appropriate training eventually concluded, it was time for him to complete his legal education at the Edinburgh Law School.

During these revelatory years, George had studied the works of various famed 'Radicals', such as the respected English-American philosopher, political theorist and revolutionary, Thomas Paine.

His intrinsic passion for fairness, truth and justice would come to the fore and

permeate his entire being.
He became the living embodiment of their principles.
As a result, he would henceforth become stoic and absolute in his conclusions regarding the insidiousness, corruption, control and redundancy of church, state and monarchy.
He was also a firm and true Scottish patriot.
Needless to say, George obviously abhorred the concept and practice of human slavery and held appropriately strong abolitionist views.

Upon the successful completion of his legal studies, George, in his 21st year, returned to Montrose.
The money inherited from his first employer allowed George to set up in business for himself as a legal Writer, or Attorney.

Due to his natural benevolence, compassion, generosity, and amazing wit, he was a bright, shining light in Montrose society and was accepted wholeheartedly by members of every class, to an equal degree.
Beloved and popular souls will always bring out the worst in certain people of weak character; be they 'users', 'takers', or, most commonly, the bitter and envious.
Ultimately, George would most assuredly feel their 'sting'.

As the years passed, in startling juxtaposition with George, his father and elder brother adhered to a 'royalist' mindset.
This division of viewpoints and precepts inevitably resulted in a considerable measure of estrangement between them; however, the essence of familial love remained intact regardless.

When young David Beattie was old enough, he was invited by George to join his prosperous law firm, which already employed several other clerks.
George held David in great esteem, love, and affection and was more than proud to be his mentor.

As fate would have it, back in St Cyrus, his family's old friend and benefactor, the 7th Laird of Kirkside, Joseph Straton, offered George the position of 'factor' to the Kirkside estate (a factor or estate manager is a person or firm charged with operating a property for a fee, when the owner is unable to personally attend to such details, or is not interested in doing so).
This would result in George being a frequent visitor to his treasured birthplace and landscape.

George was not only the life and soul of gatherings, he was also a visually impressive figure.
He had become a handsome, gentlemanly man; approximately five and a half feet tall, and around fourteen stones in weight; with black curled hair, dark blue eyes, and always immaculately dressed.
His ever-smiling countenance, his humour, his fun, and his endless jokes ensured he would always be surrounded by a delighted and admiring audience.

George's love for elaborate, harmless practical jokes was demonstrated on several occasions; one of them taking place on an evening, in the eerie twilight, when the Old Church was casting its deep and gloomy shadow over the churchyard. He happened to come up the 'church-way path', which led through the middle of it, when John Petrie, a grave and douce 'Seceder' was strolling down to the 'Links' (The word 'links' comes via the Scots language from the Old English word 'hlinc' : 'rising ground', 'ridge' and refers to an area of coastal sand dunes and sometimes to open parkland) wearing a broad Kilmarnock bonnet. George stooped behind a tombstone, and, as John passed, he leapt up behind him, whipt off the bonnet, and promptly vanished again. John, startled, looked round and, seeing nothing and hearing nothing, took to his heels in fright, and ran like the wind. The following day, George saw his friend in the street with his 'Sunday' bonnet on, and went down from his office to speak to him.

"You're looking great there today, John!" he proclaimed, enthusiastically.

"Oh aye, Geordie, thanks," replied John, looking rather perturbed, "but if this were the proper time and place for it, I would tell you a right queer story."

He however, still proceeded to tell him, in a low and deadly serious tone, how his bonnet had been carried off by some unearthly being as he passed through the church-yard, but had, fortunately, been able to escape himself.

"Well," says George, "one of my clerks was out at the Crancil braes, and found a bonnet… I wonder if it could be yours?"

They both went up to George's office, and, to be sure, there was the identical bonnet.

The question now was, how the bonnet got to the Crancil braes.

George advanced a theory to account for this extraordinary circumstance.

The Great Plague of 1666 and its victims, had been buried in these sand-hills due to fears that, if buried in the churchyard, it could return again and reinfect the inhabitants should the graves be opened.

George said that the folk who had died of the plague had gone down to see their former neighbours in the Old Churchyard, and had taken John's bonnet on their way past; but being unable to carry it with them to another world, had left it above ground at the Crancil braes, where his clerk had found it.

George, so well known in public life, went extensively into general society, and wherever he went a play of light humour, and even of boisterous mirth, circled around him.

No wonder that he was the life of every company.

Where he shone most was in small dinner, or supper, parties.

There his wit sparkled with particular brilliance, and then, most of all, he delighted his friends with his humorous sallies.

He had a talent, few men possess, for keeping people laughing for an entire evening, at nothing.

At the evening parties, it was usual to insist on every individual attending to give a toast, a sentiment, or a song. As George could not sing, he was regularly compelled to tell his story of 'Mark-Monday'.

This often repeated story afforded endless delight, and was told year after year in the same circle, at the evening festivities held during the season of Yule.

The scene of the story was set in Montrose, on the day of a total eclipse, which was called 'Mark' Monday from its being murk, or pitch dark. A number of speakers were brought in, who were well-known characters, and the humour of the story lay in George's mimicking of their voices, their tones, their attitudes, repeating their expressions, and humorously hitting off all of their peculiarities.

One speaker was a baillie (civic officer), who could not grope his way down to the salt-pans, through the Links, and said the lamps should be lighted. There were two yarn-merchants, one of whom had a short cough, and the other a long one, who met, and coughed, and coughed, and coughed until both parties, after vain attempts to speak, shook hands to meet another day; and an adjutant in the Militia, who had a funny walk; plus many others, too numerous to mention.

Needless to say, George bore no manner of ill-will towards any of the characters in 'Mark-Monday'. They were all well known to the rest of the guests, and that gave zest to the story.

George was a perfect mimic, and his talent in taking-off the characters with such drollery afforded such profound pleasure and mirth that his friends heard the story over and over again with unwearied delight.

One of the most elaborate practical jokes carried out by George and his friends became almost legendary in Montrose.

On one grey autumn morning, back whilst George was still clerk to Mr Colin Alison, the Procurator Fiscal, the citizens of the town awoke to discover that all the High Street lamp posts were missing their lamps.

John Findlay, the town officer, was ordered to roam about banging his drum and proclaiming the offer of a reward to anyone providing information as to their whereabouts.

As planned, little Annie McMurtrie, the Procurator Fiscal's servant girl, 'earned' the reward when she found the missing lamps stacked in a corner of the cellar when she went down to fetch coal for the office fires.

On another occasion, during a performance of 'Macbeth' being held in Montrose's Theatre Royal, being accompanied by his friend, John Tweedale (landlord of the Red Lion Inn), just upon the nerve-wracking climax of the play, George suddenly jumped to his feet and yelled:

"Stop! Stop!... John Tweedle's scared!"

During the uncomfortable pregnant silence that followed, John, indignant and embarrassed, blurted out loudly:

"It's a damnable lie... John Tweedle's not scared... NOT scared!"

Chapter Three

It is November 11th, 1815.

George is now in his twenty-ninth year.
Having an ever-growing passion for the written word, George was a regular 'contributor' to the local newspaper, the 'Montrose Review'.
In this month, he completed the first draught of an epic poem based on the deluded boasts and rants of a boorish Montrose town officer, named John Findlay (or Finlay) of Arnhall (John o'Arnha').
This work was an homage to the celebrated Ayrshire bard, Robert Burns, who was first-cousin to George's best friend and confederate, James Burness, Esquire.

Life at this time was extremely social.
Citizens would habitually gather in groups throughout the streets to discuss events of the day, and things in general.
With its broad, roomy High Street, Montrose was ideal for this purpose.

Although George was noted for his social qualities, he was simple in his habits, and extremely temperate; a thing unusual at this time.

As in the case of every man, who is decidedly individual, his personal appearance was in perfect harmony with his character.
With his ever-smiling countenance, his warm-heartedness and good humour, literally, shone from his eyes.

Besides his habitual wit and drollery, he was a humourist in the proper sense.
There are two types of humourist: the broad sarcastic, and the low comic.
The former has keen insight into character, great breadth of view, and a clear perception of the moral weaknesses and follies of mankind. His power lies in irony, sarcasm, and satire, and sometimes in dry humour.

George wrote a number of satires, which were extremely deserved, focused and profoundly acerbic in nature, and observation.
In him, the creative does not lie primarily in the region of thought, but moreso in that of imagination and feeling.
The use of occasional halting spondaic and trochaic lines in the middle of regular iambics, is a marked characteristic of his Muse.

We can conceive that his winning smile and kindly disposition would gain him many friends, but there was something deeper which endeared him to the people, always being quoted along with his name. As a lawyer, the poor and oppressed found in him a kind and sympathising friend.
He achieved redress for their wrongs, and furnished them with legal advice, for which services he would take no payment or reward.
His conduct in this respect had obviously made a great impression on the people, as it was so frequently alluded to.
It would form a striking contrast to the behaviour of far too many of his professional brethren.

The law firm which George had begun, now assisted by his younger brother, David, and several clerks, was situated on the first floor of a building in the High Street of Montrose, at the east side, not far from the church and Town House (Town-Hall).
He and the family initially lived in a substantial dwelling to the left of the office before relocating to a relatively large house in a nearby area known as New Wynd, close to the 'Starr Inn' tavern.

As a boy, George had always loved having a pet, and as an adult, he was no different. At this time he possessed a, beloved, green parrot, called 'Katie', which he, for the most part, kept in his office.
He would sit Katie's cage on the window ledge, allowing her fresh air and to observe the townspeople as they engaged in their daily pursuits.

To all who knew him, George's friendship was generous, warm, and sincere. Few had so large a share of early happiness as he.
None of the outward elements were wanting.
Nature wore for him unfading charms.
He loved to visit every romantic spot, and there, in the sweet musings of contemplation, to hold converse with the unseen.
He lived amid a circle of warm friends, and had the consciousness of being universally liked and respected.

After all, it is this communion which constitutes the chief ingredient in the cup of human happiness. Fine scenery, mystic woods, and ivy-mantled ruins count for much; but this world and all that is in it would be nought without the friendship of man.
Such were the outward elements of good which he possessed. Of the inner, he had even more. In him the spontaneities of happiness were extraordinary. The common things of life gave him a more exalted pleasure than they do to others, because he had a higher sensibility.
This keener sensibility, however, if it confers a greater happiness, necessarily carries with it a capability of greater misery, which will develop under certain negative conditions.

Chapter Four

It is February 14th, 1820.

George IV (George Augustus Frederick) has now reigned as monarch for sixteen days; since the death of his father on January 29th.

Sir Joseph Muter Straton is the current owner of the Kirkside estate in St Cyrus after inheriting it from his unmarried uncle, in 1816.
Formerly known as Sir Joseph Muter, he is the youngest son of William Muter of Annfield in Fifeshire and Janet (née Straton) of Kirkside, in Kincardineshire.
In order to legally inherit his late uncle's title and property, he had to adopt his mother's maiden name of Straton.

Muter joined the British Army as a cornet (originally the third and lowest grade of commissioned officer in a British cavalry troop, after captain and lieutenant) in the 2nd Dragoon Guards in December, 1794.
On September 5th, 1801, he was promoted from captain to major by purchase, in the 13th Light Dragoons.
Then, on May 6th, 1808, he transferred in the same rank to the 23rd Light Dragoons.
He later saw service in the Peninsular War with the 13th Light Dragoons and was present at the battles of Campo Maior, Albuera, Usagre, Arroyo de Molinos, and Alba de Tormes.
At the Battle of Waterloo, and by then a Lieutenant-Colonel, Muter commanded the 6th Inniskilling (Irish) Regiment of Dragoons.
During the battle, in response to the French Infantry assault on Wellington's left centre, the Union Brigade moved forward. Unobserved until late in their advance, they caught the French by surprise and took around 1,000 prisoners, despite the two British heavy cavalry brigades losing half their numbers at the hands of the French Lancers and Cuirassiers.
Following the death of Major-General Sir William Ponsonby, command of the 2nd Union Cavalry Brigade devolved upon Muter.
At around 6pm, after La Haye Sainte farm had fallen to the French, Muter was struck by a musket ball in the right wrist. The injury quickly became infected

with pieces of glove, and pus oozing from the wound, although he subsequently recovered without the need for amputation (He was succeeded by Clifton, of the Royals, who, oddly enough, followed him in the colonelcy of the 17th Lancers. The command of the regiment, such as remained, was with a Major Philip Dorville).

After Waterloo he was awarded the Russian Order of St Vladimir and served in Ireland in 1819.

In the absence of Sir Joseph, George continued to fulfil his duties as factor to the Kirkside estate.

Membership of the long established radical institution known as the 'Montrose Club' was inevitable for George.

Five of his closest friends, also members, were: Provost Charles Barclay, James Burness, Esquire (Dean of Guild), Dr Gibson, Alex Thomson, Mr James Bisset.

On occasional Sunday's, when the weather permitted, this 'band of brothers' would make their way to a picturesque spot they favoured, called the 'Den of Ananise', in the nearby parish of Maryton.

Here the friends would relax and discuss their mutual distain for the 'Establishment' in general.

All were of the same mind; being determined to see social reform become a reality.

George was closest to James Burness (first cousin to the Ayrshire bard, Robert Burns), who was six years his senior, and also practiced Law in Montrose. Already a 'Dean of Guild' (under Scots law, was one of a group of burgh magistrates who had the care of buildings) on September 23rd, 1818, he was elected provost.

On April 13th of that same year, he had proudly announced to the Montrose Town Council,

"That at a public meeting the Guildry had unanimously declared they had heard with satisfaction that Joseph Hume, Esq., a guild brother of the burgh, had, at the invitation of his townsmen, offered himself a candidate to represent the district of burghs in the next Parliament; and, taking into account the well-known talents, principles, and conduct of that gentleman for years past, they thought him a proper person to be their representative in Parliament, and therefore recommended him to the magistrates and town council for their votes on the occasion."

Joseph Hume was the younger son of a shipmaster in Montrose, a Scottish radical politician, surgeon, scholar, and aspiring reformer whose agenda and ideals were profoundly supported by George and his confederates.

Prior to entering into politics, Joseph, born January 22nd, 1777, was apprenticed to a local surgeon. After three years he was sent to study medicine successively at Aberdeen, Edinburgh, and London, and in 1796 became a member of the College of Surgeons of Edinburgh, and on February 2nd of the following year, an assistant surgeon in the sea-service of the East India Company. This post was obtained for him by the influence of David Scott of Dunninald, Forfarshire, a director of the East India Company and M.P. for Forfar. He made his first voyage out in 1797, became a full assistant surgeon on November 12th, 1799, and was posted to the ship, Houghton. On the voyage out he discharged satisfactorily the duties of the purser who died. He was then transferred to the land service of the company, and devoted himself zealously to the study of the native languages and religions.

Having rapidly mastered Hindostani and Persian, he was employed by the administration in political duties. In 1801 he joined the army at Bundelcund on the eve of the Mahratta war as surgeon to the 18th Sepoy regiment, and was at once appointed interpreter to Lieutenant-Colonel Powell, commanding one of the forces. In 1802 he rendered the government an important service by devising a safe means of drying the stock of gunpowder, which was found to have become damp. During the war he filled several high posts in the offices of the paymaster of the forces, the prize agency office, and the commissariat, and, at its conclusion, was publicly thanked by Lord Lake.

His opportunities of enriching himself had not been neglected, and in 1807 he was able to return to Bengal with £40,000 and to quit the service. He landed in England in 1808, and spent some years in travel and study. He visited the whole of the United Kingdom in 1809, more especially the manufacturing towns, and travelled during 1810 and 1811 in the Mediterranean and in Egypt.

In the same year he began a political career at home. On the death of Sir John Lowther Johnstone, he was returned in January of 1812 to Weymouth, having purchased two elections to the seat; but when upon the dissolution in the autumn of 1812, the owners of the borough refused to re-elect him, he took proceedings for the recovery of his money, and succeeded in getting a portion returned.

Before re-entering parliament, Hume took an active part upon the central committee of the Lancastrian schools system, and studied the condition of the working classes, publishing a pamphlet on savings banks. He also devoted great attention to Indian affairs, and tried strenuously, but without success, to obtain election to the directorate of the East India Company. He was indefatigable at proprietors' meetings in exposing abuses, and published some of his speeches at the Court of Proprietors.

He re-entered parliament under liberal auspices in 1818, as member for the Border burghs, joining the opposition in 1819.

He was re-elected for the same constituency in 1820.

Chapter Five

It is January 5th, 1821.

George is in his thirty-fifth year.

History, in her ample pages, has enrolled the names of many lovers, of whom poets have sung, and whose story has impassioned the hearts of the youthful and the feeling.
Yet, none of these records has the romantic interest, or the fascinating power and intensity of the story of George Beattie.

Time, like the Evening, softens all the tints and mellows all the colours; and the twilight, in which the past is seen, wraps all the events of history in obscurity, and the well-known and familiar, as the story of human affection must ever be, gains an enchantment by being dimly seen across the bourne which parts us from the unknown and the long forgotten.

Once again, snow has transformed the streets of Montrose and moonlight reflection illuminates the darkness.

Just outside 'Adam Macpherson's' tavern, just opposite the Starr Stables in New Wynd, George met one of his more recent acquaintances named Squire Robert Gibson, whom, having refreshed himself effectively with a large glass of whisky punch and two pints of 'nappy' ale, was more than merry.

"A HAPPY NEW YEAR TO YOU GEORGE!" proclaimed Squire Gibson enthusiastically, but with slightly slurred speech. *"You really must come up to the house one evening soon George... you've never met my wife, Isabell and my daughter, William... have you?"*

"*Indeed not sir... I've not yet had that pleasure,*" replied George, somewhat concerned that this invitation was offered merely through the influence of alcohol.

"*You're probably wondering why we named a girl William... I'm guessing... eh, am I right George?* Squire Gibson mumbled, almost incoherently.

"*Well, er... yes... possibly... a little curious I suppose,*" George answered, cautiously.

"*Her uncle you see... my wife's brother, William... in Grenada... pots of cash!... We thought the baby was going to be a boy... for some reason... anyway, we'd intended to name it after him, hoping he'd look upon us generously in his Will... rather embarrassing actually... I mean... for her, especially... having to live with a boy's name and all that... still... hmmmm... what's done, et cetera, et cetera,"* he explained, his voice trailing off bemusedly. *"Anyway George, Friday today... how would this Sunday suit you... about 4pm?"*

"Eh, yes, yes... excellent sir... excellent... thank you most sincerely, I'll look forward to it!" replied George, still harbouring an element of uncertainty.

Squire Robert Gibson was a 'gentleman farmer' who lived with his family in a mansion house which stood near a large megalithic monolith known as the 'Stone of Morphie'. The house was referred to by this title.
Ironically, this area is not far from George's birthplace and former home at 'Hill of Morphie' in St Cyrus.

George, being a natural scholar and a student of history, whether general or local, must have been aware that the Gibson family, as with so many other north-east Scots gentry, had surely derived the majority of their finances, in some way, from proceeds gleaned from Caribbean plantation slavery; however, in this instance, he demonstrated an extreme degree of cognitive dissonance.

Upon his visit, George was graciously welcomed by Squire Robert, whom immediately introduced him to his wife and youngest daughter.
For George, it was 'love' at his first sight of Miss William Gibson.

Miss Gibson was tall, sprightly, and dashing; fascinating rather than beautiful, with light brown hair and hazel eyes. She had entered her twenty-third year in the previous autumn.

Through regular visits to the 'Stone of Morphie' household, George and Miss Gibson had developed an ever-growing friendship, and by August of that same year, he considered himself warranted in paying his addresses to her, and though they were not nominally rejected, he was strictly enjoined by her not to cease or lessen his visits.

It soon appeared that Miss Gibson's refusal was not sincere.
Their intimacy continued to grow till the spring of 1822.
This was the blooming season of the year, when 'summer first unfolds her robes', when the woods resound with the songs of the singing-birds, and the primrose, with all the other plants of early summer, are in bloom.
The lovers spent many happy hours wandering in the gloaming among the woods of Kinnaber.
This spot is three miles from Montrose, on the south bank of the North Esk river, near the ocean.
Leaving the town by the highway going north, you pass the woods of Charleton on the left hand, while on the right a series of woods and sandy downs stretch to the sea. Between the second and third mile-stones the woods of Kinnaber come into sight, away down to the right.

A mansion known as the 'House of Kinnaber', at this time, was owned by the

Gibson family, but whilst renovations were being carried out, it remained, as yet, uninhabited.

Miss Gibson, coming from Stone of Morphie, would walk a mile down the other side of the North Esk, cross by the bridge, and meet her lover in the garden.
For a considerable part of this summer the lovers met at least twice a week at the House of Kinnaber.
This is a plain, white house (originally built in 1680) which, at this time, could barely be seen from the highway for thickly growing trees.
The garden is surrounded by a wall and is full of bushes, and of fruit-trees, some of which were grown to a great size and extremely old.
This was their favourite haunt.
Many were the vows of fidelity and solemn promises which passed between them.
In certain points of character, there was a wonderful contrast between them.
She was proud, aspiring in her ideas, and ambitious; he was unreserved, affable, and much more humble. At first sight, it is surprising there should be so strong an affinity between natures so different; but when there is a strong common sympathy, and each is weak where the other is strong, there is a leaning on both sides, and these differences are sources of true attachment, since in them, lies the secret of mutual dependence.
Often did they discuss the points of differences in their character, a hundred times told, did they conclude that their union would be the beginning of a life-long happiness, and that nothing but death would part them.
They gilded the future with beautiful imaginations, and one would have thought that a love so hallowed, so pure, and devoted, would have lasted forever.
It was strong on both sides.
Miss Gibson was much more demonstrative, as well as more sensitive and jealous, whilst George's love was deeper, and more serious.
Their relationship continued and their friendship increased the following summer of 1822, till the spring of 1823.
Throughout this time, the couple kept in regular contact via letters and notes using pseudonyms to preserve their privacy, being either posted, or delivered by the hand of servants.
George visited often at Stone of Morphie, and whenever Miss Gibson was in town, they arranged to walk out together.
As an example of their vows of fidelity, George, on one memorable occasion, had called at Stone of Morphie, and when they were alone, she complained that he had been jaunting without her. George explained that it was not on pleasure, but business, and that the weather had been disagreeable.
On his rising to leave, Miss Gibson positioned herself between him and the door, and urged that they both must repeat their vows.
She then laid her hands in his, and proposed they both repeat a solemn oath.
He said that he had no objections whatsoever, but to bear in mind that it bound

them, whether her parents might be agreeable or not.
She insisted that her parents were most definitely agreeable and emphatically stated that she had already informed them of their engagement, and that they had expected no less.

"Go on then my love, just tell me what you wish me to say," said George, compassionately.

"Please repeat after me these words," she said solemnly, with her eyes fixed firmly on his. *"May I never know peace in this world, or see God in mercy, if I marry another than you; or if I ever go south again without taking you along with me as my wife!"*

George repeated, exactly as requested, and then Miss Gibson took a similar oath herself.

This was perhaps the most marked of their oft-repeated vows on former occasions. Whatever may be thought of the propriety of taking such oaths, it is certainly a dreadful crime to break them, ratified as they are with such a sanction.

Chapter Six

It is May 1st, 1823.

The Gibson family received accounts of the death of William Mitchell, the uncle, and namesake, of Miss Gibson, and brother to her mother, Isabell.
He had succumbed to malaria at fifty-seven years of age.
He gained considerable wealth in Grenada (Grenada is an island country consisting of Grenada itself and six smaller islands at the southern end of the Grenadines in the southeastern Caribbean Sea. Grenada is located northwest of Trinidad and Tobago, northeast of Venezuela, and southwest of Saint Vincent and the Grenadines) and had apparently bequeathed a large portion of it to his close relatives in Scotland.

Reluctantly, Robert Gibson had formerly agreed at the behest of his formidable wife to promulgate the story that William Mitchell held the prestigious post of 'Governor of Grenada' (gubernatorial official, appointed by a king or other monarch) and was an honourable, loving, and generous man.
The truth however, was vastly different.
William Mitchell, Esquire, was in fact the owner/agent of the Mount Nesbit sugar plantation in St John.
He held ownership of over one hundred black slaves.
Needless to say, William Mitchell was at no time a governor of anything, other than that of human misery, bondage and exploitation.

Most of the wealth accumulated by the British 'landed gentry' had been garnered not simply through tenant rent, but, primarily, through Caribbean plantation slavery, illegal trade... and smuggling.
Dishonourable conduct and corruption are frequently, if not exclusively, the means by which great wealth is amassed.
This particular case was to be no exception.

In the written communications between Miss Gibson and George, Miss Gibson had adopted the pseudonym of 'Sarah Brounker'; the name of her uncle's black housekeeper; or so she possibly thought, and, most definitely, led George to believe.

Sarah Brounker was in fact no 'housekeeper', but rather, a slave-owning 'quadroon' (a person having one-fourth black ancestry; the offspring of a mulatto and a white) **woman of** independent wealth.

She and William Mitchell shared an intimate relationship which led to the birth of an octoroon daughter, whom they named Hannah.

William Mitchell had indeed initially bequeathed a huge sum of money to his relatives in Scotland, as well as naming his niece, Miss Gibson, as residuary legatee, but this Will did not reflect his financial status at the time of death, nor was it the only one which existed; an unregistered and unwitnessed updated version was found by Sarah Brounker.

There had also been some West India property.

His plantation was mired in debt to the extent that he had been forced to borrow three thousand pounds from Sarah Brounker.

On Sunday, May 4th, George visited Stone of Morphie.

Although Miss Gibson was currently aware of her apparently enhanced financial wealth, George apprehended no change in her affections, and in this he was not mistaken.

Old matters were talked over, and all their pledges and vows renewed.

Miss Gibson declared that the fortune she had become possessed of could not alter her feelings, but, on the contrary, make them more lasting.

Their conversation culminated with George offering to give Miss Gibson a little time to reflect on her 'change' in circumstances and perhaps reassess her affections for him.

She indignantly replied, *"Nothing has changed; I wish no time; I am yours for ever!"*

Thus once more did these lovers interchange vows of unalterable fidelity, in spite of her 'fortune'.

Later that same evening, George and the Gibson family had adjourned to the parlour after dining.

Whilst nursing a curiously excessive glass of brandy, George graciously declined a cigar offered by his host.

It would very quickly become obvious that an agenda was about to unfold.

As Robert Gibson strangely began staring sheepishly at the floor, his wife, Isabell glared intently at him, as if to urge the raising of some particular topic.

Following a peculiarly strained interlude, Robert briefly glanced uneasily at his wife, before 'laying his cards on the table'.

He opened by first acknowledging he and his wife's awareness of the existing engagement between George and his daughter, and professed great delight at the prospect of having George as a future son-in-law.

He then suggested that in light of him soon becoming part of the family, that he should hold no objection to being of 'assistance' in aiding his new family in

possibly resolving a pressing and important issue.
George listened intently, albeit apprehensively, to what was being said.
Robert momentarily hesitated before leaning forward and, at last, declaring his request.
Basically, George was asked to acquire, in his official capacity as a trained legal writer and solicitor, a copy of William Mitchell's Will, duplicate it somewhat, but have it dated just prior to William's date of death, and, most importantly, exclusively favouring his Scottish kin.
Utterly baffled and bewildered by this request, George, becoming increasingly offended at this obvious attempt to exploit him, categorically, but nevertheless, politely, declined to participate in anything even remotely unprofessional in nature.
Apologies were made and the topic of conversation quickly changed.
Isabell Gibson furtively exited the scene.
Believing all to be well, George left about nine o'clock that evening.
Unbeknown to him at this time, 'alea iacta est' (the die is cast) and his fate is now sealed.

On the the following day, profoundly influenced and cajoled by her mother, Miss Gibson wrote to George informing him of her change of heart and requesting an immediate end to their engagement and relationship; callously and unjustly alluding to the notion of she and her family's 'concern' that her fortune may hold too great a charm for him.

In what extraordinary light does this show the human heart.
Yesterday the sincere and devoted lover, now, suddenly resolved to cast her oaths and vows to the winds.
Only a woman with the heart of a serpent could write such a thing to a man like George Beattie, knowing, absolutely, that the mere insinuation of him being 'after her money' was not only ludicrously cruel and untrue, but would cut him to the core of his very being.
None knew better than she, that his guileless, unmaterialistic simplicity was incapable of such a thing.
This tactic was undoubtedly intended to gall him into giving her up.
It was also made clear that she wished the return of all the letters she had sent to him; her manoeuvres even stooping to emotional blackmail by referring to his honour as a gentleman.

Soon after this he saw Miss Gibson, and, unfathomably, all the unpleasantness which had occurred, was buried in oblivion.
Miss Gibson claimed that she made the request merely to test him, and laughed at the idea of his having taken the matter seriously.
She also said that she wanted a document from him on the subject of their engagement, and that his two last letters were quite sufficient... and bound him completely.
She then 'voluntarily' took a most solemn oath that she would punctually and faithfully fulfil her engagements with him, and never think of retracting while she

drew breath. Miss Gibson then said she wished to reside a short time at the House of Kinnaber, which she had newly come to, and that as soon as arrangements could afterwards be made, their union would take place.

It is almost incomprehensible from what motive she now acted as she was also now courting the addresses of another man... whom had previously never shown the slightest interest in her.
The greatest likelihood was that this entire charade was simply yet another manoeuvre to regain her letters.

The man who began to pay marked attention to Miss Gibson, now that her 'fortune' had become notorious, was William Smart of Cairnbank, a partner with his brother, George Smart, as a firm of grain merchants.
He was a somewhat handsome man, but a foppish, conceited fool, whose ends were merely mercenary.
In truth, he cared nothing for her herself, only for her 'money'.
Miss Gibson welcomed his attentions, and it soon became evident that her last solemn oath and her engagements with George at their 'reconciliation', were all a lie.
Yet, there was some curious acting on that occasion. After some conversation had taken place between them, she asked George why he was looking so ill. He made no immediate answer, but eventually confessed that he had been greatly affected by her recent actions. She, actually looked rather poorly herself.
Miss Gibson suddenly burst into tears, and said she never could forgive herself for having latterly acted towards him the way she had done. She then promised to meet him soon.

After all this, only two days had elapsed when she set off for Edinburgh without informing George, and it was now evident she now shunned him.
While she was there with her father, George wrote out a statement of facts in regard to the entire connection between Miss Gibson and himself, and sent it to Squire Gibson.
Despite having written it in despair, he truly felt that he had done nothing improper, as Robert Gibson was his close friend.
Miss Gibson took the statement from her father and destroyed it.
Upon returning home she wrote extremely offensive and cruel letters to George in retaliation for this perceived 'threat'.
A short while after this, she went to Pitcaithly (famous in Scotland for its five mineral springs. Hotels and tea rooms were built to accommodate the tourists coming there to take and to bathe in the waters), William Smart being one of the party.

On Tuesday, July 29th, Mr George Neill of Borrowfield, who was also a close friend of George, and married to Helen Gibson (Miss Gibson's half-sister), called on George with a view to securing Miss Gibson's letters.
George graciously, but adamantly declined to surrender them, and was not at all impressed that the Gibson family had forced George Neill to accept this errand by

exploiting he and George's long-standing friendship.

He thought of seeking legal redress; and perhaps the only fault which is attachable to him, is saying he would.

Although, hugely entitled to, and guaranteed of success, that he was utterly incapable of seeking or of accepting money damages, is evident from his 'known' character.

George even found it unthinkable just getting a decision recorded in a court of law against the perjury of which he had been made the object, where the sole punishment would be exposure.

He was driven to the idea of seeking such a redress by the insults offered to him on the part of the Gibsons, and by the vulgar triumph of his rival.

This, however, was never done, and never attempted.

Chapter Seven

It is August 11th, 1823.

The summer was hastening to a close.

It was early May, when nature had put on her mantle of living green, that the first rude shock awoke him from his dreams of happiness, and he felt the first pangs of a broken heart.

The trees which had budded and blossomed, now hung with ripe fruit; the birds had sung their sweet songs and fledged their tender brood, and now were gathered to wing their way to sunnier climes; the wild flowers bloomed and faded; the golden harvest was reaped from the fields; but all had been unheeded by this true lover of nature. Peace had fled from his once happy mind, and he was too much absorbed with his own misery to heed the changes in the face of nature.

It had now become notorious that Miss Gibson had abandoned him, and was to be married to another.

Weighed down by crippling grief, and crushed by despair, George, on Friday, August 8th, executed a Will, and afraid he could not survive Miss Gibson's wedding-day, and apprehensive that his Will would not hold good unless he lived sixty days after making it, he sent a letter to Miss Gibson asking that her forthcoming nuptials be postponed for a short time.

This letter was answered in the negative by her father, who appeared to exhibit no indignation at the perfidy of his daughter.

Nevertheless, Robert Gibson may have appeared callous and heartless, but he was the least guilty of the family.

He had always liked George, and would not have done anything against him.

In a way, he could also be regarded as a victim, as he too was at the mercy of his second, and current wife, Isabell.

It was Isabell Gibson who instigated and abetted her daughter to discard George. She was no better than a 'Medici' tyrant, who held a grudge against George for not complying with the request to aid in her corrupt agenda.

She also was acutely aware that George could now expose her criminal intentions, should he ever choose to do so.

William Smart had been socially known to the Gibsons for quite a while. He and his brother George, had purchased the Cairnbank estate, near Brechin, in 1821. They were a cold and calculating pair of opportunists who, as with most of the upper class, were willing to do anything to obtain or maintain social position, power and wealth.

Again, it was Isabell Gibson who convinced William Smart to enter the picture, with assurances of financial gain, regardless of her being aware that he would never love her daughter in the slightest. The Smarts and Mrs Gibson were cut from the same cloth, and were adept in manipulation and deception.

A vehement campaign of harassment against George was now embarked upon. Not content with trampling on all her solemn engagements and oaths, Miss Gibson made public George's last appeal, and held it up to ridicule and mockery.

George sat in his parlour with his head resting in his hands.

This is the picture of a man whose heart is torn with jealousy and devastated with insult.

Those places, people and pursuits which had once brought him such happiness, were now devoid of all effect. Dark shadows obliterated his every thought.

Being deeply ashamed that he could have been dragged to such depths by circumstances so ignoble in nature, combined with reluctance to burden others with his troubles, he would not seek solace or support through confiding the details of his heartbreak to any of his close family or friends.

Everyone may have known the general outline of what had been perpetrated against him, but his exhausting efforts to disguise his pain were sufficiently successful.

In his chaotic and tormented state of mind, George took a coach to Aberdeen in order to purchase a flintlock pistol; whether to use on himself, or in an 'illegal' duel with William Smart, he had not yet decided.

On Saturday, September 20th, he left in the morning and returned at night.

His going so far was evidently to avoid attracting notice.

The following day, with the newly acquired pistol carefully hidden, he walked his usual route to St Cyrus. There arriving, he began testing the weapon on the south wall of the Auld Nether Kirkyard.

Being dissatisfied with its performance, he concluded he must replace it and resigned himself to a repeated journey.

His contemplation of suicide, now gave way to serious alternate intent.

That evening, of Friday, September 26th, aware that William Smart was attending a Montrose council meeting, he waited in the Loggia beneath the Town House (which ironically, was the setting for the famed fight scene in George's epic poem, John o' Arnha').

Upon his eventual departure from the building, George calmly confronted him and assertively demanded a private meeting, alone, somewhere devoid of prying eyes and ears… in order to settle their situation once and for all.

Strangely, Smart readily agreed; simply asking George, where and when.

The first place which sprang into George's mind was, of course, the Auld Nether Kirkyard at St Cyrus.
Three o'clock at the Auld Kirkyard on Monday, September 29th, was promptly arranged.
   The weekend passed so slowly that it felt like an eternity to George.
On the Sunday evening, he sat by the fire in the parlour of his home with his mother, Elizabeth and his two younger siblings, David and Catherine.
His father, William and elder brother, James, only returned home every third weekend, as they were still employed as Excise Officers at the Perthshire based, 'Ruthven Printfield Company' where they had been assigned to thirteen years previously.
The atmosphere was, under the circumstances, peculiarly peaceful.
As the sky bruised and the evening drew to a close, he rose from his armchair, wished everyone a goodnight, gently kissed his mother and sister, ruffled his young brothers hair, and, serenely, retired to bed.
   Since the middle of August, George had been writing, with the utmost clarity, astonishing disclosures concerning the state of his mind, which he had entitled, 'The Last', so that, whatever occurred, a detailed record would exist.
He had finished it earlier that afternoon.
He had thought he was finished several times before, but restarted again, causing repetitions which reflected the erratic nature of his thoughts and emotions.
In George's usual fashion, the sheets on which he had written it, were folded up, like lawyers' papers, with the title on the blank outside page.
   Due, primarily, to his Will still requiring a further eight days before becoming legal, George knew that its meticulously detailed contents were vital to the future security of his young siblings.
His relationship with his elder brother had deteriorated beyond repair caused, mainly, through their political and religious beliefs. However, without a legally binding Will, as the eldest, James would be the sole beneficiary.
George had no idea what the following day would hold, but for the time being, at least, self-destruction was no longer his imminent and solitary intention.
   He awoke long before the sunrise, which he especially wished to witness.
George was immaculately groomed and dressed when he came down for breakfast.
Later that morning, approaching noon, Catherine asked George if what she had planned for dinner that evening would be appealing to him.
   "No thanks Kate, not for me… I'm off to the country and may not be back till late; I'll get something myself if I come… if I come."
This response concerned her.
The brother she had known all her life had changed so much; his bubbly personality and cheery disposition had gone.
When ready to leave, with his pistol concealed under his coat, he again softly kissed his mother and sister on the cheek, smiled warmly at his brother, and walked

down the hall to the door.
When he opened it, he gazed at the sky and said,
 "Looks like it may rain."
Then he left.
A dreadful feeling of impending catastrophe descended over the household.

As he stepped into the High Street, the children were happily playing, and the busy hum of city life went on as usual.

He had three hours until his rendezvous with William Smart, so before beginning his journey to St Cyrus, he went down to the Links, made general conversation with various people, and ate a couple of apples whilst sitting outside James Duke's 'heckle-house' (where flax was teased and combed out); a shipload of which had just come in, as it was the end of September.

Just over an hour later, he then went along the links northwards from Montrose towards the woods of Charleton, on his way to the Auld Nether Kirkyard.

He unhurriedly wended his way toward the scenes of his childhood, and the lonely, silent, melancholic place in the kirkyard where, on Saturday afternoons, he would sit on the grass, leaning against the short thick stone wall (dyke) next to the spot where his departed young siblings were laid to rest.

By this road he had often gone before in far different moods, when he accompanied a friend on an evening walk, or went to the 'meeting places' in the woods and the garden of Kinnaber, or when he walked alone to enjoy, in sweet musings, the beauties of nature. But now a gloom darker than 'Erebus' overshadowed his soul.

As he walked over the lonely sward, leading to the dark pine wood of Charleton, the sea is hidden from his sight by the range of sand-hills, but the cliffs of St Cyrus beyond the North Esk… his boyhood paradise, are in sight the entire way.

The skies now gloomed, as the sun struggled to shine through the darkening clouds. The last ears of the harvest had now been reaped, the fields were empty and bare, and the leaves were falling from the trees. Nothing now yielded him the sympathy for which he craved.

 Leaving the Links, he proceeded along the high road and crossing the North Esk by the bridge, hastened towards the braes of St Cyrus.

The scenes of youth have, for everyone, an inexpressible charm. Nature is then responsive, and everything reflects our ardent feelings; even when we come to see, that the charm lay not in them, but was a projection from our own minds, they retain their place in our sympathies on account of the feelings they recall by early associations. Here among those sunny braes by the sea, George had spent the happiest days of his youth. From his childhood's home he had gone out into the world and commenced the struggle of life. He had risen from a comparatively humble origin to a position of influence and honourable independence. He had done something as a poet to make his name remembered. Many warm friends had he gained; while the poor and downtrodden blessed him as a kind benefactor.

Within the last two years he had formed an attachment, which wielded over him a malignant spell; and now, after a summer of such humiliations and such anguish as were more than his wounded spirit could bear, he returned desolate and alone to the home of childhood.

The thought of all these things crowded in upon his mind. The vista through the valley of life, when he first started on its path, had been lit up with the rays of hope, and everything as he went on, enchanted him with its novelty.

He had now come to a point where he saw the same things, in reverse.

He had gone through almost every experience which a mere earthly life can give. The charm of novelty had fled. Those gilded imaginings of the future, like the memories of the past, were now tinged with despair.

It seemed to him but a moment since he was here as a boy.

The many events of those past years, had now faded from his view. He had returned, as it were, to the beginning of the race, and found himself at the point from which he had started.

Was all this the price of an unusually happy childhood, where he whiled away the long summer days sporting among the braes; or was it because he'd risen to fame and honour?

The blasting of his hopes and the treachery of which he had been made the object, with all the complications, had brought on a struggle which threw him back on his last resources; what a man lives by and lives for… involves his very manhood.

   As the Auld Nether Kirkyard came into view, George briefly grasped the handle of the pistol hidden beneath his coat. At first he could see no-one.

As he approached the kirkyard stile, his eyes darted from side to side as he scanned the area. He still saw nothing.

George removed the pocket watch from his waistcoat and checked the time.

It was just past three o'clock.

His heart was beating evermore rapidly as he spun around to see in every direction, when he heard a voice call out his name.

It came from inside the kirkyard watch-house (most communities near the Scottish schools of medicine in Edinburgh, Glasgow and Aberdeen employed some means of protecting the dead, such as a watch-house for the relatives of the deceased to keep vigil), which was built into the north-east corner of the kirkyard, forming part of its walled enclosure.

As its door opened, from out of the darkness within the watch-house, slowly emerged William Smart.

He held up his hand in an oddly beckoning gesture. As George climbed and crossed the stile, he felt himself engulfed in an air of sinister apprehension.

William Smart hovered, barely visible, in the doorway whilst George proceeded cautiously towards him, keeping close to the wall.

Nearing the little stone watch-house, George paused as Smart now began slightly advancing.

   "I really didn't think you'd come," stated George with a caustic tone.

   "Why would I not… Geordie… old chap? answered Smart arrogantly, wearing

his quintessential condescending smirk. *"What is it I may do for you this fine day?"*

"Your permanent emigration to the colonies would suffice nicely... Willy... old boy," George replied, with matching contempt.

Studying George carefully, Smart's demeanour suddenly changed.

"Geordie... George... let's be civilised about this... we've no need to be enemies, no need whatsoever. The Gibsons and I merely have a business arrangement... that's all... business... just business." Smart stated placidly. *"Come George... please... walk with me for a moment."*

Somewhat taken aback by his sudden altered attitude, George bewilderedly acquiesced to his request.

With an ushering arm extended, William Smart motioned forward.

Seconds after George turned away from the watch-house, he was struck violently across the back of his head, and fell forward, completely unconscious.

Smart had been accompanied by two hired thugs who had obviously been laying in wait amidst the darkly shadowed interior of the watch-house.

With 'cosh' still in hand and assisted by his equally vile partner, George was roughly carried towards the south-east corner.

Because Miss Gibson had previously described to Smart, how and where George regularly sat whilst visiting the grave of his siblings, he had already decided exactly what was to happen next.

Upon reaching the intended spot, George was set down in the exact position he would normally have sat; with his back against the wall and his head resting in a perfectly shaped, and naturally formed, little niche.

Verbally guided by Smart, they carefully arranged his body with appropriate detail in accordance with the specifics of their plan.

The pistol carried by George was discovered, and promptly seized.

They had brought pistols of their own, but this one, was more than ideal.

George's hat was placed back on his head; his pistol, already loaded, was moulded correctly into his right hand, the muzzle then placed near his opened mouth... and the trigger pulled.

The killer's coat sleeve had slightly ignited on fire through having partially obstructed the gunpowder flash.

Apart from the absence of the normally inevitable powder marks on George's face and the somewhat unnatural angle of the shot... it now truly 'looked' like a suicide.

The final touch, was the placement of a professionally forged, but peculiarly worded, suicide note, which contained fine details unknowingly furnished by Miss Gibson through interrogative conversations she'd had with her odious, Machiavellian mother.

Samples of George's handwriting had been easily acquired by William Smart, and, being no stranger to the criminal fraternity, knew exactly the right individual to whom he should assign the task.

With his hat now crushed over his eyes, a loosened gaiter, and a large pool of blood forming behind him and on his lap… George was dead.

Even the initial wound on the back of his head had been conveniently obliterated. William Smart and his mercenary hirelings stealthily fled the scene of their monstrous crime in a carriage which had been calculatedly concealed in a nearby secluded grove.

As evening fell, the darkness towards the north-east was something more than common; the clouds gathered over St Cyrus until the rain began pouring down in torrents… while the east wind was wuthering round the trees and tombstones. George's lifeless body was, almost lovingly, sheltered to a great extent by the kirkyard wall.

William Reith, was herd-boy of his father's cattle that season, and whilst putting them in the adjacent pasture, at noon the following day, Tuesday the 30th, saw the body, whom he took for the local minister, Reverend Alexander Keith, lying apparently asleep.

Believing it to be the minister, he took no further notice at the time; but on returning to let out his cattle at about two o'clock that afternoon, he saw that the body of this person was still lying in the same position.

He then went to examine the matter more carefully, and was horrified in looking over the kirkyard wall, to see a large pool of coagulated (lappart) blood lying in the lap.

The pistol lay with its muzzle resting on George's lower lip, and the thumb of his right hand was close to the trigger. His face was not touched in the slightest degree by the powder.

The boy ran home and told his father, who, along with others, hastened to the kirkyard, but by the time they got down, a number of 'salmon fishers', who had been taking a stroll in their dinner hour, were already there, and had also discovered George's body.

The first of the squad of fishers who discovered it was William Balfour, who had been for many years the respected blacksmith and veterinary surgeon at Bruce Mill.

The mournful intelligence of George's death was communicated to his family by his friend, the Reverend Dr Keith of St Cyrus. His family and friends were naturally devastated in the extreme.

The body was transported to Montrose for examination at the local morgue. Nothing too unusual was discovered, and the death was recorded as self-inflicted. Under the general circumstances, the verdict of suicide remained primarily unchallenged, thus, William Smart and Isabell Gibson, had successfully removed their 'problem'… and gotten away with murder!

The people of the town, who had loved him in life, knew better.

The untimely death of George Beattie awakened the most intense feelings in St Cyrus and Montrose. It was a mingled feeling of pity for his fate, and stifled indignation against the guilty cause of it.

George had indeed been the victim of Miss Gibson's perfidy and cruelty, but she was unjustly blamed, almost in entirety, for George's death.

Ironically, with George being out of the way, William Smart decided that there was now no hurry to marry Miss Gibson, and the marriage was repeatedly delayed, until late November.

After the marriage took place, she and William Smart travelled down south.
On their return, they landed publicly in Montrose, but she had sadly misreckoned public opinion, for the people rose on them, and they were forced to take refuge in the Starr Inn of New Wynd, from the violence of the mob.

Ultimately, however, these manifestations of popular indignation ceased to be shown, and the turbulent feeling settled down into something altogether different. Her impiously trampling on the most solemn oaths, her refined cruelty towards her tragic victim, and her defiance of every obligation held sacred by man, came to be well known, and the feeling of people toward Miss Gibson may be summed up by the words… horror and disgust.

It was remarked of her that, after her marriage, she walked in the streets of Montrose with a defiant air, as if she scorned public opinion.

This demonstrates that she was well aware of the general feeling.

Despite her marriage to the loathsome William Smart, she was only ever referred to as Miss Gibson.

She had made a shipwreck of her happiness, and her future held not a happy day. Smart, not having received the degree of wealth he had anticipated as Miss Gibson's inheritance was in consols (consolidated annuities/government bonds) and paid out annually, treated his wife with great carelessness and neglect.

On one occasion, they were travelling to Edinburgh on one of the steamers, and Miss Gibson was sitting in a seat on the quarter-deck, wretchedly sick and cold, while her husband walked up and down with other male passengers, paying no attention to her whatsoever. There happened to be a horse-hirer from Montrose, who went by the name of 'Babylon' also heading to Edinburgh. Seeing her so miserably cold and abandoned, Babylon offered her his cloak, and no creature according to him, was ever more grateful, even although it was from a man she would not have deigned to look at in any other circumstances.

In the face of such cold and unloved treatment by an ignoble and mercenary troglodyte like William Smart, over time, Miss Gibson gradually regained her soul and senses. The love of her life was George Beattie, and she became agonisingly aware of this fact and reality.

When residing at Castlested, a mansion at the top of the Montrose High Street, where the castle had once stood, the unhappy couple could be seen every afternoon driving through the town in a dog-cart at a furious rate, with a groom riding a considerable way ahead, to clear the way. They would return from the country about an hour later, driving in the same manner.

The ladies in Montrose stood aloof, and did not associate with Miss Gibson. She was often in the society of the late Lady Panmure, and of course she had a circle of

her own in which she moved.
Her life stretched to a point seventeen years later than the death of George. That tragic event, and the romantic friendship of the two preceding years, with her own subsequent conduct, had become indelibly fixed in her memory, ever haunting her remaining days.

For the last two years of her life she was confined to the house by a lingering illness, and, latterly, was unable to leave her room. A circumstance which had existed before, now became too dreadful to be borne. She had always had a horror of being in the dark and thought she saw the image of George Beattie in it. Now, when she was altogether unable to leave her bed, she could never endure to be left alone for even a moment, and required one of the maid servants always to stay with her and to sleep in the same room.

For two long years the dark clouds gathered and hung over her with perpetual gloom. The selfish apathy of William Smart was cold cheer to a hopeless sufferer, and formed a painful contrast to the devoted kindness and love of George Beattie. Her heart would now sink at the thought of what a dupe and fool she had been; how she had destroyed all her bright dreams of happiness, and been guilty of such wickedness for the sake of an object of ambition… and what a poor paltry thing it had turned out to be.
Horror of conscience, remorse and despair, filled her tormented mind.
At the moment of her death in her forty-second year on January 22nd, 1840, it is recorded that she cried out the name of her true love… George Beattie.

On the death of his 'wife', William Smart made the appearance of being overwhelmed with grief, although it was palpable to everybody that he had been the opposite of kind to her.
Wearing a white cravat, weepers, a long crape hanging down to the middle of his back, and a rueful countenance, for a long time, he went almost every day to visit her grave in the new Cemetery at Rosehill, of which she had been the very first internment.
For over a year he went about the streets in this garb, making himself an object of attention; but every one disbelieved him.
In going into the Old Church of Montrose, he would walk along the passage with a slow and solemn air in the same deep mourning, and come in late with the view of attracting attention, letting his 'grief' be known to all men.
He even went to the continent to wear away his sorry.
He wished to create the impression that between himself and his wife there was a mutual and endearing affection, but everybody knew that this was a lie.
On her tomb he inscribed the words: 'William, the beloved wife of William Smart' etc. However, the story of their life was too well known for the popular mind to be deceived by lying monuments.

The abominable Isabell Gibson, the mother of Miss Gibson, survived her daughter by five years, expiring on December 25th, 1845, and though William Smart had been neglectful of his wife... knowing where the money lay, he paid extraordinary attention to the old woman, who had been alone in the House of Kinnaber since the death of her husband, Robert, on May 8th, 1828, and thus became heir to *her* money as well.

He thus succeeded in feathering his nest as he had always sought to.

His memory will be disdained by every noble mind.

He died, with all his sins, at Montrose in 1853, aged sixty-seven, a miserable withered wreck.

'For what shall it profit a man, if he shall gain the whole world, and lose his own soul?'

What indeed?

Due to his 'supposed' suicide, legally, George could only be buried between the hours of nine o'clock and midnight, without religious ceremony.

However, Reverend Dr Keith felt privileged and honoured to give service to his respected and lamented friend.

On Friday, October 3rd, George was tenderly laid to rest at the spot he had departed this world, in the same grave as his siblings: Joseph, Elizabeth and Mary. With those who loved him the most, silently gathered in the cold, misty autumn moonlight; it was a heartbreakingly solemn event.

One year later to the day of his burial, when the earth around George's grave had settled sufficiently, his closest friends had a beautiful and impressive monument of polished granite erected upon it, surrounded by a three feet high stone enclosure, with iron railings surmounted by 'chevaux de frise' (a protective row of spikes set into the top of a wall to prevent intrusion). A marble tablet on its north-east face bears an inscription (penned by James Burness, Esquire) which could not be more profoundly impassioned or panegyrical, but sadly, having not been commissioned by his own family, omitted the names of the siblings with whom he now shared eternity.

Until the death of William Smart (and five years later, his brother George), the true story of George Beattie was totally suppressed by these, and other, socially powerful, elitist reprobates in Montrose.

George's family were pressured, harassed and threatened into silence, with every possible measure being taken to erase his memory; but thanks to a concerted effort by his friends and confederates, to preserve the truth, George's written statements were, laboriously and meticulously, duplicated, by hand, numerous times.

It is customary and natural to say a last word over our departed friends when they are committed to the dust. At George's funeral service, the Reverend Dr Alexander Keith relayed a poignant, albeit perceivably trifling story, which demonstrated George's inherent goodness and the kindness of his heart.

There was a poor man, named Jamie Calder, nearly blind, who often sat in the Montrose churchyard brae asking alms. Every day George remembered to give this poor man some money, and if any day he happened to be engaged elsewhere, the next day, he made it up.

George Beattie was universally beloved, and this cannot be without cause. He who made himself loved by all must have had a warm and generous nature, and the very finest spontaneities of heart and mind.

This fact was profoundly, and sincerely, immortalised in an obituary written by the impartial public journalists of the 'Montrose Review'.

Certain Souls are incarnated on the physical plane in order that 'others' may be Spiritually and morally tested… and ultimately… proven as positive or negative in essence.

As with so many… George Beattie was a literal martyr to the virtues of integrity, honour, compassion and love… and no regressive agenda, intent or machination will ever alter that fact.

For the duration of his relatively short lifespan, this bleak and harsh world was brighter… enlightened, enhanced and blessed by his presence.

He died beloved by the right people and persecuted by those who were devoid of the virtues he had himself epitomised and embodied.

The tapestry of his life may be viewed with innumerable loose threads from this earthly perspective… however, when ultimately viewed from the 'other-side'… a picture depicting immense beauty and divine revelation will be surely be beheld… by all.

Biographical Research

Overview

George Beattie, Esquire, was an early nineteenth-century poet, legal writer, philanthropist, truth-seeker, freethinker and man of superior intellect, temperance and spirit, who became one of the most well-known, beloved and respected people ever to have graced the community of the Scottish east coast town of Montrose.
His memory and story, for the most part, have strangely been lost somewhere in time and due to an unusual lack of information, as well as the circulation of a substantial amount of misinformation and disinformation down through the years, this is an extremely complex and difficult biography to accurately piece together.

To begin with, there is no mention of George Beattie's day and month of birth to be found on his memorial, in the 1863 biography, or anywhere else for that matter, only the year of 1786 (MDCCLXXXVI).
Our extensive research, with invaluable aid from the representatives of the 'National Archives of Scotland', regarding this anomaly has, we hope, uncovered the reason for this unusual omission.
Thus, it would seem that it is more than likely, that 'George Beattie' was born/baptised on Monday, September the 18th in 1786.
The problem is, that only the name 'William' appears in the Old Parish register entry for the year 1786, rather than 'George'*† :

* (Reference 18/09/1786 Old Parish Records of Births 267/00 0010 0151 ST CYRUS / BEATTIE, WILLIAM / Whitehill / William Beattie and Elizabeth Scott).

† It is, in our opinion, unlikely that George's mother, Elizabeth Scott, had two separate births in the same year; twins, or that George was born in the first few months of 1786 and NOT registered, therefore, we feel compelled to conclude, as do the representatives of the 'National Archives of Scotland', that the name 'GEORGE' was either an adopted middle name

(after his paternal grandfather) or that 'WILLIAM' was merely a clerical error made at the time of Parish register entry, being confused with the father's forename.

George's parents, WILLIAM BEATTIE and ELIZABETH SCOTT lived in a humble croft which nestled at the base of the 'Hill of Morphie' in an area known as 'Whitehill' on the Kirkside Estate, in the parish of St Cyrus, Kincardineshire.

※ St Cyrus was named after Ciric, the Latin name of Giric, Grig or Gregory the Great, son of Dungail, who succeeded to the Pictish throne about A.D. 877, he was also known as Circius, Ciricinn or Crig.

In an adjoining dwelling also lived GEORGE BEATTIE (Senior), the father of William Beattie and grandfather to young George and his siblings.

Thus far it is unknown whether George was the third eldest of seven children, two of which (Joseph and Elizabeth) having died before 1798, or the second eldest of five children, with 'David' possibly having been originally baptised as 'Joseph'.

In the first case scenario, it being the most likely by far, the names in descending chronology would be as follows :-

JAMES : born/baptised on 10/12/1780 - (O.P.R. reference 267/00 0010 0133 ST CYRUS);
JOSEPH : born/baptised on 16/05/1784 - (O.P.R. reference 267/00 0010 0148 ST CYRUS);
GEORGE : born/baptised on 18/09/1786 - (O.P.R. reference 267/00 0010 0151 ST CYRUS);
MARY : born/baptised on 27/02/1789 - (O.P.R. reference 267/00 0010 0153 ST CYRUS);
CATHERINE : born/baptised on 19/03/1791 - (O.P.R. reference 267/00 0010 0156 ST CYRUS);
ELIZABETH : born/baptised on 08/05/1794 - (O.P.R. reference 267/00 0010 0159 ST CYRUS);
DAVID : born between 1796-1798   (Unfortunately no specific date can be traced).*

* All the surviving Beattie children are listed in a volume of Kirk Session minutes for St Cyrus (ref. CH2/590/1) in a 'List of Inhabitants of the Parish of Ecclesgreig or St Cyrus' on p.29 under 'Whitehill' which was drawn up on the 25th of October 1798.

George Beattie experienced a simple, but very happy childhood. He loved the wonders of nature and wandering the stunningly beautiful hills and braes of his east coastal paradise of St Cyrus with his pet Jackdaw (kae) on his shoulder.

He received a good, but ordinary education at the local school, taught initially by a Mr Todd and subsequently by a harsh disciplinarian, a Mr Alexander Anderson.

In 1797/98, when George was eleven years of age, his father William and older brother James attained positions as 'Officers of Excise' in Arbroath (salt) (1798-1800), due in part to their obvious intelligence, but due mainly to the influence of and endorsement by the '7th Laird of Kirkside', Joseph Straton, uncle of the future '8th Laird of Kirkside', Lt General Sir Joseph M. Straton.

Lt General Sir Joseph M. Straton, CB (Companion of the Order of the Bath), KCH (Knight Commander of the Royal Guelphic Order of Hanover), FRSE (Fellow of the Royal Society of Edinburgh), etc., was regarded as a Peninsular and Waterloo hero, formerly known as 'Colonel Joseph Muter'.

☞ Exactly WHY the 'Beattie family' were aided by the 'Lairds of Kirkside' remains unclear.

☞ It is important to note, that General Sir Joseph M. Straton's surname was originally 'Muter', as he was actually the son of the 7th Laird's sister; but in order to inherit his unmarried uncle's title and become the '8th Laird of Kirkside' in 1816, his name HAD to be changed to 'Straton'.

General Sir Joseph M. Straton was the youngest son of William Muter of Annfield (in Fife) & Janet Straton of Kirkside.

LT GENERAL SIR JOSEPH M. STRATON

※ His K.C.H. star was auctioned by 'Spinks' in 1998.

In 1800, father and son were re-assigned consecutively to 'Officers of Excise' positions in the nearby east coastal towns of Usan (1800-1802) and Montrose (1802-1810), then in 1810 to the 'Ruthven Printfield Company' near Perth.*†

* Ruthvenfield, is a village, in the parish of Tibbermore, Perthshire.

† Due to fire, no further records now exist (Reference RH4\6\1-2).

The Beattie family appear to have left their croft and relocated to Montrose around 1800, possibly following the death of William's father, George (Senior), at St Cyrus.

※ Montrose sits between the mouths of the North Esk and South Esk rivers and is a historic seaport and market town on the Angus coast between Dundee and Aberdeen.

After an extremely short lived and undesired apprenticeship as a mechanic to a local tradesman, financed by his father, George was sent to Aberdeen to a situation as a clerk, but after only six weeks his benevolent employer died bequeathing him the sum of fifty pounds (which would be approximately seven thousand pounds today).

Upon returning to Montrose, young George entered the office of the Procurator Fiscal, Mr Colin Alison, who also treated him very kindly.
There he received the normal training one would expect and subsequently went on to complete his legal education in Edinburgh, which ultimately resulted in George setting up his own business as a writer, or solicitor, in his home town of Montrose.

He was an intellectual, philanthropic, warm and sincere man of true spirituality and although being a 'practical' , but non-churchgoing 'Christian' (very possibly of Gnostic Deistic thought), radical, slightly risqué and occasionally prone to bursts of profanity when frustrated...
he became extremely beloved and respected by the great majority of the populace, not only because of his unusual degree of profound kind-heartedness and benevolence in all aspects of life, but also because of his brilliant comedic wit, natural talent for impersonation and love of harmless elaborate practical jokes.
People eagerly sought to be in his company.
With his ever-smiling countenance, George Beattie was considered to
be very handsome despite being short of stature and somewhat stout. He had curled black hair and dark blue eyes and would generally be
seen wearing a black frock coat, neat fitting ribbed pantaloons and black gaiters. He also wore a gold watch and chain with several seals attached to it.
In his spare time he penned his own unique form of satirical, subversive and humorous poetic verse.

In November, 1815, when around 29 years old, he wrote a poem which would become his most enduring and renowned, the satirically comic epic 'John o' Arnha'' which was first published in a basic short form in a local weekly newspaper, the 'Montrose Review', before eventually being further enriched and lengthened by almost four times.
In a later, more illustrious printed edition, upon being demanded by its Publisher to provide a 'Preface' regarding the epic poem, George Beattie wrote the following extremely insightful words for the purpose :-

' Gentle and Courteous Reader,
THE following Tale was originally written from mere frolic. It was first published in 'The Montrose Review', and afterwards in a small Book, which, being low in price, met with ready sale. As my Pegassus, however, was somewhat restiff, and the Rider both awkward and impatient, to save time and trouble, nearly one half of it was composed in plain prose. After this, some sketches were drawn from the scenery, and the Publisher, in his wisdom, had these engraved. I was again commissioned to render the prose into verse, for another edition, which I did, such as it is, with great alacrity. I was told, however, that the Poem behoved to be lengthened, so as the Plates might be placed at proper distances, and not come in contact with each other. With much good nature I again set to work, and dilated as far as leisure and patience would permit: to this extension Mr. Southey, and some other gentlemen, owe the honour of being introduced in the following pages. Having wrought at the instigation of another,

without fee and without reward, neither expecting praise, nor dreading censure, I have not that tender and paternal regard for the work, which almost every author has for the offspring of his brain. The public may treat it as they please, without in the least hurting the feelings of the Author. This will appear pretty evident, on reading the work itself. At the same time, although the Publisher has brought it forth in a style much more elegant than it could have any title or pretension to, I should not wish him to be a loser by his folly; which, however, I much dread: at all events he cannot say he has been burdened with payment of 'copyright'.

I now see I could have made the Poem more bulky, without being at the trouble of adding more lines to it.

This could have been done by dividing it into 'Cantos'. By the modern method of book-making, the termination of one Canto, and the beginning of another, generally swallow up four full pages.

Six Cantos, therefore, would have made it twenty-four pages longer, without the addition of a line. Dividing into verses, or sections, and filling up the spaces with numerical letters, is another expedient for extension. The Spenserian stanza has always been considered entitled to this; but it is quite an innovation in 'namby-pamby'. The introduction of episodes, in the shape of songs, sonnets, &c., preceded by blanks, and titled in Saxon letters, is for the same reason resorted to by the "Hireling Harpers" of the present day. Indeed, it is by these means that our modern Bards and Publishers fill their pockets, and gull the public.

After having finished the Tale, in some shape or other, I really was somewhat astonished on being again told by the Publisher that it was necessary to write a 'PREFACE'; and, moreover, that he "must have it immediately," as he had advertised for publication on a certain day. I had no wish to renew my labours in the vineyard of folly; and, besides, I considered the request to be a most ridiculous one. "This is not the time," said I, "for writing a 'Preface': if you had wished anything of that nature, you should have informed me at the commencement; I never saw the 'Preface' at the end of a book, except when printed in Ireland." Printers, it appears, however, can commence at the beginning, middle, or end, of a work, as it best suits them. "That is of no consequence," said the Publisher, "I have left eight pages at the beginning for the Title and the Preface: the Title takes up two, the remaining six are for the Preface; but if you think you cannot spin as much out of your brain, in the course of an hour or two, as stain these, I can reduce them other two pages, by adding a 'bastard' Title." All this was quite unintelligible to me; and now that I have commenced writing a 'PREFACE' or something else, I really feel at a loss what to state in it, more indeed as to quantity than 'quality'. The six pages, it would appear, must be filled, and no more. I must, therefore, go on; and the Printer must stop at the end of the last page whether a sentence may happen to be concluded or not. If it wants anything, let him fill it up with a blank page, like one of those in "Tristram Shandy."

It will be pretty evident that, in writing this Tale, "Tam o' Shanter" was kept in view; at the same time I know well it can no more be compared to that inimitable production than Southey's "Carmen Triumphale" could be to "Homer's Iliad," or I to Hercules.

It ran so much in my head, however, that I was more cramped in avoiding palpable imitation, and involuntary plagiarism, than I was benefited in any other respect, by attempting to adopt it as a model; for, no sooner did I set about brewing my storm, and setting it a blowing, than the original and expressive lines of the immortal Bard came wildering across my brain:

> "The wind blew, as 'twad blawn its last;
> The rattling showers rose on the blast;
> The speedy gleams the darkness swallow'd;
> Loud, deep, and lang, the thunder bellow'd:
> That night a child might understand,
> The deil had business on his hand."

When I attempted to moralise on the fleeting nature of pleasure and glory, how quickly these vanish, and are followed by misfortune, stripes, and disgrace, then I was haunted by the four beautiful similies, proving the fact in such an original and striking manner:

> "But pleasures are like poppies spread,
> You seize the flow'r, its bloom is shed;
> Or like the snow-falls in the river,
> A moment white - then melts for ever;
> Or like the borealis race,
> That flit - ere you can point their place;
> Or like the rainbow's lovely form,
> Evanishing amid the storm."

Show me any thing that can be compared to this in your modern poems! When the fleshless Harper came into the field, and with his wild music stirred up Witches, Warlocks, Ghosts, Devils, and Demons, to trip it "on the light fantastic toe;" then jingled in my ears the forcible and firmly clenched lines of Burns:

> "He screw'd the pipes and gart them skirl,
> Till roof and rafters a' did dirl," &c.

> ".... Hornpipes, jigs, strathspeys, and reels,
> Put life and mettle in their heels," &c.
>
> "As Tammie glowr'd, amaz'd and curious,
> The mirth an fun grew fast and furious
> The piper loud and louder blew;
> The dancers quick and quicker flew;
> They reel'd, they set, they cross'd, they cleekit,
> Till ilka carlin swat and reekit," &c.

Have we any thing like this now-a-days? This most original, comic, and horrific poem, I am aware, is not so much read in the drawing-room as the modish performances of a new race of poets; but it will tickle the risible muscles, and raise the hair on the crowns, of generations yet unborn, when these ephemeral performances will sleep as sound as their authors. The muse of 'humorous poetry' seems to have been entombed with Burns. His predecessors, Ramsay and Fergusson, were also peculiarly in the good graces of that buxom lady. We have nothing now like "Christ's Kirk on the Green;" "The Monk and the Miller's Wife;" Fergusson's "Leith Races," "Hallow Fair;" Burns' "Tam o' Shanter," "Death and Doctor Hornbook," "Halloween," or "The Jolly Beggars," the last was fastidiously rejected by Dr Currie, in his edition of Burns' Poems. I by no means wish to insinuate that these are the best poems of the Bards I have just now mentioned: they are the best of their particular class - the humorous; and I speak chiefly of poems in the Scottish dialect. "The Gentle Shepherd," "The Farmer's Ingle" "The Cotter's Saturday Night," and other poems of the same authors, have their peculiar merits and beauties. The incidents and descriptions in these are exquisitely natural, and truly pastoral. Burns and Fergusson, in particular, had the happy knack of leading their readers, in the very best humour, to the "wee bit ingle and clean hearth-stane," "the cosh and cantie housie," of the Scottish peasant, where the inmates are brought before us, and viewed, not through the medium of caricature, or the mist of time, but in a way so simple, natural, and chaste, that they are instantly recognised as real, living, generick characters.

Such descriptions must be read with pleasure by every one who is not so miserable as to be refined above enjoying the beauties of nature a disease not uncommon amongst the critics, and those who gratuitously rank themselves in the higher classes of society.

The descriptions of our present poets are very different from those I have just mentioned. They usher us into the Gothic Castles and Halls of Barons bold, and to the presence of princely dames, and warriors clothed in steel. These beings may be made to speak and act as best suits the convenience of the author; for as no person *living ever had the pleasure of seeing the originals, they cannot, consistently, take upon them to condemn the pictures. Anxious, at all times, to shelter myself under the wings of my betters, I have also presumed to bring forward some characters not known in common life, for which I shall plead no excuse to the gentle and courteous Reader. The Hero himself is drawn from a living original in this neighbourhood, already well known to fame. As to the second personage, the 'Water Kelpie', whose only ambition is, and has been, for centuries past, to wallow in the Ponage Pool, and take the benighted and way-worn traveller off the hands of the treacherous 'Spunkie', to plunge him in a watery grave, good breeding, or court etiquette, could not be expected to emanate from such a quarter. As to the "grewsome" appearance of the Ghosts, poor fellows, no blame attaches to them, it was none of their doings. Let the other characters speak for themselves there is 'one' that I have no great inclination to meddle with at all - "let sleeping dogs lie." As to the Tale itself, I shall "speak lowne," particularly as I am not prepared to say any thing in its favour: if I had been possessed of more leizure, and endowed with more patience, I think it might have been made better. The scenery, however, I mean the natural scenery not as described by me, is certainly not inferior to the "Banks of the Doon" and "Alloway Kirk." The lone and dreary situation of the Old Kirk of Logie, in the vicinity of the dark and gloomy Den of St Martin, long reported to have been the sinful haunts of "Warlocks grim and wither'd Hags;" and the Ponage Pool, on the North-Esk, at a little distance, the well-known rendezvous of the 'Water Kelpie', are objects of terror to the superstitious, and of more than ordinary interest to those who may at times take delight in amusing their minds with the traditionary legends of this part of the country.*

Presuming my allotted space is not yet filled, I take an opportunity to state (although it has little connection with the called-for Preface), that I am extremely partial to the language of Caledonia. From its expressive simplicity it is peculiarly adapted to the pastoral, the natural, and pathetic; and since the year 1490, when Maister William Dunbar, the chief of ancient Scottish poets, wrote "The Twa Mariit Wemen and the Wedo," and "The Mirrie Aventure of twa Quhyte Friers of Berick," and uther ryghte mirrie and wittie tales, down to the death of Burns, it has been constantly and most successfully employed in the humorous and ludicrous.

That it is equally well adapted to the martial and heroic, is strikingly illustrated in "Bruce's Address to his Army," by Burns.

Let the 'petit maitre', and the fine lady, who cannot hear a sentence pronounced in Scotch without fainting, remember that this "vulgar jargon" was once the language of heroes; and that those who yet understand it, find it richer, and more expressive, than the English.

As to errors, whether of the pen or the types, let them be pointed out by others.'

* At this point it should be noted, that George Beattie made no secret of his disdain for the 'Lake Poets'; the Poet Laureate of the time Robert Southey in particular, whom he regarded as "a prostitute of his muse", among other things, going on to state that 'Lake' poetry was *"a farrago of merghless, foisonless, farrachless nonsense"*. George was obviously disgusted by 'pretension' of any kind and on any level.

JOHN FINDLAY or FINLAY
JOHN o' ARNHA'

'John o' Arnha" (Arnhall), was based on a local town officer named John Finlay or Findlay (both versions have been cited), who was infamous for his boorish arrogance, oak cudgel, multiple marriages to young girls and tall-tales of imagined heroism around the globe, despite the fact that he is said to have never left the vicinity.

☞ John Finlay/Findlay and his cronies met in various taverns throughout Montrose, where, after he had partaken of his favourite beverages: 'whisky punch and nappy ale', he could be easily overheard by George Beattie, boasting of his imagined heroic adventures. These taverns included 'Adam Macpherson's' in the New Wynd (opposite the Starr Stables) and, most notably, Fraser's 'Ship Inn', better known as "Strippie's", which stood in the area now known as 'Queen's Close'.

Almost three years after George Beattie's death, the poem was translated into a play and performed by theatre actor/manager Charles Bass with poet James Bowick, at the Montrose Theatre Royal, in Bridge Street, on Monday the 19th of June in 1826.

Already being somewhat displeased at the poem in of itself through being aware that he was its inspiration; Finlay/Findlay* apparently did not appreciate the further heightened humour apparently gained at his expense in this particular new version and, ultimately, went berserk, assaulting various people in the process.

Being a local success however, Bass also took the play to the Dundee Theatre Royal later that year and then finally to Edinburgh's Caledonian Theatre in 1829.

* John Finlay/Findlay died on Saturday, the 11th of October in 1828, aged 91 years.

The legal business which George had established on the first floor of 114-116 High Street in Montrose, included his younger brother David and was extremely prosperous.

☞ On a light-hearted note, we would like to briefly mention the whimsical fact that George possessed a 'treasured' green parrot named 'Katie'; and whenever the weather permitted, George would put 'Katie' out on the window ledge of his office in her cage, and it is recorded that when people passed by she would repeat (as taught by George) aloud the phrase:
"Geordie and his Katie!". On one occasion, a local fisher also called George, was passing beneath the aforementioned office window whilst carrying a Skate (fish) over his shoulder and upon hearing 'Katie' screeching this particular phrase from above, he apparently thought the bird was intentionally mocking him, whereby he began shouting death threats and general abuse at her in return.

George employed several clerks and was also factor to the Kirkside Estate, now owned by the 8th Laird of Kirkside, General Sir Joseph M. Straton.

George possessed a town house in 'New Wynd', Montrose, where he lived with his family.

Despite a very busy life, George always found time to perform free legal services for the poor and oppressed, along with his usual charitable acts, which endeared him even further to the community.

☞ It should be mentioned, that a picturesque spot near Montrose called the 'Den of Fullerton', was generally known at that time as 'Ananise' or 'Ananias'.
It was at the 'Den of Ananise' that George and five of his like-minded friends would meet on occasional Sundays to discuss their mutual ideas on the evils of organised religion, monarchy and state; a mindset probably resulting from the 'Age of Enlightenment' and very possibly inspired by the works of Thomas Paine (1737-1809), who was a participant in the American Revolution.
Of the two opposing political parties at the time, the Conservative and the Progressive, George Beattie's sympathies lay overwhelmingly with 'Progressivism', which stood against the greed and selfishness of the privileged classes, as well as the sterile, heartless dogmatism of the 'Church'.
'Conservatism', stood merely for the preservation of 'draconian tradition'.

As a result of his passionate beliefs, he became a member of the radical, long established, 'Montrose Club'.

In a 2012 publication by a Montrose 'historical society', George Beattie and his companions are slandered by the accusations of being merely atheistic, troublesome alcoholics, in a 'volume' containing a significant amount of other verifiably ill-researched and erroneous 'facts' and details.
When we respectfully requested a source for the slanderous assertions from the 'historical society in question, the reply received by us was, that there was NO recorded source whatsoever... and thus, merely petty malicious heresay (entirely unsubstantiated 'slurs' in other words) at best!
In this particular publication, the slanderous statements are coupled with a 'rant' by the Church of Scotland minister and religious zealot... Rev. William Ruxton Fraser, quoted from his 1896 publication, 'St Mary's of Old Montrose'.
The question once again being... WHY ?
The understanding and exposure of this continued 'blackening' and dismissal of George Beattie's memory and literary legacy is the crux of our 'Project'.

In juxtaposition, a quote regarding the celebrated and eminent doctor, Radical and Reformer, Joseph Hume, M.P. (1777-1855), from David Mitchell's 'History of Montrose' (1866), is as follows :

" *The pear was ripe, too, and fell into his hand; for at the time he was first made member for the burgh, there was a noble band of Reformers in Montrose, who prepared his way. These were Provost Charles Barclay, James Burness, Esq., Dean of Guild, Dr Gibson, Alex Thomson, Esq., Mr James Bisset, and Mr George Beattie.* "

This quote obviously contrasts sharply with the 'historical society' sub-heading, from a profoundly 'flawed' book...
"A den of atheists at Fullerton"

At this juncture, we feel morally justified in stating the astounding fact, that in spite of all our non-profit efforts to restore a more 'accurate' version of events regarding the story of George Beattie into the annals of the Scottish historical canon... that in five years, we have received ZERO aid, endorsement or encouragement whatsoever from the relevant local historical societies... in fact... quite the opposite would be a much fairer assessment.
A searing indictment perhaps... but, as far as we are concerned... unequivocally, entirely and sadly... deserved.

☞ George Beattie also ran for town council in Montrose; losing only by a single 'casting' vote.

The Romance

In 1821, at the age of thirty-five, George Beattie was the most popular soul in Montrose and at the peak of his life when he met Miss William Gibson, the twenty-three year old daughter of one of his 'socially superior' friends, squire Robert Gibson.

It was love at first sight for George.

Miss William Gibson was a tall, vivacious and pretty young woman, very pale, with light brown hair and hazel eyes.

Her parents, gentleman farmer, squire Robert Gibson and his wife Isabell (née Mitchell), occasionally referred to as 'Isabella', owned and occupied a large house at the 'Stone of Morphie', which is about a mile up from the bridge on the North Esk.

STONE OF MORPHIE

※ The 'Stone' from which their home takes its name is an eleven foot un-sculptured and un-inscribed monolith said to commemorate the burial place either of the Danish/Scandinavian general Camus, or that of one of his sons, slain in the 'Battle of Barry' in 1010 AD by a 'Chatti' warrior OR in honour of a member of the noble 'Graham' family, whose lineage once owned the lands of 'Morphie'.

Being the factor for the 'Kirkside Estate' brought George back to St Cyrus on a regular basis and he became a frequent visitor to the Gibson residence at 'Stone of Morphie'.
Despite his being, 'technically', of a 'lower' social status, George felt that it was permissible for him to initiate a relationship with Miss Gibson and despite a short initial period of her playing 'hard to get', it quickly became apparent that Miss Gibson held reciprocal feelings for him, in her own 'particular' way.

Until the spring of 1822, their intimacy delicately grew until it began
to bloom at this most appropriate time of year, at which point Miss Gibson was openly courting and inviting the attentions of George by requesting of him, by note, to extend his usual evening strolls from Montrose towards St Cyrus and meet with her either inside the Gibson owned, but then uninhabited, 'House of Kinnaber' or, weather permitting, outside in its beautiful walled garden.

HOUSE OF KINNABER
WALLED GARDEN

※ The 'House of Kinnaber' is a large white house, barely visible from the highway for heavy tree growth.
It is a three storey mansion built in 1680, possibly incorporating an earlier house and altered in 1790, which is close to the ocean about three miles from Montrose on the South bank of the North Esk.

HOUSE OF KINNABER

During that summer, supposedly in secret, Miss Gibson would, at least twice weekly, make her way down from 'Stone of Morphie' and cross the bridge from the opposite side of the North Esk to meet her lover at their favourite spot in the flourishing walled garden of the 'House of Kinnaber'.
George would walk from Montrose and take the highway going north, passing on his left, the 'Woods of Charleton' and on his right was a tree strewn landscape stretching towards the sand dunes and beach of the North Sea shoreline.

Many promises, vows and affirmations of fidelity, undying love and lifelong happiness were endlessly made by them both and they became unofficially engaged to be married.
However, due to the social barrier which still remained as an obstacle, her parents were supposedly not made privy to their plans, but obviously they must have suspected something was developing.
Their personalities and characteristics, although drastically opposite, seemed almost complimentary.
Her idealism, haughtiness and ambition, contrasted with his affability, openheartedness and humility. Basically, where one was weak the other was strong.
In their love, Miss Gibson was demonstrative, sensitive and jealous whereas George was much deeper, more serious and true.
As time passed, their romance and friendship continued to grow.

It was recounted by Beattie that on one occasion whilst he was visiting 'Stone of Morphie', when they were alone, Miss Gibson complained about the fact that he had gone to Edinburgh without taking her with him and despite his explanation that it was strictly on business and in unpleasant weather, she not only insisted that they remake their prior vows to each other but, laying her hands in his, requested that he repeat aloud the following solemn oath...

"May I never know peace in this world, or see God in mercy, if I marry another than you; or if ever I go South again without taking you along with me as my wife"

… following this by a similar oath made by herself just before announcing to him the assurance that her parents actually approved and expected their engagement to be married. Grand plans and beautiful imaginings of eternal bliss increasingly filled their minds and whether at 'Stone of Morphie', at Kinnaber or in Montrose, the couple would meet whenever possible

… until the spring of 1823.

The Maelstrom

The course of true love never yet ran smooth and for poor George Beattie; the darkest of clouds hastily approached.
In the spring of 1823 a sudden and fearful "change came o'er the spirit of his dream".

George had no idea that a 'maelstrom' lay ahead, which would consume him, entirely.

News arrived that a wealthy uncle, William Mitchell, Esquire, who had supposedly been a 'Governor of Grenada', residing in the town of St George, had died leaving a considerable fortune to be divided between William and her mother Isabell.
This apparent legacy would, in every way, prove to be a curse.

☞ There is however, NO evidence to be found that he EVER held such a prestigious post, but rather, that he was an 'Agent' for the Mount Nesbit Estate (Plantation) and a slave owner in St John, Grenada.

He owned over one hundred slaves.*

* Sourced from the Slave Registers of former British Colonial Dependencies, 1812-1834; Colonial Papers, volume XXX, nos 42,42.1.

☞ The 'original' biography author 'A.S. Mt Cyrus, M.A.', emphasised that there was a superior legal claim to the estate of William Mitchell in existence, namely that of his brother, Mr James Mitchell of Montrose (actually, St Cyrus).
James Mitchell, being the oldest, was the legal heir to his brother William Mitchell's estate.

※ William Mitchell was born in 1766 to parents : William Mitchell and Jean Deas of Maryton, Kincardineshire.

Andrew Smith (A.S. Mt Cyrus, M.A.), in all the editions of his 1863 biography of George Beattie, basically states, that 'correspondence' had been entered into by Miss Gibson with her uncle William Mitchell, whilst he was in Grenada, that had 'poisoned his mind with prejudices' against his brother James, to the extent that, as 'supposedly' manipulated, he ultimately changed his Will in favour of his sister and niece.

Apparently, it was the intention of William Mitchell to return to Scotland where, no doubt, the 'truth' would have then been revealed, however, death, unfortunately and conveniently, prevented him from doing so.

☞ It appears that William Mitchell had initially left a share to his mother, Jean Deas, before changing the bequest

in favour of his sister, Isabell.
Miss Gibson was bequeathed thirty-five hundred pounds.
The total amount of the monetary legacy to his relatives in Scotland being approximately TWELVE AND A HALF MILLION POUNDS in present-day currency.
Immovable assets possibly being another matter entirely.

Our research has established that this money, whatever the actual final amount, was in the form of 'consols' (consolidated annuities/government bonds), being paid out accordingly. NOT as a lump sum.

☞ This fact MUST be clarified :

that FAR from being his ' black housekeeper ', as was apparently believed by George Beattie, Sarah Bronker/Brounker and William Mitchell appear in the 1817, 1820 and 1821 Slave Registers. She owned at least seventeen slaves and he owned over one hundred.
She was bequeathed over three thousand pounds by William Mitchell in his Will (approximately TWO AND A HALF MILLION POUNDS at the present time); it being recorded that this sum was OWED to her for repayment of a LOAN which she had given to him.
She was also bequeathed a further three thousand pounds.*†

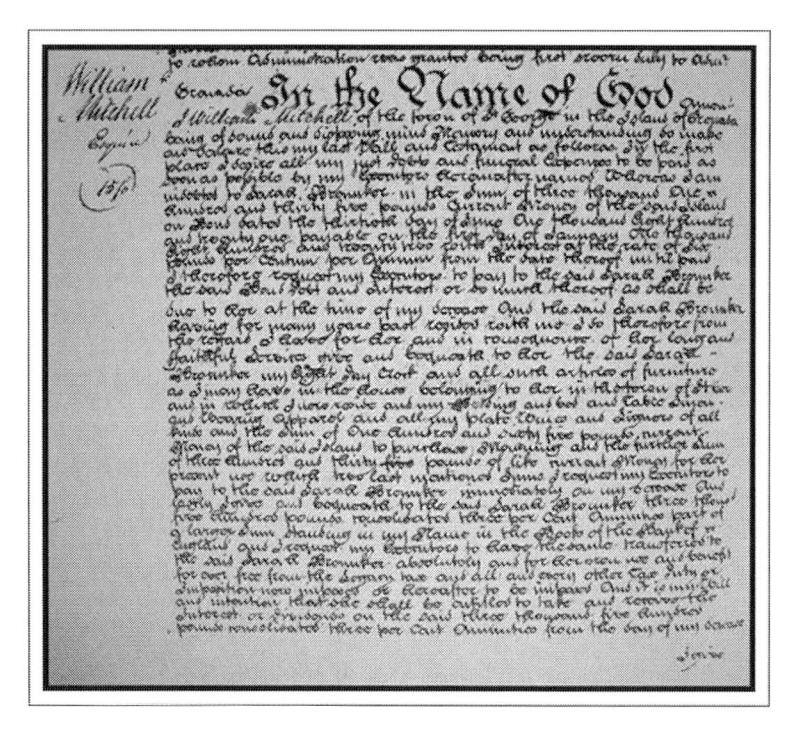

FIRST PAGE OF
WILLIAM MITCHELL'S LAST WILL AND TESTAMENT

* Sourced from William Mitchell's Last Will & Testament (MITCHELL, WILLIAM: Reference PROB 11/1674/80) & (BROUNKER, SARAH: Reference PROB 11/1689/359).

† Sourced from Slave Registers of former British Colonial Dependencies, 1812-135 / Class:T71; Piece: 265. Office of Registry of Colonial Slaves and Slave Compensation
Commission: Records; (The National Archives Microfilm Publication T71).

☞ Initially, the Gibsons had requested of George that he 'officially' write to acquire a copy of the uncle's 'Will' for them. We speculate that the evidence suggests that George Beattie would have remained an acceptable suitor for Miss Gibson, in her parents eyes, had he acquiesced to performing some particular task for them; a task and agenda which he refused to be any part of, believing it to be morally and financially corrupt. He and his 'acquired knowledge' had, from that moment, become a serious threat to their plan, of which, we also speculate, William Smart was already involved in... among others, almost certainly... all, of an equally sinister disposition.

On Sunday, the 4th of May, George nervously visited 'Stone of Morphie', where, to his relief, vows of endless love and fidelity were once again wholeheartedly renewed.

☞ According to the version of events in the 'A.S. Mt Cyrus' biography in 1863... the amount left to Miss Gibson was thought to be about thirty-five hundred pounds, however, by the following Tuesday, the amount had apparently increased to around ten thousand pounds after a 'supposed' final reckoning of the estate.

George was promptly extricated from the scenario and henceforth furnished with no further details, other than what was contained in a brief note sent to him by his 'friend', Robert Gibson, which suspiciously contained the very minimum of detail.

For Miss Gibson, no doubt 'powerfully' swayed, by her mother in particular, this sum is said to have been a game changer and supposedly, her prideful ego took over entirely.

The solemn oaths, the vows, the promises of true love, were all scattered to the winds and Miss Gibson invoked the loss of peace in this world for the sake of paltry lucre and pride.

Her superficial capacity for true love cooled immediately, becoming cold, false and cruel. She began to shuffle and to prevaricate with the brave, honest, true-hearted man who loved her so well and after several months of treachery and duplicity, finally cast him off after engaging herself, with her mother's encouragement, to an ambitious, mercenary, conceited and foppish corn/grain-merchant named 'William Smart of Cairnbank' (the apparent 'playboy' brother to and business partner of Alexander & George Smart of 'AW&G. Smart - Grain Merchants').*

* George's feelings toward this particular individual are beautifully summed up by the following quote from Emily Brontë's timeless novel, 'Wuthering Heights';

"If he loved with all the powers of his puny being, he couldn't love as much in eighty years as I could in a day."

☞ 'Cairnbank' was a mansion house and estate near Brechin, formerly known as 'Bothers'. It was purchased around 1821-22 by the 'Smart' brothers from a Mr Alexander Ritchie.
It is now known as the 'Templewood Estate' due to the former ownership of its lands by the Order of Knights Templar.
The 'Smart' brothers obviously relished their newly purchased 'title' and permanently adjoined it to their names thereafter.

George Beattie, the poor distracted lover, slow to believe in her utter perfidy and his own ruin, gradually sank under the savage blow which hit him like a thunderbolt. He became engulfed by grief and despair.

He made a 'Last Will and Testament' on Friday, August 8th and settled all his property among his remaining relatives.

He wrote to the false woman the most heart-broken letters of touching agony, but her heart was stone.
He declared with the most profound emotion and tears that without her, life was unbearable.
She was deaf alike to the call of honour; to her own solemn imprecation and to the voice of love.
And as the traditional story goes…
nothing therefore remained, so thought the wretched man, but to destroy himself and put an end to the existence he found unendurable.

" When hope is killed, a man no longer desires to live. He who would yet live, either has still a ray of sweet hope, or he dreads to die."

He supposedly travelled to Aberdeen, where he would be less known, to secretly purchase a pistol (which could easily have been acquired in order to practice for an arranged 'illegal' duel with William Smart).
After some alleged testing of the weapon on a bothy door at St Cyrus beach and on the south wall (dyke) of the Auld Kirkyard, it was found to be wanting, and so a second trip to the 'Granite City' to acquire a second pistol was embarked upon.

Despite his overwhelming black depression, as in the case of many
reconciled to imminent death, George summoned the strength to smile through his pain, and accepted an invitation to a party at the home of his friend, Mr William Gordon.

This was to be an event which, ironically, saw George Beattie succeed in simulating the high spirits in which he had once so often been.

On Monday the 29th of September in 1823, George was well-dressed and groomed.
He had put his affairs in order as best he could.
Upon leaving his dwelling in Montrose, George Beattie uttered his final words to his sister Catherine as she informed him of what meal she had planned to make him for dinner that evening :-

" Na, Kate, ye'll not do that, I'm going to the country, and I'll maybe no' be back to dinner, but I can get something if I come… if, I come, "

… which he, supposedly, repeated twice.

After looking back several times, he spoke of the likelihood of rain, then he left.
Away wandered the lonely and stricken man by the shore of the bleak and moaning sea.

Having just recently turned 38 years of age, he was never to be seen alive again.

At what exact time on that fateful day George Beattie actually pulled
the trigger on himself (assuming he actually did), will never be known.
What we do know, is that it would turn out to be an appropriately wild and stormy night.

Upon the following day a young herdsman found Beattie lying dead in the Auld Nether
Kirkyard of St Cyrus beside the grave of his sister Mary and more than likely, also that of his other lost siblings, Joseph
and Elizabeth, to which he had wandered in his agony.

The Old Lower Churchyard of St Cyrus was situated in the west end of a field or haugh belonging to the farm of Scotston of Kirkside. The field was generally in grass, or a least was so on that particular season. The young cattle, in the summer months, pastured it, and were then enclosed nightly in a pen or fold adjoining the Churchyard, its dyke forming part of the enclosure.

William Reith, was herd boy of his father's cattle that season, and while putting in his cattle, about midday on Tuesday the 30th, saw a person, whom he took for the local minister, Rev. Alexander Keith, lying apparently asleep, resting his head and shoulders on the east wall of the graveyard.
Believing it to be the minister, he took no further notice at the time; but on returning to let out his cattle at about two o'clock in the afternoon, he saw the person still lying in the same position.
He then went to examine the matter more carefully, and was horrified
in looking over the dyke, to see a large pool of coagulated (lappart) blood lying in the lap, the hat crushed over the eyes, a flintlock pistol in the hand with the muzzle resting just inside the mouth on the lip... in short, a dead man.
There was no apparent signs of struggle, except for one loosened gaiter. It is however, EXTREMELY strange, that there were NO gun powder marks visible on George Beattie's face.
The boy ran home and told his father, who, along with others, hastened to the Churchyard, but by the time they got down, a number of 'salmon
fishers', who had been taking a stroll in their dinner hour, were in the yard, and had also discovered the dead body.
The first of the squad of fishers who discovered the body was William Balfour, who had been for many years the respected blacksmith and veterinary surgeon at either Langley Park or Bruce Mill, who subsequently wrote a highly graphic letter, detailing the entire circumstances of the discovery, so far as he was concerned, to a Mr George Duthie of Dundee.

Another of the fishers identified at the scene was a Mr James Graham.

Beside George, supposedly, lay a suspicious and strangely worded letter with many apparently heartfelt and solemn words to his brother, David :-

DEAR DAVID,
you will see me no more in life. My exit can not entail disgrace on you. I hope it will not even do so on my memory.
It will be accounted for on a perusal of the Papers at the "right" end of my desk connected with John Walker's box, in which you will find several letters. I have tied a string round the box and papers. Take care of them and use them cautiously and discreetly. They are necessary for my justification, if I can be entitled to such. None of you need regret the want of me. You must have observed for some time that I have been totally unfit to attend to business. This has proceeded from (what I consider) wrongs done to me, as will in so far appear from these letters and pages. I entreat you to be of good cheer. I am confident I will be happy. I think I have left Catherine and you what will keep you from want if well guided, which I need not advise you about.
You will get on with the business. I think you should collect the accounts. There is a very considerable sum due on the books. If you think it for your interest, you may take any body you choose into partnership with you. You are in possession of my settlement.
There is no use for sealing up my repositories or letting any person into my desk but yourself. You need be the least disheartened, for I would only have been a burden upon you and on myself. You may safely convince my father and mother of this. I need not say more. The papers, letters &c., may be used freely in any way you may think proper in rebutting any charge that may be brought against one who can not answer for himself. You can take advice as to this from any of my friends and acquaintances who are qualified to give it. I am sure they will not refuse their good offices under the circumstances.
May God bless you, and I am, dear David, your loving brother;

George Beattie

THE EXACT SPOT IN THE AULD NETHER KIRKYARD
WHERE GEORGE BEATTIE DIED
ON MONDAY, 29TH OF SEPTEMBER, 1823

THE EXACT SPOT ON THE AULD NETHER KIRKYARD WALL
WHERE GEORGE BEATTIE DIED
ON MONDAY, 29TH OF SEPTEMBER, 1823

The news of the tragic death was brought to the family by the Rev. Dr Alexander Keith (1791-1880), a 'Church of Scotland' minister and friend of George Beattie.

REV. DR ALEXANDER KEITH

George's body was taken to Montrose and after several days, was returned for internment at the spot in the south-east corner of the Auld Nether Kirkyard where he had tragically left this world, joining at least one of his siblings, if not three.
Contrary to the belief of some, George Beattie was indeed buried inside the Auld Nether Kirkyard.
At that time, in the 'Church of Scotland', those unfortunate souls committing suicide could be denied a Church burial service, but not a burial itself, as the ground was apparently NOT owned by the Church.

※ In the year 1823, it was enacted that the body of a suicide should be buried privately between the hours of nine and twelve at night, with no religious ceremony. In 1882, this
law was altered by the Internments (felo de se) Act, 1882, where every penalty was removed except that internment could not be solemnised by a burial service, and the body may now be committed to the earth at any time, and with such rites or prayers as those in charge of the funeral think fit or may be able to procure.

One year later, after the earth had settled, a beautiful monument was erected by his friends.

Of the woman who helped send him thus broken-hearted in mad despair to an early grave, he takes leave in some lines of touching intensity of feeling within his final poems, 'The Appeal' and 'Farewell Sonnet', if not sublime, they are at least full of sad and sincere beauty.
Thus came an end to all the bright, golden visions of a courageous, honest and true heart.
Besides the letters from Miss Gibson which Beattie had kept, he left
written documents which give a full account of the final tragic chapter in his life called the 'Statement of Facts', 'Supplement to Statement of Facts', 'Additions to Supplement' and 'The Last'.

The untimely death of George Beattie evoked much intensity of feeling
in St Cyrus and Montrose.
There was a volatile mixture of sadness and pity for his fate combined with outrage and indignation directed against those deemed responsible for the tragedy, namely, the Gibson family and William Smart.
As George Beattie was now no longer a possible threat to his mercenary machinations, William Smart, with a clear field and now exhibiting an agenda FAR from his former haste to marry Miss Gibson, repeatedly delayed the event (probably waiting for an acceptable 'dowry').
Upon their eventual marriage in November of 1823 and return from 'honeymoon' to Montrose, the pair were chased and stoned from the harbour by a waiting 'angry mob' and forced to seek refuge in the 'Starr (or Star) Inn' of New Wynd.

The immense and obvious social power held by the Smart and Gibson families is undeniable.

Despite the common public knowledge that George Beattie had been used and abused by these families and their cohorts… their overwhelming effectiveness in suppressing and subverting his story and legacy is blatantly and disturbingly obvious to anyone who elects to analyse the remaining evidence.

That being said… there is nothing new or unique about the lengths to which those whom possess the lust for power and status will go to.

What an ignoble reason for living… is greed.

Mr and Mrs William Smart purchased one of the most historic houses in the town of Montrose, 'Castlested' or 'Castlestead'; once owned in the fifteenth century by Sir David Wood, the friend and Chancellor of King James V.
It was also subsequently owned by several other wealthy notables, including the Earls of Montrose.

The famed great James Graham, 1st Marquess of Montrose., was born in it in 1612.

Sadly and ironically, 'Castlested' is now the Montrose 'Job Centre'.

CASTLESTED or CASTLESTEAD

※ William Smart of Cairnbank, was a 'Land Tax Commissioner of Angus & Kincardineshire' in 1836.

Now, metaphorically, bearing the 'mark of Cain' as it were, Ms William Gibson (Smart), lived, for seventeen years after George Beattie's death, a life of cold, loveless, privilege and comfort, with a man she now was painfully aware, never did nor ever would, love her.
We believe that the primary reason for this was because the inheritance from William Mitchell's estate was probably consumed by outstanding debts in the West Indies, thus, he never achieved the degree of wealth he had anticipated.

As the years passed, her regret and realisation grew.
It was said that Ms Gibson (Smart) was so afraid of the dark, believing she could see George Beattie's apparition in it, would not
sleep alone if her husband was away, requiring one of the maids to stay with her and a candle always to be kept burning.
The undying devotion she would have received from George Beattie was starkly contrasted with many years of continual merciless neglect and indifference by her 'chosen' husband.
After a lingering illness for the final two of those years, Ms William Gibson (Smart) died in her 42nd year on the 22nd of January, 1840 at Castlested, whilst, ironically, crying out the name of whom she had become, once again, aware, was her 'true' love, the
man who had unconditionally given her his heart… George Beattie.

She was the first burial in the then new 'Rosehill Cemetery' of Montrose.
Although it was common knowledge, to most people, that William Smart never loved his wife and had only married her to gain her fortune, he 'acted' as though he was overwhelmed with grief through various forms of public display.
He wore mourning attire for over a year.
Upon returning from the continent, where he went to 'deal' with his 'sorrow', he proceeded to pay 'extraordinary' attention to his dead wife's ageing mother, Isabell Gibson, he being aware of the significant fortune she possessed, especially after the death of her husband Robert at Kinnaber on May 8th, 1828.

☞   Robert Gibson left four thousand, five hundred and ninety pounds upon his death.

In his Will he states the following :-

" Helen Gibson, spouse of George Neill of Borrowfield, and Williamson Gibson, my son, are now the only surviving children of myself and the deceased Margaret Beattie, my former wife."

" £318.10 was formerly lent out on a Bond granted by the late Lieutenant Colonel Hercules Scott of Brotherton and payable to me and Isabella, my spouse, and to whomever lives the longest, and at our death, to the child or children procreated by our marriage. The said sum having been realised under the settlement of the late William Mitchell (Senior) of the island of Grenada of date, the twenty-fifth of August and registered in the Sheriff Court books of Kincardineshire on the first of September, 1797."

This could also explain why Miss Gibson was, strangely, named 'William'.
We believe that the Gibsons were merely attempting to ingratiate themselves with their wealthy relative in Grenada.

Ultimately, especially having 'always' been in her favour, she died on Christmas Day in 1845, supposedly, leaving all her property to him.

So, in the end, William Smart of Cairnbank, apparently inherited the 'Gibson' estate in its entirety.

Probably because 'Smart' had total control at her death, Isabell Gibson was not buried with her husband Robert (possibly at Spa Fields, Islington in England), but rather, with her daughter William, in what was to become the 'Smart' family burial plot in 'Rosehill Cemetery' of Montrose.

His daughter Helen (from his first marriage to a Margaret Beattie) and her husband, George Neill of Borrowfield are also buried in Rosehill Cemetery, very near the 'Smart' family plot.
We would just like to add at this point that Robert Gibson had two children with his first wife, Margaret Beattie; Helen and Williamson, thus being half-siblings to Miss William Gibson, as she was the only child of Robert Gibson's marriage to Isabell Mitchell (Gibson). It is strange that Helen and George named their firstborn child, Isabell Mitchell.
This daughter married a Jamaican plantation owner named Alexander Cauld.

☞   The accounts of Williamson's death in Jamaica (due to the climate), stated in a letter to George Beattie from

Miss Gibson, our research suggests to be incorrect, if not a deliberate fabrication; the reason for which, thus far, remains unclear.*

* Sourced from Robert Gibson's Last Will & Testament : 1831. GIBSON, ROBERT (Reference SC47/40/7 FORFAR SHERIFF COURT).

He may have succeeded in achieving his goals, but Mr Smart, the deciding factor in the fate of George Beattie, died at Castlested in Montrose in 1853, aged 67.

Since there is no record or evidence that William Smart had any children, we can quite confidently and educatedly speculate that his brother, George Smart of Cairnbank, was the major, if not sole, inheritor of the estate.

We speculate that George Smart may possibly have already been in possession of 'Kinnaber House' at this time.

Whilst William Smart was living, George Beattie's 'Memorandum' was 'blocked' against dissemination or 'officially suppressed' in some way; however, at least one 'copy' was being circulated and laboriously re-copied repeatedly by hand, but after Mr Smart's death, this became no longer necessary and the documents were eventually printed and published by W.P. Nimmo in the A.S. Mt Cyrus biography of George Beattie in 1863 entitled, "George Beattie of Montrose: a poet, a humourist, and a man of genius".

☞ We believe this 'biography' to have been, primarily, an exercise in 'damage control', commissioned by 'remaining influences', good or bad. The book served not only to focus blame and vilification mainly on Miss Gibson and promulgate a good deal of misinformation, but it also allowed its author...

Andrew Smith, to indulge his 'true' passion, which was botany. We believe that the book also helped finance his relocation to South Africa.
It should be noted, that the third edition had no author attributed to it.

As to the author of the 1863 biography; A.S. Mt Cyrus, M.A., was a pseudonym for an Andrew Smith of Lauriston Mains, who went to the South African Province of Natal, and eventually died in Queenstown, South Africa in 1898 of heart disease, in his early 70's. He was a native of St Cyrus and an avid follower of the works of the Rev. Dr Alexander Keith, especially his publication on 'Prophecy'.
He was also lifelong friends with Dr Keith's sons.*

* Andrew Smith had three brothers: the Hon. Charles Abercrombie Smith, a Vice-Chancellor of the University of the Cape of Good Hope;
the Rev. David Smith and the Rev. Robert Smith of Carsock. He also had
a sister who was the wife of the Rev. W. R. Thomson of Balfour.

Mt Cyrus is another name for the Ecclesgreig Estate which was originally known as the 'Lands of Mount Cyrus' and 'Lands of Criggie'.

Ecclesgreig Castle was built in 1844 from the remains of Mount Cyrus or St Cyrus House. The name was changed to 'Ecclesgreig' (Eglise Grig) by the ancestral owners, the Forsyth-Grants, to avoid confusion with the village of St Cyrus.

ECCLESGREIG CASTLE

The Irish novelist Bram Stoker stayed at Ecclesgreig Castle and reputedly, it inspired his classic and iconic work… 'Dracula'.

Our research has uncovered, as stated earlier, that George's father, William and brother, James, left Montrose and relocated to Perthshire, where they continued their careers as 'Officers of Excise' at the Ruthven Printfield Company (Cotton).

We have not been able to establish whether William Beattie and his wife, Elizabeth Scott remained together.

We know that James married and eventually relocated to Glasgow.
He fathered two children, William and Elizabeth, named obviously, after his parents.*

George Beattie had ultimately died intestate, due to the timing of his death and his Will not having become valid.

The validation period was sixty days.

He died only <u>eight</u> days before his Will would have become valid.

His property therefore passed to his elder brother, James; who in point of fact, honoured George's wishes and passed the house etc., back to David and Catherine.*

It appears as though there had been estrangement between George and James, but we have been unable discover if this was the case or not.

William Beattie died in 1843, aged 80 years.*

David Beattie died, after an apparently successful life, in 1848, about 52 year of age.*

We have found no records pertaining to James and Catherine Beattie's dates of death.*

* Sourced from George Beattie's Inventory : 1823. BEATTIE, GEORGE (Reference CC3/5/7 BRECHIN COMMISSARY COURT) ;
Sourced from George Beattie's Inventory : 1823. BEATTIE, GEORGE (Reference CC3/3/16 BRECHIN COMMISSARY COURT) ;
Sourced from George Beattie's Inventory : 1824. BEATTIE, GEORGE (Reference SC47/40/1 FORFAR SHERIFF COURT) ;
Sourced from Miss William Gibson's Last Will & Testament : 1835. GIBSON, WILLIAM (Reference SC47/40/10 FORFAR SHERIFF COURT) ;
Sourced from William Beattie's Last Will & Testament : 1844. BEATTIE, WILLIAM (Reference SC47/40/15 FORFAR SHERIFF COURT) ;
Sourced from William Smart's Inventory : 1853. SMART, WILLIAM (Reference SC47/40/7 FORFAR SHERIFF COURT).

We are unaware if any descendants of George Beattie are still living.
All we actually know for sure is that an 'anonymous' donation for 2/6 (two shillings and six pence, usually said as "two and six" or "half a crown"), stated in the 'Montrose Review' to be from a "Descendant" was made in 1923 towards a centenary 'Renovation Fund' for George's grave, in order that it may be improved and then maintained in a "creditable condition" henceforth.

※ It may be noted, that the fatal flintlock pistol that deprived George Beattie of his life, was last known to be in the possession of a Mr James Fraser, who owned the "Curiosity Shop" which once occupied No. 123 Nethergate, Dundee.
At the present time, these premises are known as the 'Cafe Rodi'.

☞ Regarding the accusations of insanity which were, and still are, directed at George Beattie; we are NOW aware that exogenously induced endogenous 'major depressive disorder' is NOT in fact insanity, but merely the paradoxical reaction of a sane moral mind trying to adjust to an insane immoral world.
It can only be speculated upon, that had a greater understanding of his condition and circumstances been prevalent at the time, then maybe his cruel fate could possibly have been altered.

A RARE OLD PHOTOGRAPH OF
GEORGE BEATTIE'S GRAVE

A RECENT PHOTOGRAPH OF
GEORGE BEATTIE'S GRAVE
AFTER IMPROVEMENTS UNDERTAKEN BY 'THE GEORGE BEATTIE PROJECT'

The Conspiracy

The fact cannot be ignored, that the 'absence' of George Beattie was extremely beneficial, if not vital, to the machinations of certain people.

☞ Great insight as to this fact may be gained from George Beattie's own words:

> *"That plots were laid by others to oust me and secure Miss Gibson's fortune, I know well from the inquiries that were made at myself from a certain quarter. Those who interfered were far too many for me."*

Contrary to the traditionally accepted version of events… we personally believe that our research will reasonably establish that George Beattie was mercilessly railroaded into suicide (virtually, if not actually, and morally murdered) by certain socially powerful individuals apparently attempting to shield themselves from the consequences of their immoral agenda and actions… being motivated solely by greed and their lust for power!

As a result of our extensive research, we can only conclude that, for whatever specific reason, the evidence points overwhelmingly to a cold-blooded conspiracy to remove George Beattie from the picture.*

*All was well with the relationship when George Beattie was requested by the Gibsons to become 'professionally' involved in the legalities of the 'Mitchell legacy'.

- Without warning, he is abruptly, illogically and inexplicably ousted from a long-standing romance and engagement, being immediately replaced by William Smart of Cairnbank; who had previously never shown the slightest interest in Miss Gibson.

- He is abruptly ousted, in all respects, from his 'legal' services to the Gibson family.

- A campaign of ridicule, scorn and harassment is directed against him by the Gibsons and Smarts.

☞ George Beattie specifically stated that he was also being badgered by a relation of William Smart. We believe that this individual was George Smart of Cairnbank, who obviously had a vested interest in all of his brother's dealings.

- He is renowned for his devotion to the care of his family and makes an elaborate Last Will and Testament to ensure their protection, but ultimately dies intestate only eight days before the end of the required sixty day legal validation period, despite there having been no marriage between Miss Gibson and William Smart.

- The outraged public directly blamed the Gibson and Smart families for the death of George Beattie.

- George Beattie's 'Statement of Facts' was being painstakingly hand copied by many people who obviously believed that its preservation was extremely important.

- The 'Statement of Facts' was suppressed from publication for forty years, until after the death of all those involved.

- Despite the fact that the public journalists of the 'Montrose Review', at the time of his death, proclaimed in their obituary :

    > "*We have no right to intrude with our own private feelings, in lamenting the death of this worthy and valuable member of society; but it would have been doing injustice to the public, whose concern is deep upon this occasion, to have said less; and we are assured that none will contradict us when we declare, that no man in this town and neighbourhood was ever more generally beloved in his life... or more universally lamented in his death.*"

    there is no public memorial to his memory to be found anywhere in the Burgh of Montrose, even although a plethora dedicated to a multitude of other 'selected' notables are prominently displayed throughout.

- The A.S. Mt Cyrus biography of George Beattie in 1863, was not only written under a pseudonym, diluted with unnecessary botanical and geographical detail and replete with inaccuracies; but it also made strangely inflammatory statements, coupled with one particularly elaborate fabrication regarding the long-distance 'mind poisoning' of William Mitchell against his brother James, supposedly by his niece, Miss Gibson.

※ A 'Residuary Legatee' is entitled to the residue of an estate after payment of debts and distribution of specific bequests.

- To this day, we personally believe, an 'agenda of obfuscation' is still in place and being adhered to.
  This conclusion being based on the general lack of support and the apparent 'snubbing' and 'stonewalling' we are encountering from relevant and necessary individuals, institutions and organisations.

- Not a single personal item directly or indirectly belonging to George Beattie appears to exist.

- George Beattie died a relatively wealthy man.
  Today, he would have had almost one million pounds in the bank;
  with a great deal more still owed to his Legal business from various clients.

- Lt General Sir Joseph M. Straton, alone, owed six hundred pounds to George... which would be over 'half a million' pounds at the present time.

☞ George instructed his brother David to write off much of the debt owed.

David did however, receive two hundred and seventy pounds via David Carnegie of Craigo, Trustees of the late Lieutenant General Sir Joseph Straton's estate.

We sincerely believe that the evidence based, not only on our own original and extensive research, but on the 'first' biography of George Beattie by Andrew Smith (A.S. Mt Cyrus, M.A.), can more than 'justify' our assertions and the use of the term… 'conspiracy'.

Caribbean Slave Trade

For over 300 years, enslaved Africans were forced to work for Europeans.

In the Caribbean, many laboured on sugar, coffee and cocoa plantations owned by North East Scots.

Many North East families owned plantations in the Caribbean in the eighteenth and nineteenth centuries. In some cases, the young men who went to the Caribbean had no land or money to their name when they left Scotland. If they did well in the Caribbean they bought one or more plantations there. When they had made enough money, they sold up their properties there and bought an estate in Scotland, where they retired to live as landed gentlemen.

A complete list of the Caribbean properties owned by North East Scots would be very long indeed.

Generations were born into this slavery. Millions died young because of poor diet, cruelty and relentless hard labour. The survivors lacked the most basic freedoms, such as the right to care for and protect family members.

Many sugar labourers were women. A girl began work around age four, collecting grass to feed the mules and oxen. By ten she was weeding the cane fields, and by 18 she was planting and harvesting

the canes. By 40 she was worn out, and was sent back to feeding the livestock. If she survived a few years more, she became a nurse to the babies on the plantation, a new generation of workers that probably
included her own grandchildren.

When enslaved Africans arrived in the Americas, they were often alone, separated from their family and community, unable to communicate with those around them. The following description is from 'The Interesting Narrative of the Life of Olaudah Equiano' :

"When we arrived in Barbados (in the West Indies) many merchants and planters came on board and examined us. We were then taken to the merchant's yard, where we were all pent up together like sheep in a fold. On a signal the buyers rushed forward and chose those slaves they liked best."

A SLAVE AUCTION

On arrival, the Africans were prepared for sale like animals. They were washed and shaved: sometimes their skins were oiled to make them appear healthy and increase their sale price.
Depending on where they had arrived, the enslaved Africans were sold through agents by public auction or by a 'scramble', in which buyers simply grabbed whomever they wanted. Sales often involved measuring, grading and intrusive physical examination. Sold, branded and issued with a new name, the enslaved Africans were separated and stripped of their

identity. In a deliberate process, meant to break their will power and make them totally passive and subservient, the enslaved Africans were 'seasoned'. This means that, for a period of two to three years, they were trained to endure their work and conditions, obey or receive the lash. It was mental and physical torture.

Life expectancy was short, on many plantations only 7-9 years.

It was a life of endless labour. They worked up to 18 hours a day, sometimes longer at busy periods such as harvest. There were no weekends or rest days.

The dominant experience for most Africans was work on the sugar plantations. In Jamaica, for example, 60% worked on the sugar plantations and, by the early 19th century, 90% of enslaved Africans in Grenada, Nevis, Montserrat and Tobago toiled on sugar slave estates.

The major secondary crop was coffee, which employed sizeable numbers on Jamaica, Dominica, St Vincent, Grenada, St Lucia, Trinidad and Demerara. Coffee plantations tended to be smaller than sugar estates and, because of their highland locations, were more isolated.

A few colonies grew no sugar. On Belize most enslaved Africans were woodcutters; on the Cayman Islands, Anguilla and Barbuda, a majority of slaves lived on small mixed agricultural holdings; on the Bahamas, cotton cultivation was important for some decades. Even on a sugar-dominated island like Barbados, about one in ten slaves produced cotton, ginger and aloe.

Livestock ranching was important on Jamaica, where specialised pens emerged.

By the 1760's, on mainland North American plantations, half of enslaved African people were occupied in cultivating tobacco, rice and indigo.

Children under the age of six, a few elderly people and some people with physical disabilities were the only people exempt from labour.

Individuals were allocated jobs according to gender, age, colour, strength and birthplace. Men dominated skilled trades and women generally came to dominate field gangs. Age determined when enslaved people entered the work force, when they progressed from one gang to another, when field hands became drivers and when field hands were retired as watchmen. The offspring of planters and enslaved African women were often allocated domestic work or, in the case of men, to skilled trades.

Children were sent to work doing whatever tasks they were physically able. This could include cleaning, water carrying, stone picking and collecting livestock feed.

In addition to their work in the fields, women were used to carry out the duties of servants, child minders and seamstresses. Women could be separated from their children and sold to different 'owners' at any time.

The plantation owners may have controlled the work and physical well being of enslaved people, but they could never control their minds. The enslaved people resisted at every opportunity and in many different ways.

There was always the constant threat of uprising and keeping those enslaved under control was a priority of all plantation owners. The laws created to control enslaved populations were severe and illustrated the tensions that existed. The laws passed by the islands' governing Assemblies are often referred to as the 'Black Codes.'

Any enslaved person found guilty of committing or plotting serious offences, such as violence against the plantation owner or destruction of property, was put to death. Beatings and whippings were a common punishment, as well as the use of neck collars or leg irons for less serious offences, such as failure to work hard enough or insubordination, which covered many things.

SLAVES CUTTING THE SUGAR CANE

The sugar cane plant was the main crop produced on the numerous plantations throughout the Caribbean through the 18th, 19th and 20th centuries, as almost every island was covered with sugar plantations and mills for refining the cane for its sweet properties. The main source of labor until the abolition of slavery was African Slaves. These plantations produced 80 to 90 percent of the sugar consumed in Western Europe.

In the 19th century sugar dominated Martinique, Grenada, St Croix, Jamaica, Barbados, Leeward Islands, Saint-Domingue, Cuba, Guyana and many other islands that were run by French or British owners.

Sugar was the most important crop throughout the Caribbean, although other crops such as coffee, indigo, and rice were also grown. The sugar was best grown on relatively flat land that was near the coast where the soil was naturally yellow and fertile, so mountainous parts of the islands were less likely to be used for sugar.

In the mid-17th century sugar cane was brought into the British West Indies by the Dutch from Brazil. Upon landing in Barbados and other islands, they quickly urged local farmers to change their main crops from cotton and tobacco to sugar cane. With depressed prices of cotton and tobacco due mainly to stiff competition from the North American colonies, the farmers switched, leading to a boom in the Caribbean economies. Sugar was quickly snapped up by the British who used the sugar for cakes, and sweetener in teas.

During the colonial period, the arrival of sugar culture deeply impacted society and economy in the Caribbean. It not only dramatically increased the ratio of slaves to free men, but also the average size of slave plantations. Early sugar plantations made extensive use of slaves because sugar was considered a cash crop that exhibited economies of scale in cultivation; it was most efficiently grown on large plantations with many workers.

A SLAVE OVERSEER

As a result, slaves were imported from Africa to work on the plantations. For example, before 1650 more than three-quarters of the island's population was white. In 1680, the median size of a plantation in Barbados had increased to about 60 slaves. Over the decades, the sugar plantations became larger and larger. In 1832, the median plantation in Jamaica had about 150 slaves, and nearly one of every four bondsmen lived on units that had at least 250 slaves.

For about the next 100 years Barbados remained the richest of all the European colonies in the Caribbean region. The colony's prosperity remained regionally unmatched until sugar cane production grew in geographically larger countries such as Saint-Domingue, Jamaica and elsewhere. As part of the mass sugar production, the process gave rise to other related commodities such as rum, molasses, and Falernum.

The West India Interest was formed in the 1740's when the British merchants joined with the West Indian sugar planters. The British and West Indies shared profits and needs. This organisation was the first sugar trading organisation which had a large voice in parliament.

In the 1740's, Jamaica and Saint-Domingue (Haiti) became the world's main sugar producers. They increased the production by using an irrigation system that French engineers built.

After the abolition of slavery in Saint-Domingue as a result of the Haitian Revolution, Cuba became the most substantial sugar plantation colony in the Caribbean, outperforming the British islands.

After slavery, sugar plantations used a variety of forms of labour including workers imported from India under contracts of indenture. In the 20th century, large-scale sugar production using wage labour continued in many parts of the region.

By the early 21st century many Caribbean islands were no longer producing sugar. However, sugar is still grown in Jamaica and Cuba, among other countries.

In 1833, Grenada became part of the British Windward Islands Administration and remained so until 1958.

PORT OF MONTROSE

WILLIAM MITCHELL'S
MOUNT NESBIT ESTATE
PLANTATION

A Timeline
of the
Atlantic Slave Trade

16th Century

1562 Sir John Hawkins, backed by Gonson and other London merchants, leaves Plymouth with three ships, making him the first English slave trader. He takes 300 Africans and trades them with the Spanish and Portuguese for sugar, hides, spices and pearls.

1564-65 Backed by Queen Elizabeth I, Hawkins makes his second slavery voyage trading 500 Africans for precious metals, pearls and jewels.

1567 Hawkins makes his third and final slavery voyage, again with the Queen's investment, involving six ships, including one captained by his cousin Sir Francis Drake. After trading 500 Africans in the Caribbean, Hawkins sought refuge from storms in the Mexican port of San Juan de Ullua, where he is ambushed by the Spanish. Many of Hawkins' crew is captured; some face the Inquisition, others forced into slavery and some taken back to Spain to be hung. Only three ships return to Plymouth, carrying seventy out of the original four hundred men.

17th Century

1607 Colony of Virginia is founded and is the first permanent English settlement in North America; soon becoming one of the main areas for the arrival of enslaved Africans.

1618 King James I establishes The Company of Adventurers of London Trading into the ports of Africa, more commonly known as The Guinea Company; the first private company to colonise Africa for profit.

1619 Beginning of trade in enslaved Africans in Virginia to grow tobacco.

1623 The first English settlement on St Kitts is established by Thomas Warner.

1625 Barbados becomes an English Caribbean colony.

1626 First ship of enslaved Africans arrive on St. Kitts.
1649 Slave rebellion takes place in Barbados.
1655 England takes control of Jamaica from Spain.
1655 Escaped slaves in Jamaica create 'Maroon' settlements in the mountains.
1656 Slave rebellion in Guadeloupe led by Angolans.
1657 Juan de Bolas, a Jamaican leader of escaped slaves ('Maroons') surrenders to the British but on terms of pardon and freedom. Other Maroons continue to fight British rule.
1660s Demand for African labour for the Barbados sugar plantations intensifies.
1672 The Royal African Company is re-formed after its collapse in 1667 to regulate the English slave trade. By the 1680s it is transporting approximately 5000 slaves per year.
1675-35 slaves are executed for plotting to rebel in Jamaica.
1668 'Lobby's rebellion' in Jamaica; 200 slaves escape to the mountains.
1685 Slave conspiracy in Jamaica uncovered 1685-86 Slave rebellion in Jamaica suppressed.
1690 Major slave revolt in Jamaica.
1692 Slave conspiracy to slaughter whites discovered in Barbados.
1698 Royal African Company monopoly ends.
The slave trade is officially opened to private traders causing a dramatic increase in Africans being transported on English ships.
1699 80% of Caribbean inhabitants are enslaved Africans.

18th Century

1702-13 War of the Spanish Succession.
1713 Britain gains all of St. Kitts, and the right (asiento) to import enslaved people to Spanish America is granted to the South Sea Company.
1727 Quakers in Britain officially express their disapproval of the slave trade in their London Yearly Meeting Book.
1729 Slave rebellion in Cuba 1730 Britain becomes the largest slave trading country.
1730-39 First Maroon War in Jamaica. British agree a treaty with the Maroon leader Cudjoe in 1739 giving the Maroons 1,500 acres of land in return for helping to capture other escaped slaves.
1735-36 'Tackey's rebellion' in Antigua.
1745 Olaudah Equiano (author of The Interesting Narrative of the Life of Olaudah Equiano, or Gustavus Vassa, the African) is born 1746 Slave rebellion in Jamaica.
1752 Slave rebellion in Martinique.
1756-63 Seven Years War. Britain gains Dominica, Grenada, St Vincent and Tobago.
1759 William Wilberforce, the abolitionist, is born in Hull.
1760 Slave revolts in Jamaica last for several months, up to 400 rebels are executed.
1760 Thomas Clarkson, the abolitionist, is born 1765 Granville Sharp begins legal challenges to the British slave trade with the case of Jonathan Strong.
1770s The abolitionist campaigner Granville Sharpe collects evidence showing that slavery is incompatible with English Law.
1772 John Woolman, an American Quaker and early anti-slavery campaigner comes to England to gather support from English Quakers.
1772 The Somerset case in London. Chief Justice Lord Mansfield rules that enslaved people in England cannot be forced to return to the West Indies. This ruling does not entitle slaves in England their freedom.
1772-73 John Stedman joins a military expedition to suppress a slave rebellion in Surinam, South America and is appalled by the inhumanity shown to Africans. In 1796 he publishes 'The Narrative of a Five Years Expedition against the Revolted Negroes of Surinam', a full account of his experiences that becomes a classic of abolitionist literature.
1774 John Wesley, an early leader of the Methodist movement, publishes anti-slavery tract Thoughts Upon Slavery.
1775 Royal Commission is set up to take evidence on the slave trade.
1775-83 American War of Independence. France seizes Grenada, Tobago and St Kitts from Britain but retains only Tobago after the Peace of Versailles.
1778 The Knight vs Wedderburn legal case in Edinburgh rules that enslavement is incompatible with Scots law.
1781 The Zong case causes outrage and strengthens the abolition campaign: 470 Africans are forced onto the slave ship Zong. The cramped conditions are so appalling that seven crew members and sixty Africans died from sickness; the remaining 133 sick Africans are thrown overboard and left to drown. The case is heard as an insurance dispute not a murder trial.
1783 London Yearly Meeting present to Parliament the first petition against the slave trade signed by 273 Quakers.
1786 Thomas Clarkson's 'An Essay on the Slavery and Commerce of the Human Species' is published and makes an immediate impact.
1787 The Society for the Abolition of the Slave Trade is founded.

1788 Due to the growing concern about conditions in the 'Middle Passage' the Dolben Act limits the number of enslaved people a ship is permitted to carry. Even with these restrictions, conditions remain appalling.

1788 First public abolitionists meeting held in Plymouth Guildhall - Plymouth Committee of Abolitionists leaflet is produced.

1789 Olaudah Equiano's 'The Interesting Narrative of the Life of Olaudah Equiano, or Gustavus Vassa, the African' is published.

1790 William Wilberforce presents the first abolition bill to the House of Commons, although it does not pass.

1790 Thomas Clarkson pays another visit to Plymouth.

1791-1804 A slave rebellion in St Domingue in 1791 sparks off the Haitian Revolution, led by Toussaint L'Ouverture with an army of ex-slaves. The revolution eventually leads to St Domingue becoming independent Haiti in 1804.

1792 House of Commons votes in favour of the abolition of the slave trade but the bill is rejected by the House of Lords.

1793-1802 French Revolutionary War between Britain and France delays the abolition campaign.

1794 France abolishes slavery and frees all enslaved people in her colonies. Legislation is passed by US Congress to prevent US vessels being used in the slave trade.

1795-96 Second Maroon War in Jamaica, ending in defeat for the Maroons.

1795 Fédon's Rebellion in Grenada causes enormous damage to plantations. Enslaved people seize control of large parts of the island before being defeated by British troops in 1796.

1795 Rebellion in St Vincent results in expulsion of Black Caribs from the island in 1796.

1796 Napoleon seizes power in France and soon restores slavery in the French colonies.

19th Century

1802 First West India dock opens, initially dealing solely with the produce from the West Indies.

1803-15 Napoleonic Wars between Britain and France. Vienna Settlement confirms British control of St. Lucia, Tobago and the Guiana colonies.

1804 On January 1, St Domingue is declared the republic of Haiti, the first independent black state outside Africa.

1807 The Transatlantic Slave Trade is abolished by the British Parliament. US also ban the slave trade, to take effect the following year. Britain declares Sierra Leone (in West Africa) a crown colony.

1808 The British West Africa Squadron is established at Sierra Leone to suppress any illegal slave trading by British citizens.

Between 1810-65, nearly 150,000 people are freed by anti-slavery squadrons.

1810 Britain negotiates with Portugal for the abolition of the South Atlantic slave trade.

1816 'Bussa's rebellion' in Barbados, inspired by the Haitian revolution, causes huge damage in the harvest season before being brutally crushed.

1817 Spain signs a treaty with England agreeing to end the Spanish slave trade north of the equator immediately, and south of the equator in 1820.

1817 Slave Registration Act forces all slave owners to provide a list of all the enslaved people they own every two years.

1820 US law makes slave trading a crime equal to piracy, punishable by death.

1823 Slave rising in Demerara is brutally suppressed by British forces: 250 enslaved people die, and Rev John Smith of the London Missionary Society is sentenced to death for his part, causing outrage in Britain.

1823 Anti-Slavery Committee formed in London to campaign for total abolition of slavery.

1831 Major slave revolt called 'The Baptists' War' breaks out in Jamaica, led by Baptist preacher Sam Sharpe, and is brutally suppressed.

1831 Nat Turner leads a slave rebellion in the Virginia, United States.

1831 The History of Mary Prince, the first narrative of a black woman, is published in London and becomes an important part of the anti-slavery literature.

1832 The Great Reform Act introduces new Members of Parliament from groups who are more likely to oppose slavery.

1833 Abolition of Slavery Act 1833 – Britain abolishes slavery and provides for the emancipation of enslaved people in the British West Indies, to take effect in August 1834. The Act declares that the former enslaved people must serve a period of 6 years apprenticeship before receiving full emancipation. Originally this period was set at six years, but it was later reduced to four.

1833 Uprising on St. Kitts in opposition to the new apprenticeship system.

1833 William Wilberforce dies on 29 July, three days after the bill to emancipate enslaved people is passed.

1838 The apprentice system is abolished following peaceful protests in Trinidad, so guaranteeing the complete emancipation of all former slaves in the colonies.

1839 A group of 49 enslaved Africans on board the slave ship Amistad revolt off the coast of Cuba. The ship lands

at New London, USA, where the Africans are taken into custody. American abolitionists take up their cause and in March 1841 the Supreme Court upholds their freedom.
1840 The Royal Academy in London exhibits J.W.M. Turner's controversial painting 'The Slave Ship' (also called 'Slavers Throwing Overboard the Dead and Dying – Typhoon coming on'). The same exhibition also includes Auguste Biard's painting 'Scene on the Coast of Africa'.
1865 The Thirteenth Amendment marks the abolition of slavery in the USA following the American Civil War.
1865 The biggest and most famous revolt by black Jamaicans. 17 Europeans are killed and 32 injured after a riot in Morant Bay which sees the crowd attack the police station and the local militia. Over a few days a number of plantations are also attacked. The authorities react violently and declare martial law. The ringleaders are executed and around 400 blacks are killed.
1886 Abolition of slavery in Cuba.
1888 Abolition of slavery in Brazil.

PALMISTE LAKE
ON THE
MOUNT NESBIT ESTATE PLANTATION

Slave censuses were taken regularly by the owners noting names, ages, and distinguishing marks, presumably for identification if a slave tried to escape, plus an annual return of decreases in numbers due to deaths, and increases due to births.
These can be found in the National Archives.*

The prosperity of Scotland in the 18th and 19th centuries came directly from Caribbean slavery.

Our wonderful buildings and their lavish architecture are in fact monuments to the unspeakable cruelty and greed of those who are now immortalised in stone, bronze and street names throughout the nation.

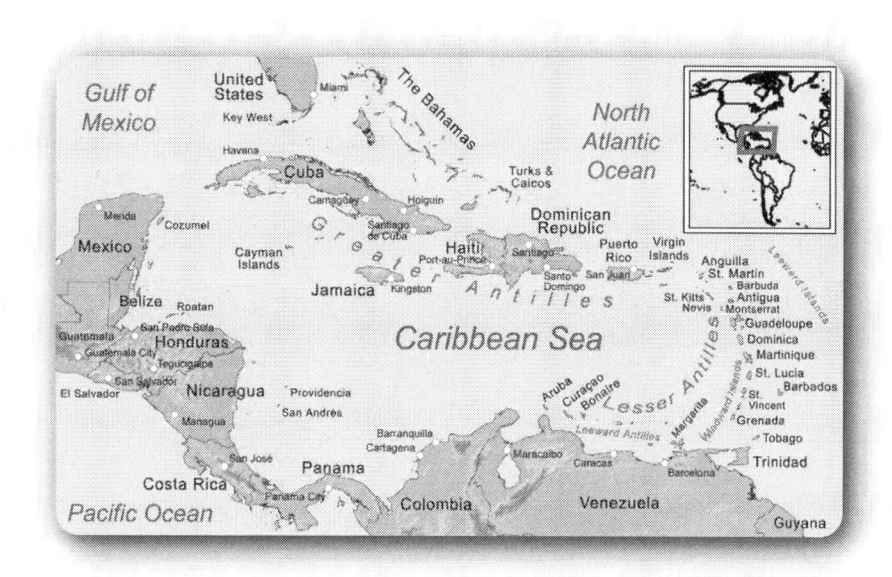

AN EXTREMELY RARE EXAMPLE OF
GEORGE BEATTIE'S HANDWRITING

You teach me now how cruel you've been …

cruel and false!
Why did you despise me?
Why did you betray your own heart, Cathy?
I have not one word of comfort.
You deserve this.
You have killed yourself.
Yes, you may kiss me, and cry; and wring out my kisses and tears:
they'll blight you …
they'll damn you.
You loved me …
then what right had you to leave me?
What right … answer me …
for the poor fancy you felt for Linton?
Because misery, and degradation, and death,
and nothing God or Satan could inflict
would have parted us!
You …
of your own will, did it.
*I have not broken your heart … **you** have broken it;*
and in breaking it … you have broken mine.

~ Heathcliff

Emily Brontë

Wuthering Heights

Original

Memoranda,

Statements & Letters

*As written personally
by George Beattie in 1823*

Statement Of Facts

In drawing up an account of the connection between Miss Gibson and myself, I shall confine myself to facts alone, without making comments or drawing inferences.
This most distressing task has been forced on me by occurrences of a late date, by which I have been much injured, and for which, I say it with sorrow, I have determined to seek redress.
I need not attempt to describe the anguish of mind which has compelled me to make the following disclosures.
   Some years ago an intimacy and friendship commenced betwixt Miss Gibson and myself, little known I believe except to ourselves. From what passed betwixt us, I conceived myself warranted in paying my addresses to Miss Gibson.
In this I may have been wrong, and it may here be necessary to admit this, as in a letter written by me to her, just to be mentioned, I invest, if I reflect right, that I had "unauthorisedly" formed an attachment.
This, at all events I stated from motives of delicacy.
This letter was written in August, 1821, and forwarded to Miss Gibson at Pitcaithly.*

---

* Pitcaithly, Perthshire (near the Bridge of Earn), was famous in Scotland for its five mineral springs. Hotels and tea rooms were built to accommodate the tourists coming there to take and to bathe in the waters.

I have no copy of it; the answer is so mislaid. In effect, my addresses were rejected; at the same time, I was strictly enjoined not to give over visiting at Stone of Morphie. I felt disappointed, but from the way in which Miss Gibson soon afterwards conducted herself towards me, I began to suspect that she was not serious in her refusal. I, however, studied not to intrude myself, and as I felt delicate in speaking on the subject, and knowing that her parents had been made

acquainted with my application, I wrote Mr Gibson asking his forgiveness, if I had done anything that was improper.
I continued visiting Stone of Morphie as I had formerly done.
Truth here compels me to state, that Miss Gibson now began to honour me with more attention than she had formerly done.
When in Town she seldom failed to allow me the pleasure of accompanying her so far on her way home; indeed, it would be more agreeable to truth to say, that she always told me, when she was to allow me that honour. (I need not premise that the purpose of stating these facts, is to show, that I never at any time paid my addresses to Miss Gibson, with the most distant view to the fortune, which she lately received, and to show that the engagements latterly entered into betwixt her and me, needed not to be matter of surprise.)

   Our intimacy continued increasing till the spring of 1822, when Mr Bell left Kinnaber.
Shortly after this period, the following note was brought me from Miss Gibson, by one of the servants at Stone of Morphie :-

If Mr Beattie feels inclined to extend his evening walk, A Friend will have pleasure in showing him some birds' nests in the garden of Kinnaber.* -

   Monday morning.

* It may be observed that at this time no person resided at Kinnaber, at least in the Mansion House.

   It need not be doubted that I willingly obeyed. I have some other Cards of similar import. I need not repeat my regrets for mentioning these matters, I am determined to tell the precise truth, as far as I do tell at all, it has been extorted from me by cruel injustice.
   Mr Gibson, shortly after this, unfortunately became indisposed.
I frequently visited him during his illness, and at these times Miss Gibson made appointments with me as to meeting at Kinnaber.
For a considerable part of the summer we met at least twice a week in the House of Kinnaber. I need not state that on these occasions promises were made, and vows of fidelity and attachment passed betwixt

us.

Upon the approach of autumn, and when we were interrupted by masons repairing the house, I continued again to visit Stone of Morphie.

Miss Gibson proposed at this time to visit at Cononsyth, and that her absence should not interrupt our correspondence, it was agreed that we should write to each other.
At this time I received the following letter from the Post-Office :-

Montrose, 30th August, 1822. -

Particular circumstances have occurred, which prevent my going to Cononsyth this week. I therefore will not trouble Mr Beattie to be my correspondent at present, but as I intend to make out my visit a few weeks hence, I still propose troubling him to write me. I hope Mr Beattie will pay us a visit at Stone of Morphie, within these few days, and he will very much oblige William Gibson. - Mr Gibson's spirits are affected by the damp weather; none can raise them so well as Mr Beattie; do come and see him.

I still continued visiting Stone of Morphie, our intimacy increased, and promises and vows were repeated over and over. Shortly after this I received the following letter by a servant :-

We have received accounts of the death of my brother, Williamson, he has fallen a sacrifice to the bad climate of Jamaica. As I am afraid his loss will affect my father's spirits, could you, my Dear Sir, make it convenient to call on us some evening soon. You may think it strange in me to ask you to come out at present,

but I trust in your good nature excusing it, and there is not another, out of my own family, that I could apply to so readily, and believe me,

your much obliged,

Stone of Morphie,

Tuesday.

Wm. Gibson

I never failed to give my good attendance, and from what passed between Miss Gibson and me, I conceived by this time, that nothing could prevent our union. Miss Gibson complained if I was absent, and her parents did not discountenance my frequent visits.

The next letter I received was through the Post-Office, addressed to Mr Smellie,* to my care.

* A name deliberately chosen by George Beattie at a happy time, reflecting his natural self-effacing wit, humility and absolute lack of ego.

This was a suggestion of my own, when I first wrote Miss Gibson, to prevent the letters being opened by any of my clerks. It is of the following tenor :-

Stone of Morphie,
Wednesday Morn.

My father is disappointed that you do not now spend an evening with him, and I am afraid that I am the cause of you being such a stranger here. I suppose you cannot be ignorant of the report the good folks of Montrose have raised, and that it has prevented your coming to Stone of Morphie, for fear my parents should adopt the Dougald system; but allow me to inform you that they have not, and may never hear that report; and they have too few
daughters to force them on any man, against his will. On my account they do not give young men a general invitation, for fear they should suppose they courted them; but those who do come are not the less welcome, and none more so than you.
I expected to have got words of you in Montrose that would have saved me writing, but I know you have too much honour to expose me.
Will you spend an evening here this week?
And if you will, let me know by putting a note in the Post-Office, addressed to me, before 2 o'clock to-day. I shall take care to be out or in the way as you choose, for I begin to think you wish to shun me, and believe me always, you much obliged,

William Gibson.

When I received this note, I had not been a week from Stone of Morphie, and I went there immediately on receipt, and found an opportunity of

telling Miss Gibson how very far she was mistaken as to the cause assigned by her, for my short absence, and left her
convinced that although I might unavoidably be absent for some time, she needed never impute this to the cause assigned in her letter.
My visits were still continued, and both parties were satisfied that a union was to take place. The storm prevented my visiting for a short time, I was also in a bad state of health, and had fallen back with business in consequence of having been for a considerable time at Aberdeen, and twice at Edinburgh.
I attended at Stone of Morphie, however, always when I could possibly get away, and our intimacy continued and increased.

   Miss Gibson now received accounts of the death of her uncle, William Mitchell, Esquire, of Grenada, and that she and her mother had been left considerable sums by his Will, and that Miss Gibson was his Residuary Legatee.
After this I visited as formerly, and, from the opinion I had formed of Miss Gibson, I apprehended at first no alteration in her affections or behaviour toward me.
In this I was not mistaken, I found her the same way as formerly.

   On Sunday the 4th of May I called at Stone of Morphie, as I before had intimated to Mr Gibson by letter, and found Miss Gibson at home.
Old matters were talked over, and all our pledges and vows renewed. Miss Gibson declared that the fortune she had become possessed of could not alter her affections, but, on the contrary, make them more lasting.
On my asking, as formerly, Miss Gibson declared herself willing to become my bride. As I had done before, I asked Miss Gibson if she held the consent of her parents to be a condition. She most unequivocally declared the contrary, and the compact was solemnly sealed betwixt us.
It may here be necessary to state (as Miss Gibson attempts to give it another meaning in her letter) that Miss Gibson said,

" I mean to say yes, but will you allow me a little time."

I said,

"Certainly, as much as you choose, it is nothing new, you have thought of it before, and something may intervene."

She replied,

"Nothing can possibly intervene, I wish no time, I am yours forever."

Miss Gibson then mentioned where she meant to reside, which house she wished purchased or taken, &c., and asked how far my means would go in such a purpose, mentioning that she would have cash of her own very soon.
I, with the utmost candour, gave a state of my finances. A condition was even made as to my going to church. It may be necessary here to remark, in relation to what is afterwards stated by Miss Gibson, as to her being allowed a few hours consideration, that our last engagement took place betwixt eleven and twelve, and that I did not leave Stone of Morphie till about nine at night.*

* From the manner I had all along been treated by them, I had not the least reason to expect opposition from them, and Miss Gibson assured me I had nothing to fear there.

My happy moments, however, were now broken in upon and interrupted. Upon the Monday following, Miss Gibson received accounts, from one of her uncle's executors, of the extent of the fortune she would succeed to in this country, as Residuary Legatee of her uncle, and that the extent of the property in India could not be ascertained until the executors there wrote.

~ I commenced by stating facts without comment, and I shall continue that course. ~

On Tuesday at twelve o'clock, Miss Gibson (who had now become very particular as to the hour) wrote me the following letter* :-

* This letter, as will afterwards appear, did not reach me till Thursday.

Can you, will you, forgive me, if I ask you to give me back that promise which I gave you on Sunday.†

† Miss Gibson displays considerable address here, in referring to "one" and her "last" promise, supposing that if it were given back, the others previously given would follow, and by this time she wished to make lightly of the matter. We were as much engaged "before" as after the Sunday engagement here referred to.

I then asked for a few hours consideration, had you given me that, it would have saved me this to-day.
I then boldly declared, that my mother's consent was of small consequence, but that is not the case, and she will never, I fear, consent; but you know I never mentioned your last letters, and I hope this correspondence may be kept as quiet.
That this will give you pain, I do not doubt, but better give it now than afterwards; and believe me, you have little to regret in the want of a nearer connection with me, unless my money, and this is not one tenth part of what they call it at Montrose.‡

‡ This is pretty knowing, she had "by this time" learned, that it was much more than she or others expected.

That no one can like me better than you do, I do not doubt, yet surely in that case you might have come oftener and seen me this Spring, particularly when I heard of your being at Kirkside; but it is needless for me to say more. I shall only add, that there breathes not a man in Europe I at present prefer to you; but I still consider that we may be better apart. That you will always possess my best wishes, be assured, and I hope God will grant you every happiness.
Do not absent yourself from this house, my father has little need to be deprived of his friends. Do answer this, and address it to Miss Sarah Bronker.*

* The name of Mr Mitchell's black housekeeper in the West Indies.

Post-Office, Montrose, and a servant will call for it on Thursday. If you grant my request, enclose this billet in it.

Thursday, 12 o'clock noon.

This letter was addressed to *J. Smellie*, to my care, and was received by me on Thursday, the 8th May, at 11 o'clock.

Far from expecting such a letter, indeed it was impossible to anticipate any thing of the kind, after all that had passed, I could scarcely therefore credit my senses, next I thought it must be a jeu d'esprit to vex me.

I was fortified in this idea, from the fanciful name by which Miss Gibson wished to be addressed.

Again it struck me, if Miss Gibson wished to communicate any thing so serious, that she would have sought my attendance at Stone of Morphie, as she had often done before. From the best judgement I could form, however, after consideration, I thought she would not jest on such a subject. The answer which I wrote the moment I could get leisure, will best show my conviction at the time, and the state of my feelings. Miss Gibson says I wrote her harshly.

I am sorry I should have done so to any lady, and more particularly that I should have had occasion to do so to her; but I could not command my feelings at the time; I had no leisure for reflection, and
even if it had been otherwise, I was incapable of reflection.
This is a copy of the letter :-

Montrose, 8th May, 1823

Madam,

I only this forenoon received your letter, which is dated on Tuesday. The reason of the delay I know not. Some very urgent business, and the utter confusion of my mind, prevented my answering it in time for being received from the Post-Office to-day. Still, I must send an answer, and I hope it will come safe. You know little of my feelings when you say simply, that you letter will give me "pain." I could not express what I felt on reading it, no language "could" describe my sensations.

Oppressed as I am, I hope you will forgive me, even if I should write incoherently. I did not think Miss Gibson could have asked any thing that I would not have granted, if in my power; but I have been fatally mistaken. I would much sooner part with my existence than give you back the promise you mention, come what will.

About two years ago I paid my addresses to you, these were rejected. Still, you gave me liberty to visit Stone of Morphie.

I became resigned to my fate and contented; and, although some might not have considered their case hopeless, I would not, for the world, have presumed again to intrude myself on you.

This, you, I never did, you yourself began to raise my hopes, you yourself made appointments, and, in fact, commanded my attendance when you thought proper.
As far as I know myself, I am not presumptuous, nor, in most cases, sanguine; but could I receive letters from Miss Gibson to meet her solitarily at the garden and house of Kinnaber, without indulging hopes.
These letters I have this day looked over with a sorrowful heart.
You know you allowed me many other meetings which you yourself appointed verbally.
God knows, I have no inclination to mention any of these things, and do so in justice to myself, to show what I might reasonably suppose after all this. You spoke freely of the report of our union, rather with pleasure than disapprobation, it is mentioned in one of your letters. I would have thought
it wrong to meet you by ourselves in the House of Kinnaber, unless I had implicitly believed that a union betwixt us was to follow.
What passed betwixt us on these on these and other occasions justified this.
I leave it to yourself if you did not put questions which were answered by me, in a way where neither question nor answer could possibly admit of any other interpretation.
I am sure you cannot forget what passed that day I called at Stone of Morphie, in going to the Mills. I will say no more here on the subject.
I looked upon the promise on Sunday as a continuation and confirmation of former pledges. It was voluntary, solemn, and decisive; and you pointed out the house you wished to be purchased or taken as a residence, &c. &c.; the
jaunt the same as had been different times before mentioned by yourself.
You wrong me cruelly in speaking of your money, it never was at any time in my calculation. I freely admit I was afraid your good fortune might bring you new suitors, and I was on that account alone anxious for a renewal of our pledges; and I am certain you believed what I stated to you, that your good fortune had been to me a source of uneasiness and even of regret.
This certainly was not doing you justice, but it was a feeling of my own that I could not control.
I explained to you what prevented my seeing you for some time in Spring, a long absence at Edinburgh had thrown me far back with business, and when I was sent for to Kirkside, I was obliged to go and return with all the speed
in my power.
I am sorry you should now attempt to make this any excuse for breaking faith.
I was after this received by you with as much kindness as before; and at no time, I can honestly assert, did my affection suffer the least diminution. I need not speak of the many repeated and nameless endearments that passed betwixt us, they are all forgotten by you, money has obliterated all.
I leave it to your honour and conscience, if, for at least a year past, either

you or I could have had any idea than that a union was to take place. Sorry would I have been to have sought or taken a rash vow from you, because you had come to a fortune (which I cared nothing about), and I was the last person in the world, that would have made such an attempt, particularly with one of your acuteness and discernment.

How I am to bear this sudden and unexpected, and to me, overwhelming calamity, God only knows, but I scorn to complain.

I know I need not now do so to you; you know what has brought about this, I shall not attempt to scan your motives.

As to the keeping secret my first letter, I now care no more about it than I do for any thing in this world.

Although particulars may not be known, it will be impossible to hinder the public from giving their decision, without the least aid from me; the matter has not slept there.

It cannot, at least it should not, affront me with the world, that I have been spurned by you in consequence of your having received what is called a fortune, the extent of which never entered my mind, as you seem to surmise
in your letter.

On a review of my whole conduct and actions, as connected with you, I have nothing to blame myself with; and I have no doubt it will be conducive to your own happiness, if you can lay your hand on your heart, and say the same.

I have given you my ideas sadly out of order. You told me your good fortune would not in the least alter your affections.

What you state as to your mother's consent is ambiguous, as connected with what you said on that head on Sunday, and previously; and also with the contents of one of your letters, where you say I need not fear your parents will adopt the Dougald system, as they have too few daughters to force them on any man, against his will.

I was at all times aware that you were capable of acting for yourself. I mean, to act honestly and fairly to the last.

I cannot give you back your vow, or rather I should say vows. I cannot give you back your letters, justice, honour, truth, forbid it; the use of these letters must now be regulated by circumstances.

I will renounce no claim, but maintain and defend them to the last.

There is something so peculiar in this business, that I fear I cannot refrain taking steps to justify myself, to your parents and the world. It grieves me to the heart to write in this style, but I cannot help it. Unfit as I am for the task, I must take a copy of this before despatching it.

Wishing you much more happiness than you have left me in possession of, and improvement in your health,

I have still more to say, but cannot now proceed farther.

Geo. Beattie.

To this letter Miss Gibson sent in course the following answer :-

Stone of Morphie, 9th May, 1823.

I own the justice and truth of all you have written, and now ask you forgiveness. I had not any idea of the pain my letter had given you, but on that head we are now "quits." May God forgive you for the harshness of
yours; but I would require to take care what I write, as you are a man of law, and therefore not fairly a match; however, I hope you will answer me by the servant, and tell me whether you will or can forgive me, and believe me I shall endeavour not to hurt your feelings again.
I allowed it was unguarded, and highly unfeeling, and I am very sorry to
say, that I have no excuse for myself.
I have only one thing more to add; if you still wish me to become your bride, I beg that, previous to quitting my father's house, all the letters that have
passed betwixt us, may be destroyed. I beg you will write by the bearer, and you may address it to my father, who is from home, and as I know your hand and I shall open.

William Gibson.

This letter was enclosed in another from Miss Gibson, of the following tenor :-

The enclosed was written on Friday, and I sent it into town with orders that it should only be delivered into your hands.
You were from home; I shall now address it the same as formerly, and put it in the Post-Office, and I request that you will answer it, and tell me what you intend with regard to myself. "The former request shall never again be made," and it would be a relief, if I thought you would forgive me, and "forget it." Address to Mrs Sarah Bronker, and I will endeavour to make someone call at the Post-Office on Monday for it.

W. Gibson.

Stone of Morphie, Saturday evening.

Received Monday, 12th May 1823.

This letter I received on the forenoon of Monday, 12th May, and in case the servant should call at the Post-Office and be disappointed, I immediately wrote, and carried the following answer to the Post-Office :-

Montrose, 12th May 1823.

My Dear Miss Gibson, I have this moment received your letter. I am too happy not to forget and forgive what is past.
The trial as severe. You are an Angel still. God Almighty bless you. My already enervated frame tells me I could not live without you; you must therefore be my bride. I can prove beyond what I have stated, my continued ardent and honourable attachment for years. Make of your fortune what
you please, personally I neither wish control over, nor the smallest benefit from it in any shape, and it will be the happiest moment of my existence when I can formally renounce it. I only want Miss Gibson, and she knows I could have begged my bread with her. My anxiety for the delivery of the last,
induced me to put a note in the Post-Office, addressed to you. The meaning of it will be known to none but yourself.
Adieu, &c. I am yours for ever.

Geo. Beattie.

I should conceive this is a most solemn engagement, confirming former ones, and the lady herself only can account for her conduct after this, in immediately after shunning me, and setting out about a jaunt, without even mentioning the circumstance to me, or conferring on me the honour of *"being her correspondent."*
  The foregoing statement consists merely of facts, supported by documents, the preservation of which depended upon chance; for, till within the period of *"one little month,"* Miss Gibson's simple word would have been held amply sufficient by me in any case.
The observations which might be made upon, and the moral which might be drawn from these facts, accompanied with some additional ones, would fill a large and not uninteresting volume. This may be an after task, if my

mind ever resumes its wonted serenity.

Miss Gibson has said in one of her letters, that I have too much honour to expose her, in this she is correct.

Nothing but the most cruel treatment could have wrung this information from me, to be communicated even to her nearest connections. But has she kept her honour with me. I leave her to answer the question herself. Whatever I may feel, I feel much more than I can express; I am determined to seek whatever redress may be within my reach, and this I will do fearlessly but justly. I can say without vanity, that for at least a year past, and up to the moment of Miss Gibson's receiving the last mentioned letter from her uncle's trustee, the attachment was as strong on her part as mine, and that previous to the last period, I could not have withdrawn, with honour to myself or with her consent.*

* This ends the Statement sent to Mr Gibson.
It did not contain the notes.

Supplement To Statement Of Facts

The narrative of the "Statement of Facts" concludes with my answer to Miss Gibson's two letters, when a complete reconciliation had taken place. This statement having reference only, as there stated, to facts supported by writing.
Nothing further is stated in it, and it was not deemed necessary to state more, as I conceived that renewed engagement to be very ample and conclusive.

Soon after this, I saw Miss Gibson, who owned having received my letter, and all that had occurred of a disagreeable nature was completely buried in oblivion. Miss Gibson said she made the request merely to try me, and laughed at the idea of my having taken up the matter seriously. She also said she wanted a document from me, on the subject of our engagement; and that my two last letters were quite sufficient, and bound me very completely. She then voluntarily took a most solemn oath that she would punctually and faithfully fulfil her engagements with me, and never think of retracting while she drew breath.
Miss Gibson then said she wished to reside a short time at the House of Kinnaber, which she had newly come to, and that as soon as arrangements could afterwards be made, our union would take place.
I was happy once more, and had been so since receiving her last letters. I could not have believed that Miss Gibson could be so unjust and unfeeling as to enter into so many engagements, verbal and written, and afterwards to break them. I could not have believed, after what had passed on very many occasions betwixt her and me, that she could have been so deliberately cruel, as again and again to raise my hopes, for the purpose of blasting them, or of amusing herself by wantonly sporting with my feelings. This conduct was the more extraordinary and unaccountable, when it is known that she had been
solemnly engaged with me for more than a year previously, and which engagement had been often and often repeated in many

different ways during that period. I now, however, saw for the first time, that attention of others, at least another, had become more agreeable to her than mine; and that she now actually shunned me, the very reverse of what had happened previous to that time, circumstances so obvious, that they were noticed by the public, and were the subject of general conversation. Although she had not, at least for a year previously, moved the smallest distance from home without acquainting me, she now set off to Edinburgh, without giving me the least intimation of her intention. She, in a subsequent letter, says, she took this jaunt for the benefit of her health.

That was certainly was not a good reason for concealing the circumstance from me; I was more interested in the state of her health than any other person, herself excepted.

Unless it were possible to place themselves in my situation, no one could have any idea of the state of my mind and feelings at this time, they admit not of description.

It was at this period that I wrote out the *"Statement of Facts,"* and forwarded it to Mr Gibson at Edinburgh.

If anything may have been wrong in this, considering all, I ought to be held excusable.

After the way in which Miss Gibson had latterly conducted herself towards me, it could have served no end to address her on the subject. Feeling as I did, I certainly resolved at the moment, to seek whatever redress might be within my reach, and I thought it no more than candid to inform Mr Gibson, so as he might have no reason afterwards to say I did wrong in concealing the matter from him. I therefore forwarded the statement to him, while at Edinburgh with Mrs and Miss Gibson. The packet was delivered into his own hand, by a gentleman to whom I sent it for that purpose, and the following letter from me to Mr Gibson was enclosed :-

Montrose, 4th June, 1823.

Dear Sir, it is with sorrow I feel myself constrained to lay the enclosed Statement of Facts before you. There has already been so much writing upon the subject, that little need be said here. The enclosed explains itself. As matters now stand, it would have been un-candid not to have put you in possession of these facts, with as little delay as possible. As yet no person, but Miss Gibson, knows anything of the circumstances. This, however, cannot be the case long. That it will be distressing to Miss Gibson and her relatives, there can be no doubt. It is impossible, however, they can suffer the one hundredth part of what I have and am suffering. When you have perused the enclosed, it will be obliging if you will take the trouble of enclosing it, and in case of the parcel being opened by any person in the office, you may direct it in a fictitious name, to my care.
In case I have done anything wrong or strange, it must be imputed to my sufferings. I hope you are enjoying your jaunt, and with best wishes,
 I am, Dear Sir, yours, &c.

Geo. Beattie.

After Mr Gibson's arrival from Edinburgh, I met him at a party at Mr Neill's of Borrowfield, when he wrote in pencil, on a leaf of his pocket-book, which he handed me :

"I received your letter and Statement; William took away the Statement after she found it correct, she has kept it."

I received the following letter from Miss Gibson, after her arrival at Kinnaber :-

Your letter and Memorial my father received some days since. You have certainly proved what I never denied.
I only asked you to release me from that engagement, but I find my fortune has too many charms for you, and you are determined to prosecute me or have it. I certainly will submit to anything, rather than appear in a court of law, even to "misery" and "contempt"; therefore I have no alternative, but recollect that at present I will not leave this house.
My parents allow me to decide so far for myself. You reproach me for going to Edinburgh, on a pleasure jaunt, without informing you of it. I went for
advice concerning my health, and as I am ordered frequent sea excursions, I beg leave to inform you, that I may be off in a few days again, and that one information may

serve for all.

I am also ordered to go to Pitcaithly in a short time. I also understand when you were here, that you gave me up, and I am certain you said you would "vindicate me." Have you done so?

But at all events you have not acted towards me with much feeling. You might at least have written me before you wrote my father; but he does not interfere. You will please inform me (if I do not ask "too" great a favour), what are your determinations, and put it in the Post-Office, that I may receive it on Thursday morning, and you will oblige.

W. Gibson.

Kinnaber, 9th June, 1823.

This letter is addressed "Mr Smellie, to my care."
I must certainly have been much overcome and confused, when I sent the following strange answer :-

Montrose, 11th June, 1823.

Dear Madam, I am this day favoured with your letter of the 9th inst., I will not trouble you about my feelings. I wrote the Memorial in despair. I could do nothing else. It was sent off in a moment. I need not say whether I have repented it. I am so overwhelmed with misery, that I attempt to fall upon expedients with a view to temporary relief, and in the next instant all appears like a dream. You still speak of your fortune. I can not say more upon that head than I have already said.

So far from its having too many charms for me, I would more willingly die that you might be relieved of me; but this is an event over which I have no control, although I have suffered as much in mind, as would have broken in pieces any frame possessed of less physical health. You accuse me of selfishness.

I need not make asseverations which you may now think matters of course, but if you knew my thoughts, I am sure I would stand acquitted on that score.

My pleasures, when I had any, were of the simple kind, and could all be gratified without a fortune.

If you are not "totally" changed, I might safely refer to yourself, if you seriously think that any one in existence cares so much for yourself, and so little for your fortune, as I do. I hope at all events you will change your new opinion as to the sordidness of my disposition. If you think dispassionately on this subject, and certainly I have no right to offer better advice than I can take to myself, you would find that it is the receipt of your fortune that makes you despise me, and not the fortune that has charms for me. I know, if you choose, you can take a just view of that or any other matter.

I could mention some that would now worship you, that were very ready previously, to joke me, not in the most delicate manner, upon the report of our connection. However, this is nothing. So far from being selfish, if I could believe that I could ever enjoy a moments peace in this world, I would grant your request.

No doubt, I have little, very little, as it is, but I can not agree to extinguish hope altogether.

I know what would ensue; and I can not perhaps, prevent this, do what I will. I am different from almost any other person, that could be placed in the same situation. My affections have been so totally exclusive that I never could care for another under any circumstances. I may say, I have never thought about any other than yourself for years, whether you were absent or present; and whatever I may have written in distress, I find that it is entirely beyond my power to root out, or even in the smallest degree to abate, my affections, even though I should be despised and spurned by the object of them.

This, in the meantime, is my most pitiable case. What can I do? You bid me state my determination, at the same time you tell me your own, which, in a manner, leaves me a nonentity.

I am ready to do whatever you wish. You could not mention or think of that thing I will not do, if you only hint at it; all but just give up my interest in yourself, in mercy do not ask it in the present state of my mind.

Ask me to go to the uttermost ends of the earth, or not to see you, or anything else, and I will obey you in all but that.

I can not do business, I can not look on a book, or sleep; and what is more distressing than all, I am obliged, as far as I am able, to act my former self,

to save appearances; but this can not be done.

If Colonel Straton were away, I must retire. This can not continue long. As I have borne so much, I can bear your classing me with misery and contempt. I believe you are right after all. I never had a high opinion of myself, and I can assure you it is now low enough. If you had a year ago entertained the same opinion of me, which you have so recently adopted, I would have been comparatively happy at the present moment. I ask your forgiveness for whatever I have done amiss. You will grant I have some excuse for not acting in all respects as I ought.

I do not do wrong intentionally, I am suffering for all. It is strange that I have been plunged all at once into such a sea of misery. I stand much more in need of pity than reproach. I intended to have been at Mr Neill's on Saturday, perhaps you are to be there, and our meeting might be disagreeable. I wish you to drop a single line on the subject; I can safely send word that I am indisposed. If you want any thing stated

more explicitly, I shall be happy to do it. Your letter is certainly very acrimonious. You, however, shall hear no more reproaches from me.
I am sorry I can not consent to break our engagement.

Wishing you every improvement in your health, I am, &c., &c.

   Geo. Beattie.

  In the answer just quoted, I had by some means neglected to take notice of that part of Miss Gibson's letter, which states: *"I also understood when you were last here, you gave me up, and I am certain you said you would vindicate me."* These, like the assertions in the same letter, that I must have her fortune or prosecute her, that she would submit even to misery and contempt, &c., are all meant as direct insults.
Miss Gibson presumes that by this means she can not fail to force me to give her up in disgust.
Whatever may now be my feelings on the subject, still the treatment I have latterly experienced is such, that I can not help thinking of retribution. I can speak with the utmost certainty, that Miss Gibson could not, on the occasion mentioned, or any other, have understood that I gave her up.
She must have understood, and did understand, the very reverse, she did not wish to be given up at that time.
I particularly recollect what took place on the occasion alluded to, and Miss Gibson can not deny the truth of it.
After some conversation had taken place between Miss Gibson and me, she asked me how I was looking so ill.
I made no immediate answer, and I confess I was a good deal affected, as she looked very poorly herself.
Miss Gibson then burst into tears, and said she could never forgive herself for having latterly acted towards me as she had done. I did everything in my power to soothe her, I mentioned that all this happily was now over, and added, *"I will vindicate you, Miss Gibson, but I can not vindicate myself, my conscience does not vindicate me, I must ever blame myself for making you suffer so much and so unjustly,"* or words to this very effect.
We were both much affected, and fearing that Mrs Gibson, or some other

person, might enter the room, and find us in this situation, we took leave, and Miss Gibson asked me to come back as soon as possible, and said we would both be in high spirits at next meeting. This is the last time I called. In two or three days after this, Miss Gibson set off to Edinburgh, accompanied by both her parents.

She did not mention the circumstance to me, although she must have known it was to take place, at that time.

I had forgiven what was past, and on that head only was I to vindicate Miss Gibson; but I never meant to vindicate any after conduct, unbecoming one in her situation.

Whether her tears proceeded from sorrow for what had happened, or remorse for what was to happen, may now be problematical, after what has taken place, but I could only think of the former, and it may be supposed I would not vindicate the commission of further wrongs against myself; nor could I have any idea that such would be committed after all that had taken place.

Miss Gibson returned the following answer to my last letter :-

Kinnaber, 14th June, 1823.

I have this moment received yours of the 11th inst., and it is now unnecessary to inform you that I was not invited to Borrowfield to-day. The person who took the letter from the Post-Office had not an opportunity of delivering it to me till this morning. I know there are people in Montrose who think more of me than they once did, I am well aware; but were I "free" as air, the person you allude to, could never be more to me than a common acquaintance.

If my letter was acrimonious, recollect that you addressed a Memorial to my father, which you must be aware, was very irritating; but I beg you will make no more complaints to him of me; his health is too feeble to permit of his being agitated, without seriously injuring him. Therefore what you have in future to say, address to myself.

I think I before informed you, that I am ordered frequent change of air, and sea excursions. I am, on that account, going in a few weeks to Edinburgh, and from thence join my father at Pitcaithly. I trust when I do go, you will not think of sending such threatening letters after me. You offer to grant me any request "save" one.

Will you return me all the letters I have ever written you? If you do so, put them in the Post-Office, that I may get them on Monday morning, and you will oblige,

W. Gibson.

I never meant to class you with misery and contempt, far from it, it was your packet (which my father gave me to read before it was destroyed) that made me "miserable," and in it you mentioned me with contempt, at least I thought so; but I again beg you will not tease my parents with such things, for they will not interfere on your side.

To this letter the following answer was sent :-

Montrose, 21st June, 1823.

Dear Madam, I only received yours of the 14th "yesterday" forenoon. I cannot account for the extraordinary delay.
Not at first adverting to the date of your letter, as I could not suppose it to be so far back, I though you only wanted an answer on Monday first. I now find, however, that it was to be called for on Monday last, it will be nearly a week behind.
The letter was a good deal soiled. Being put in the Post-Office on Saturday, it would not, at any rate, have been delivered till Monday, as I seldom call for letters on Sunday, and they do not deliver them that day; but I cannot account for the subsequent delay. The request you now make is so closely connected with what I made the exception, that I consider they are one in the same; and will you tell me honestly what you meant should follow the delivery of your letters.
Had I really been disposed to grant your request, it is a task I could not perform; the enclosing these letters would to me be like shutting the very tomb upon yourself. I shall now, however, if possible, write sober sense, without moralising or troubling you with my own feelings, which to you, I doubt not, now appear troublesome and impertinent. I am sure you did not expect that I would send these letters through the Post-Office, besides, you know I had previously declared that I would not part with these, and you promised never again to make the request. I am still ready to do, however, what I previously promised, you may rest assured that I will not trouble or interfere with your parents as you seem to apprehend. This I never intended.
If I did what was wrong in this respect, I have already stated the cause, and expressed my deep regrets.
You know that no one would feel more reluctant than I would, to irritate your father, or hurt his feelings in any respect.
You may also be assured it is not my wish to be troublesome to you; but you will

allow that a person may be treated in such a manner as to induce him to sacrifice everything to obtain whatever redress might be within his reach.

As you seem disconcerted about the Memorial, I am sorry it was sent; but after it fell into your own hands, I think you should not have destroyed it. You do not mention this in your first letter. I wished to be checked if anything was wrong stated.

It was my wish to draw up a correct Statement, while the circumstances were recent, to prevent any after misunderstanding.

I beg leave, however, to mention, that I have still an exact copy of this paper. I do not mention it as a threat, or that it should operate with you as such; nor do I wish to hurt your feelings, far from it; but as you have different times called on me to state my "intentions," with regard to yourself and my determinations, &c., I would be acting uncandidly if I did not state as distinctly as I possibly can, that as I intend neither to break my word or write, I will not permit the engagement on your part to be evaded,

without seeking every redress, by every means whatever in my power. This determination I know I will never alter, and it can be of no use at any time to say more on that subject. I have honestly told you my intentions, you certainly are not so plain.

I shall not, however, attempt to draw from you any explanation, which you do not wish to communicate yourself.

I made, perhaps improperly, allusion in my letter to "some" that would now pay more attention to you than formerly, you apply this to an individual. It would have been highly improper in me to have made so pointed an allusion, and I shall not allow myself even to guess at your application. It is a subject that I should not have interfered with, and I beg you will excuse me upon grounds already stated. I most sincerely wish that your health may be benefited by your sea excursions, and change of air, and I am satisfied you have been well advised in this. I would fain say something more, but I shall refrain.

I am most unwilling to trouble you with complaints, and would wish to suffer in silence. Notwithstanding every exertion, I get worse and worse. No effort of reason, or attempt to laugh away my miseries have the least effect.

My health is now suffering much. I shall seek no remedy. Will I never be allowed to look upon you again?

In case anything may happen, I shall seal up and lock past your letters, and leave written instructions as to the delivery to yourself, so that, in the mean time, you need not be anxious on that ground.

If I could reveal my misery to any person it might give me some relief.

I was but lately one of the happiest beings in existence, and I am sure I am now the most miserable.

I am, &c., &c.

Geo. Beattie.

This 'Supplement', and the 'Statement of Facts', contain chiefly an account of what can be supported by documents.

Any thing beyond this is of little consequence. It would be of no use to enter into a long history of all that has passed betwixt Miss Gibson and myself; the letters speak so far, and the rest may be imagined.

As we never wanted opportunities of meeting, it is a chance that there was any writing at all.

It may only be necessary further to state, that whatever may now be pretended, I am perfectly satisfied her parents were aware of the intimacy betwixt us, and they did not discourage, on the contrary, they urged my attendance at Stone of Morphie. Nothing prevented our union previously, but apprehensions as to the extent of our means for living in a married state. I told Miss Gibson I was saving all I could, and she very often spoke of her prospects from her uncle, which, she said, would make all right.

When the first accounts of the uncle's death arrived, I was entrusted with all the secrets.

Miss Gibson was entitled to £3,500 consols, certain. I presume she thought this sum would not put her beyond my reach. I was appointed to write for a copy of the Will, and nothing at this time was concealed from me by Miss Gibson or her parents. As already said, upon Sunday, the 4th May, we had renewed all our engagements.

On the next day, 5th May, the intelligence arrived of what Miss Gibson would be entitled to, as Residuary Legatee, beyond the specific bequest of £3,500 consols. It was resolved on, therefore, to discard me, to set all our engagements aside, and to give me no further information on the subject; upon the following day, the 6th May, Miss Gibson wrote me, wishing to be off from all engagements, without telling me of her good fortune, farther than stating that the people in Montrose called it ten times more than it was.

Her father had the civility to write me the following letter on the occasion :-

Stone of Morphie, 5th May, 1823.

Dear Sir, We have this day heard from Messrs Barclay & Davidson, with a copy of the Testament, and about the amount of the late Mr Mitchell's subject at London. It is not worse than we expected, but he can not say anything about the West India property, until he hears from the executors there, and, how soon he hears from them, is to advise William.

I am, Dear Sir, yours truly,

Robert Gibson.

(Addressed)

George Beattie, Esq., Writer, Montrose.

Additions To Supplement

In the *"Statement of Facts,"* where my letter to Miss Gibson, of 8th May, 1823, is quoted:

"I am sure you cannot forget what passed, upon that day I called at Stone of Morphie, on going to the Mills."

As the Statement was written out, and forwarded in the course of an afternoon; it was impossible to notice all circumstances, and, as already mentioned, it refers only to what was in writing. On this occasion, I found Miss Gibson by herself, and had been immediately left by Lieut Wemyss. She must recollect what passed betwixt us, and what was spoken about, while I remained. She complained that I had been jaunting without her. I mentioned, that it was not a pleasure, but business, and that the weather had been disagreeable. On my rising to go away, after having remained past Mr Jolly's dinner hour, Miss Gibson went betwixt me and the door, and said that we must repeat our vows.
I mentioned that there could be no necessity for this, but that I could have no objection.
She said that this was needless, as to our marriage, but that something behoved to be understood as to the time, or near about it. She then laid her hand in mine, and proposed repeating a solemn oath. I said that I could have no objection, but that it bound us whether her parents might be agreeable or not. She said, *"they are quite agreeable;"* I told them of our former engagement, and it was just what they expected.
I then said *"go on;"* and she made me repeat these words :

"May I never know peace in this world, or see God in mercy, if I marry another than you;
or, if I ever go south again without taking you along with me as my wife."

She took a similar oath herself, this, I am sure, Miss Gibson will not deny. To recapitulate all the different communings and engagements,

would be impossible. From some empty envelopes, addressed to me, it will be seen that I had other letters, which were destroyed. Others were destroyed, envelopes and all. It was by mere chance any were preserved. I shall proceed no further, but state that Mr George Neill called on me, upon the 29th July, wishing up Miss Gibson's letters, which I refused to give.
I here refer to :

No. I. Copy letter I wrote to him.
I also refer to
No. II. Copy letter sent to Miss Gibson, of the 11th August, evidently written in considerable mental distress,
And
No. III. Letter from Mr Gibson, of 13th August. These are all tied together. I sent no answer.

No. I. COPY LETTER, GEO. BEATTIE, TO GEO. NEILL, ESQ., BORROWFIELD.

Montrose, 29th July, 1823.

Dear Sir; After your calling to-day, wishing up Miss Gibson's letters, which I refused to give you, I became anxious, in case any misunderstanding might exist on the subject, although I expressed myself very plainly. I beg leave to mention, and if you think proper to communicate it to Miss Gibson, you may do so, that I have never done, nor intend to do any thing evasive of, or in violation of, the engagements betwixt her and me. I shall be extremely sorry if she either has conducted, or shall conduct herself unbecoming one in her situation. If she does so, I must state candidly and explicitly, that in justice to myself, and as due to my wounded feelings, I will, if I live, take steps for my own vindication; nothing can possibly deter me from doing so. This I have explicitly stated to herself, and to her father.
I can not say more, the matter is known to her parents, and if she, with their consent, may be inclined to violate her engagements with me, it will be known who are to blame, I am not.
No person can know the circumstances, nor the extent of the injury I have sustained but myself. I hope nothing can diminish the friendship subsisting betwixt you and me.

I am, Dear Sir, yours truly.

(Signed)   Geo. Beattie.

No. II. COPY LETTER, MR BEATTIE TO MISS GIBSON.

Montrose, Monday, 11th August, 1823.

Miss Gibson, it is humiliating for me to be under the necessity of addressing you. I beg you will hear me without reference to what is past; no person knows the state I am in, nor do I wish it should be known. On Friday last I executed a Settlement. From the nature of the greater part of my small property, and from the state of my mind and health at present, the Settlement, I am afraid, would only be good, on my living 60 days after its date. In the event of my dying before that time, David and my sister might be left unprovided for. I am now satisfied it is your intention to break the engagements betwixt us.
I can not prevail on myself to consent to this; but as I can not prevent your doing so, it would be conferring a very great favour on me, if you would delay marrying another, till after the lapse of that period. By the time it expires, I will be no more; and I now look most anxiously forward to a termination of my woes, may it be the commencement of your happiness.
In earnestly asking this favour, I do not mean to excite your pity, nor do I in consequence sanction any violation of these engagements; on the contrary, should I be granted strength to support existence, which I have no reason to anticipate, I would, as I have already said, seek every redress within my reach, for these violations. A single line, though unsigned, unaddressed, and without date, will be satisfactory, and if you wish it, I pledge myself to return it immediately. This must appear strange, and it is so; I can not help it. If I could make myself otherwise than I am, I would do it. I have struggled hard, but all is unavailing; I see my fate very clearly, and it can not be avoided. My whole endeavours shall be to reconcile myself to it. O! do not do anything to hasten it!
Not upon my own account, but on account of those who are dependent on me, and never have offended you; I never intended to do so, but I do not know myself. Will you yet offer my best respects to your parents.
I will never see any of you again, nor the garden, &c.; it is better I should not, it would only make me worse. These recollections are bitter.
Will you pray for me?

COPY LETTER TO MR GIBSON, ACCOMPANYING THE ABOVE.

Dear Sir; May I trouble you, for this once, to deliver the enclosed to Miss Gibson. To the best of my knowledge, there is nothing wrong in it: and she, I have no doubt, will communicate the contents to you, if you wish it.

No. III. COPY LETTER, MR GIBSON TO MR BEATTIE.

Kinnaber, 13th August, 1823.

Dear Sir; I have perused your letter to William. Its contents surprise me very much indeed. This world is made for disappointments and trials. I thought you one of those men, that any thing of the kind would have cried buff on, and am sure you have more good sense than let any disappointment ever be known to the world, far less to interfere with your happiness or peace of mind. There is as good fish in the sea as ever came out of it.
Do let us see you as before, and believe me yours truly,

    (Signed)   Robert Gibson.

The Last

A dreadful cloud has hung over me for some time past: I fear much I shall never again enjoy the sunshine of this world. This paper will be laid down beside the Statement of Facts, &c., respecting Miss Gibson. The letters from that are in John Walker's little black box. I beg that special care may be taken of these letters, and the different papers; they may perhaps be required as a justification of my conduct, if any such can be admitted, for I have suffered, and am suffering more than I can bear. I thought myself, and I have no doubt that most people will hold the same opinion, that I would almost have been the last man in the world, that would have allowed himself to be so oppressed and borne down, upon an occasion of this nature; and I dare say, I might have laughed at any other person, under similar circumstances. None can know, however, until they are placed in the same situation, and unless they were acquainted with all the circumstances, which none can be but the poor victim himself. God knows what may happen, I have no distinct views on the subject; my feelings have been lacerated in a dreadful degree. I shall blame no person, but I have been most cruelly and unjustly treated; and no person can know the extent of this treatment, but myself. I can scarcely command resolution to look back upon the connection and intimacy that subsisted between Miss Gibson and me, and which was, at all events, as much cherished by her as me; when I have, at the same time, to bring to my remembrance, that no sooner did she acquire an accession to her fortune, and know the extent of this than (forgetting, without regret or remorse, all our former pledges, vows, &c., &c.) she immediately wished to break her engagements with me, which she has actually done; and no sooner was this done, than she instantly admitted the addresses of, and entered into engagements with, another.
Could all the circumstances be revealed, no person could believe that such could have been the case. I could not tell my ideas on the subject; they could not be expressed. Much will now be said about me.
Fain would I have lived till overtaken by death, in the ordinary course of

nature; but I have wrestled with my fate, till I can wrestle no longer. I could have suffered any degree of bodily pain, penury, privations, or hardships of any description; but the agony of my mind, contrasted with my former happy condition, can not be borne, I must submit.

I hope every person will endeavour to think as charitably of me as possible. I will not, I need not attempt to justify my past life or conduct. I wish they had been much, very much better than they have been; yet, I may not, on the whole, have been very much worse than some others, who have made greater pretensions than ever I did.

What I most dreaded was my defects and deficiencies, as a practical Christian and a good man, terms of nearly the same import. Without taking any merit to myself, I may state that I have undergone a pretty strict self-examination for some time past. I have had ample time for this, during the night, when sleep has not visited me.

I have found myself lamentably deficient; all my comfort is, I never oppressed the poor or helpless, although I had the power, and had been urged to do so. I never did a deliberate act of cruelty to man or beast. Although I sometimes got into a very temporary passion, which I never failed afterwards to regret, I never deliberately did, or wished harm to any person. Although latterly accused, when I least expected it, I never was selfish, nor did I at any time acquire cash by improper means. Any means I was in possession of I had no pleasure in squandering, and I could not justly do so, while others were depending on me; and I can say, as a dying man, that the accusation brought against me by Miss Gibson, of wishing to possess myself of her fortune, is as cruel as it is unjust and unmerited. Although her fortune had been laid before me, I would not have touched a halfpenny of it, and it would now be of no use to me.

If she really believes the accusation herself, what must she think of the individual preferred to me, who only could have paid his addresses to her, after she came in possession of it, and who never would have done so but for it.

As a dying man I may pledge myself for the truth of this. I am however, digressing, and my time is limited.

I have only to say then, that although I found myself deficient in almost every respect, and although I die the death of a wretched suicide, yet, trusting in the unbounded goodness and mercy of God, I am confident I will be happy.

I hope all my friends and acquaintances will vindicate me, as far as they can do so with justice.

I meant to have mentioned some of them by name; I have not time, however, and perhaps in the agitation of my mind, I might forget some of the best of them. May every happiness attend them through life, and may they never suffer themselves to be induced, as I have been, to place their whole happiness on one object.

I meant to have written a separate letter to my parents; this, however, I can not do. I can only think of them, with that dreadful degree of agony, that the perspiration falls in drops from the tips of my fingers on the paper. I die as I lived, their loving, dutiful and affectionate son. It gives me some consolation, at this awful juncture, to think that I have not been a bad son, or a bad brother; my parents, and David and Catherine, can speak as to this.

They are all good themselves. I feel for poor David, he must work away with the business. I hope some will employ him for my sake, and many for his own. A better young man, a more honourable, or a more punctual, does not exist.

He is well calculated, in every respect, for business; much better than ever I was myself. I hope the brethren of the profession will be kind to him.

Catherine, I know, will feel dreadfully. All this redoubles my agony, and urges me to a speedy oblivion of my woes.

We will all meet in a better world.

I have one consolation, they will not be left destitute here.

I have endeavoured, by every possible means, to conceal the dreadful state in which I have been for some time, it certainly must have been noticed. I have not slept many hours in the course of two months.

I am a complete wreck and a ruin, totally unfit to do business. I have been different in every respect from what I previously was. Instead of reading my book, as I was wont, I have sought company and even dissipation; I do not mean, that I have betaken myself to drinking, but, I have left company with regret, knowing that I had not the power, as formerly, of

retiring into myself with comfort and placidity.
Time, which flew over me with rapidity before, now lags, and wears me out of patience. I have not been the same man at all. I know myself, and I know that time, instead of giving me relief, will only increase my woes, and what impels me to fly from them just now, is the fear of absolute and total insanity. I would then be deprived of the power of extricating myself from that deplorable state of existence.
Now, when about to leave this world, I can say with truth, that before I was visited with this calamity, few enjoyed it so much, because I could delight in my earliest recreations. I had always a delight in the enjoyment of simple pleasures; the seeking of birds' nests in their season, playing games with children, &c.; but I have latterly had not even an idea of pleasure of any description. In this fatal connection, I have been true to honesty and virtue, but blind to prudence.
Still I can not blame myself. We often talked of the difference of our dispositions, &c., and Miss Gibson was so fully satisfied of our future happiness, I became of the same opinion, and she forged the chains which she afterwards broke, and along with them, my heart. The injuries I sustain are manifold, the loss of the object of my affections, after she had repeatedly owned, and given me unequivocal proofs of her attachment, the pangs which must wring one in my situation, to think that one in whom I had placed the utmost confidence, and whom I believed to be incapable of caprice or deceit, could be capable of such conduct, the affront to myself, and disgrace with the world, the humiliating idea that another should be preferred, after so long an attachment, and after solemn engagements had taken place betwixt us, and the scorn that must be borne, from one who piques himself in having cut me out, &c., &c., &c. Here I might go on for hours, but I have said enough. Who could even bear what has been stated?, and I have a thousand other feelings, many of them that I could communicate, and many of them that I could not.
After an interval of suffering, I have again taken up my pen. I find no improvement in the state of my mind. On the contrary, the more I think of the matter, I feel the more astonished an oppressed.

 The great mistake was, my allowing myself to get on an intimate footing with one who was great, or considered herself so. Miss Gibson knows what often passed betwixt us on this head; how she satisfied my scruples, and urged me on. She seemed to have convinced herself, and convinced me, that in reality our dispositions were quite congenial. I should have been like the *"Mynstrell of Dun,"* who prayed the great Lady to be allowed :

*" To hirple his waas to the cot-house doore,
And cheer with his layes ye sempelle and poore."*

The poor old man's fate somewhat resembles my own. I should therefore wish that piece preserved, particularly as it was originally written, when I was a mere boy, and before I had almost read any poetry, and lay past for years, before it was published, or supposed to be worthy of being so. I must, however, say, that till the moment Miss Gibson wished to break her engagements, and for years previous, she in all cases conducted herself, towards me, with more than ordinary affability and condescension. I can not now express myself, as I would wish, but I hope it will be distinctly understood, that it is not the breaking of written or verbal promises or oaths that troubles or astonishes me, these are no doubt the only palpable evidence that can be brought of a connection of this nature; but it is the breaking of the impalpable and continued chain of endearments that passed betwixt us for a long period, the long and uninterrupted course of interchanged affection, expressed in a thousand different modes, the meaning of which was so well known to both; it is the breaking of these that utterly confounds me. It is to me altogether unaccountable, and displays such a dreadful breach of faith and want of principle, that it shakes my resolution, and overpowers my reason to attempt to scan the motives that could have led to all this. I allow, that in many cases a female may change her mind, and, in an ordinary case, I would be ready to excuse this. I am very ready to mistrust myself, and had I not met with the strongest encouragement, I would not have continued my attentions. But the most extraordinary circumstance, after having been so long encouraged, and when so many promises had passed betwixt us, was the wish to set the whole aside, the moment the extent of Miss Gibson's fortune was known, and the instantly substituting in my place another, who had not paid the least attention to her, till she came

into possession of that fortune.
During all my visits, and they were many, I never saw that gentleman unless when a party was invited.
Miss Gibson wishes to make it one excuse for drawing back, that I had not visited often enough in the spring. That circumstance has already been explained, and I am sure that gentleman never was there in my absence during the spring.

If I could have acted agreeably to philosophy and reason, I would have shaken off this nonsense, and despised any daughter of Eve that could have acted in such a manner. I know it will be said that in not being able to do so, I have displayed a great want of spirit and pride, &c., &c.; that it was contemptible to allow myself to be troubled and depressed on such a subject, &c. I am fully aware of all this myself, and although I have been enabled at times to soar above my wrongs, still they have returned upon me with increased force, and latterly I have been totally unhinged.
The treatment I have received appears so extraordinary, that the very thoughts put me in a state of mind, that I neither can account for nor control.*

* That plots were laid by others to oust me and secure Miss Gibson's fortune, I know well from the inquiries that were made at myself from a certain quarter. Those who interfered were far too many for me.

Even if it might have been allowable for Miss Gibson to have transferred her affections to another, notwithstanding of our
engagements, &c., and after all that had taken place, it might have been supposed that, from feeling and female delicacy, she would not have immediately rushed into the arms of another.

I now most freely forgive Miss Gibson. I forgive everybody. I can not read over these papers.
If I have written any thing that may offend her, I am sorry for it.
I have it only in view, that these papers shall be used in justification of the awful step I have been impelled to take, partly from the acuteness of my own feelings, they are much more so than generally known or believed.
I do not indeed know, if such a step will admit of justification or palliation. It was inevitable. I need not say more.

I wish, however, for this purpose, all circumstances, as far as I have revealed them, known to my friends, so as they may do justice to me as far as possible.

Let none of the originals be given out. If necessary a copy may be taken.

When at Edinburgh, Mr Farquhar of the Custom house, Leith, Mr George Anderson of this place, and myself, agreed that we should attend the funerals of each other, at whatever distance we might reside from each other.

I wish Mr Farquhar to be accordingly invited, Mr Anderson will be so of course. I wish this the more so, as Mr Farquhar repeated this, the last time I saw him, and we made promises. I shall never wish to hear again of these being broken, and I never did so. None will be more astonished at my fate.

If ever I had intruded myself upon Miss Gibson, or urged her to come under engagements or promises, implied or expressed, I would have had no right to feel myself much disappointed at the violation of these; but the very reverse was the case. This Miss Gibson knows well; and also what led to the connection and intimacy betwixt us.

The attachment was reciprocal, but all the proposals as to matrimonial union came from herself, and were most cheerfully acquiesced in by me. Can any human being suppose, that I can now bear the violation of these, under all circumstances. I am certain there can not.

It is not through the madness of passion, or the love of fortune, that I have suffered, or fallen a sacrifice, but from the deep and indelible sense of the wrongs done me; and which I could not have done myself, at any time of my life, to any human being, under any circumstances. The least excuse for these has not been offered, or palliation attempted.

I have perhaps written too much, and what I have written, not free from contradiction. This proceeds from the unsettled state of my mind, and the different views I take at different times.

However, I repeat, that I most freely forgive Miss Gibson, and impute no bad motive to her; what I thought she had done wrong in, at this instant appears like a dream.

I shall endeavour to die with this impression on my mind.

No man cared less for the opinion of the world, at one time, than I did.

Now I would wish everybody to speak as well of me as they can. I recollect the concluding lines, written by Campbell, on the grave of a suicide :-

> *"Ah! once perhaps the social passion glow'd*
> *In thy devoted bosom; and the hand*
> *That smote its kindred heart, might yet be prone*
> *To deeds of mercy. Who may understand*
> *Thy many woes, poor suicide unknown?*
> *He, who thy being gave, shall judge of thee alone."*

I know my character has been a good deal mistaken. There were some things, that I have observed other people extremely anxious about, to which I was totally indifferent, but not in all things.
My feelings on other points were extremely acute; but I believe, till of late, few were so happy as I as.

It may be believed I had at first considered myself shockingly used, when I was induced to threaten one I had been so long on intimate terms with, to seek legal redress. It might have been but just to do so, under all the circumstances; but this is a step I never could have proceeded with, and even if I had done so from principle, a farthing of damages never could have gone into my pocket. Again I repeat my entire forgiveness.

Nothing has sickened my soul so much, as the being accused by Miss Gibson with having designs upon her fortune.
She no doubt puts a value upon it herself, but she reasons wrong, when she takes it for granted, that I hold it in the same estimation. God knows, if I had all the wealth in the world, I would give it all, that I were myself again; but this may not be. Nay, at times, I would give it all for a sound sleep. I am well aware, the cool and calculating part of mankind can never enter into my feelings; and many will say, it is sinful in me to let the loss of a single object have such an effect upon me. They reason wrong. In the loss of this one object, under all the circumstances, everything else is lost to me. Reason and philosophy may say

"Have you not still all the objects in nature, which you formerly delighted in; your solitary walks, &c., &c. Have you not the society of friends and acquaintances, your books, and all your former enjoyments?"

But this is not the case. I have none of all these, nothing of the kind. The objects, &c., still exist, but they are not the same to me. I see them through a totally different medium. What most delighted me formerly is now painful in the same ratio, or interests me not at all.

The smooth mirror of my mind, which formerly reflected all objects in such a pleasing and agreeable manner, and which was a continual source of happiness to me, is now broken and ruffled, and reflects everything distorted, hideous, and disgustful.

I am a being different from my former self, and support a different and painful existence.

Miss Gibson must recollect how she was in the habit of treating me, when at any time she only imagined herself neglected, and this, too, without the least cause. Nothing could be more gratifying, nothing to me could be more curious, than to know how she reconciles, in her own mind, her former with her latter conduct towards me.

From any thing that I can learn, and from appearances at least, she seems to act with a self-approving conscience.

It would now appear also, that she has in the whole matter acted with the approbation of her parents and connections.

This must be so far consolatory to her.

I have forgiven her and everybody; but, although I might have lived far beyond the space allotted to man, I could never forget my wrongs.

It is officious memory that puts me on the rack, and keeps these continually staring me in the face.

Of course, while I possess memory and consciousness, I must be miserable; and without these, I would be a second Edward Shore, and not even on a par with the beasts that perish. Beyond everything, I dread the falling into this state.

I do already find many of my faculties considerably impaired, and still getting worse. There is no remedy for this dreadful calamity but one, and may Almighty God forgive one of his poor unhappy erring creatures, for presuming to have recourse to such a remedy. Miss Gibson is not, and could not, from what has past betwixt us, be ignorant of the state to which I have been brought, I shall not say by her, and truth compels me to state, that she was evinced the very reverse of any thing like feeling or regret for my condition, a sad contrast to her former goodness. If she only but a very short time previous imagined that I was unwell or unhappy, she was all anxiety.

All this certainly could not have been feigned. There was no occasion for her latterly standing aloof.

The time was gone by, and although she had again made a tender of herself, with a fortune unheard of in extent, neither would have been accepted of by me; for she had inflicted a wound by her want of faith and feeling, that shut me out from all the enjoyments of this world.

I have already said that, in many instances, change of female affection might be excusable.

This might be the case, when the acquaintance or connection between the parties had been, and when no real attachment could be formed, when stratagem, misrepresentation, or strong entreaty had been used, or when any circumstance of importance had been concealed.

Miss Gibson, however, had none of all these excuses.

It is a delicate matter to speak of the attachment that existed betwixt us. I have avoided this as much as possible.

I do not pretend to be versant in these matters. I thought I could not possibly be mistaken; but to set that matter at rest, Miss Gibson, without any question from me, voluntarily and unequivocally declared her attachment.

This first happened in the House of Kinnaber, spring, 1822; this I am certain she will not deny: and when this attachment continued increasing and uninterrupted till the instant of time that Miss Gibson became acquainted with the extent of her fortune, I think I will stand excused for feeling as I do.

If I could have figured any excuse for her conduct after this, it would have been of some relief to myself.

No doubt an individual has now come forward since the receipt of this fortune, who was not ignorant of our previous connection, and who undoubtedly is preferred. Had this happened at a previous period, it had been well.

I admit him to be more suitable, more accomplished, and better in every respect; but as he came forward after a train of engagements had been entered into with another, and which still exist, I can see little difference betwixt this and coming forward after our marriage had followed upon these engagements. There may be some difference legally, morally none on the part of Miss Gibson; there might on the part of the gentleman, if these engagements were concealed from him, which can not for an instant be supposed.

All this now signifies nothing. I will, however, be excused, under the circumstances, for stating how my feelings have been wrought upon. I have held out till I can do so no longer. I must leave my business and home in the meantime.

I repeat my most entire forgiveness, and expect forgiveness myself.

In my Settlement, I have burdened my sister and brother with no legacies. We have poor relations of our own, and they will not forget those who have been in the habit of getting some little assistance. I have only to give the hint, and I am sure it will be obeyed. I would wish them to pay ten pounds to the Kirk-session of St Cyrus, for the poor of that parish, ten pounds to William Low, Kirk treasurer here, to be given in charity, as he shall think proper, five pounds to William Blacklaws, and one pound to each of, John Hutcheon, cooper, John Graham, Mary Aitkenhead, and a poor man nearly blind, who often sits upon the Church-yard brae.

It has arrived at a dreadful crisis, when the hand is lifted against the heart; yet it here partly deserves the punishment, for enlisting itself in a cause, which has terminated so disastrously for its unfortunate owner. That it was so far pressed into the service is true. If I had acted prudently, I should have fled temptation; but this I was not permitted to do. Miss Gibson's letters will faintly show this. What she stated verbally was of a more determined nature. I could not help myself. I sincerely think, and die in the belief, that I am not to blame in any respect, thought the contrary may be attempted to be proved, after I can not answer for myself. I had it not in my power to act otherwise.

From what I have experienced, if the proposal of breaking the connection (any time before the extent of Miss Gibson's fortune was known) had come from me, it would have been scouted with the utmost indignation; indeed I confess she had so far attained the ascendancy, that such a proposal could not have been hinted at. It was therefore ungrateful, unfeeling, selfish an cruel, to bring it forward herself, at that period only, when she thought, or perhaps had seen that this fortune has become an object to others, holding, no doubt, much higher pretensions in every respect, than ever I aspired to. However, all this now signifies nothing; it only shows that my mind has not been affected, nor my feelings wounded without cause. Miss Gibson and her fortune are now alike indifferent to me, but still the treatment has left an impression that can never be obliterated, even by time itself; on the contrary, it still wears deeper, as rivers wear their channels, as the poet aptly expresses it; and it can not wear deeper, without destroying both body and mind.

This is the inevitable issue. It has already been busy with both. It is awful to think, that I can not live, and yet can not die without shocking my relatives. They have not been out of my mind for one moment, for a very long time. It is a dreadful alternative. I will make it as little shocking as possible. I will lay down the burden which I can no longer bear, in some sequestered place, I think in that solemn, sacred, and silent spot, where my bones will be deposited.

  It was upon the 9th May, as I think, that Miss Gibson sent me a letter asking forgiveness for having asked to be relieved of her engagements, stating that her conduct had been highly unfeeling, that she had no excuse for herself, that she would not hurt my feelings again, and that she would never repeat a wish to be released.

It is well known how she conducted herself at the 'Roup of Balmakewan' only a few days after this, dates will speak for themselves, I am not in a situation for making these particular references.

I hope some person of feeling, some good Christian, will yet lend their help with a view, as far as possible, of excusing the last act of my life.

  Miss Gibson did, in a strange manner, inform me of her going to

Pitcaithly. It is known that she went there accordingly, and who was her companion.
She should at least have acted more candidly towards me.
My last letter, like some others, perhaps, was very foolish, and had evidently been written under dreadful depression of spirits,
so much so, that I had thought it necessary to execute a Will of the date mentioned in my letter. I then laboured under dreadful apprehensions. In this letter I foolishly besought Miss Gibson to do nothing for some time that might have the effect of accelerating my fate; the immediate consequence was her attendance at the theatre along with Mr Smart and her mother on one occasion, and on another with Mrs Neill and that gentleman, all of whom were acquainted with the nature of my request.
It was foolish in me to write such a letter, but it proceeded from the state of my mind and feelings at the time, and it would have been no disparagement to them to have spared my feelings for a short time; the period asked was not long.
They had laid down their system, however.
They may have thought that the word of a madman would not be believed, and that…

" a dead man tells no tales."

Be this as it may, I have been studiously treated with every want of feeling; in other circumstances this would not have affected me. I would have laughed at them all; but when the spirit is deeply
wounded, any additional unkindness sinks it beyond the power of recovery.
May God forgive them. They have been the ruin and death of me.
This will no doubt be thought of little consequence.
Mr Smart was in the use of telling, that upon one occasion Twedale's natural son*, in taking a parcel from the Mail coach, let it fall in the strand, and when challenged by the guard, he said, "what does it signify, it's only to Georgie Beattie." I believe the story to be very true, and a similar remark may be made here.

* A simple, innocent creature, named Jemmy Jamie, who carried parcels from the Mail, had one day dropped a parcel for Mr Beattie in the strand. Somebody said to him he had dirtied the parcel. "Oh," says he, "it's for George Beattie, it's for George Beattie."
Had it been for any one else, he would have paid the penalty; but Mr Beattie had been very kind to him, and the poor, simple fellow knew, that the good-hearted George would not be angry at him. Mr Smart, in retailing the story, put a false gloss on it, which was as base as it was untruthful.

It is very true, as stated by Mr Gibson in his last letter, that this world is full of trials and disappointments; but it does not follow, that one fellow-creature ought to stand acquitted for willingly inflicting these on another. Were this sound reasoning, the miscreant who sets fire to a person's house, would only have to tell the sufferer to be content, as the world was full of trials and disappointments. Mr Gibson argues as if the trial inflicted on me was a dispensation of Providence.
I certainly can not see the matter in this light, nor can I think so lightly of it, as Mr Gibson seems to do, the very reverse; and from what he knew of the matter, and from what Miss Gibson mentioned to me that she had communicated to him, I thought it would have been viewed by him in a very different light.
I have no right to exemption from trials and disappointments, but I would have looked for them from a different quarter.
Many injuries would have *"cried buff"* off me, that would have made others wince; but, in some instances, they would wound me deeper than they would do any other. That there are as good fish in the sea
that ever came out of it is very true, but this applies not to my case; it might be thought applicable by some, but my feelings will not admit the most distant application, or even meaning, here. How would a
mother feel, who had lost her first born, if this proverb were offered her, in the shape of consolation? It would be equally true in her case.
It can not now be of the least consequence to me, but I should like to know if Miss Gibson, in the midst of her nuptial preparations, allows herself to recollect of what she was in the use of talking to me, on that subject, about procuring a ring, providing furniture, &c., &c., &c.;
and if she has forgotten, that she was in the habit of making suppositions, as to how I would acquit myself in these matters. This was a subject of mirth to us both. Trifling as they are, it can not be supposed that these,

and many other circumstances, can be forgotten by me.
As I have often repeated, I am very anxious to justify myself as far as possible, and in doing so, I have no wish to throw blame on Miss Gibson. There is nothing to be apprehended on this score. Any one possessed of a fortune, and living in prosperity, can never be in the least affected by any circumstance of this nature; he would have a superficial knowledge of the world, that could think so. I have continued my remarks longer, much longer than I intended; it all proceeds from the wish to excuse myself, for the commission of an act which I can not avoid, do what I will.
I have not done this in a pet, but after making every attempt to stem the torrent, and finding to a certainty, that I really have not the power. I would not, I could not, for worlds, pass such another period of suffering and misery; rendered doubly so, by being reduced to the necessity of continually disguising my feelings, and concealing my misery and distress from the world. The punishment of attending parties, or attending to business, is distressing beyond description. Good fortune to myself in this world would now be worse to bear than any thing. This may appear strange, but it is nevertheless very true. Misfortunes and disasters are more suitable to the present state of my mind, which appears unalterable unless to the worse. The only consolation I have, and it certainly at times makes me tranquil and almost reconciled to my fate, is, that I am not suffering from any
wrong that I have committed.
It relieves me to think that I have injured no one, but that my sufferings proceed from injuries that have been done to me. The
feeling or sensation, therefore, hard as it may be to bear, is not remorse nor any thing akin to it. Had the tie been broken by a dispensation of Providence, over which mortals have no control, the feeling would have been very different.
The regret, in this event, might have been equally strong, but this must ultimately have been followed by a soothing melancholy which would have been unaccompanied entirely by the wounded spirit, the irritated feelings, the self-degradation, and the many other feelings and sufferings, which have brought about the present crisis.
I never dreamed that I could possibly have been visited by such a

calamity. I was not previously acquainted with these matters. I hope few have suffered so much as I have done, and that it is a very uncommon case. If it is not, the world is not worth the living in, and I have lost nothing by leaving it, if I could have only left it in the course of nature. This I did believe at one period I would have done, but however powerful have been the workings of my mind, they have had to operate on a frame so full of health, that it could not be pulled down but by violence. Many would have given much to be possessed of such health, but it has been my bane latterly.

My agonies and want of sleep, having no effect on my bodily health; it could not be subdued by any operation of the mind, and it is impossible these operations could have been more powerful.

My Will must be now perfectly good, for notwithstanding of my mental sufferings, I have had a very distinct, clear, and satisfactory view of the manner in which I have disposed of my property. It was my intention to make a settlement in exactly the same terms before I fell into the shade, and I am sure it will not be challenged. If it should, it would be found good, otherwise my disponees will be wronged, and my settled and unalterable intentions disregarded. I have heard that some individuals enjoy a morbid and sickly satisfaction in fancying themselves to be miserable; this is far from being the case with me. I
would fain leave miser far behind me, I would fain emerge from the the cloud, but memory makes it more dense and dark, and the almost continual sunshine of the breast which I formerly enjoyed, is no longer my companion.

I say to myself in words,

> *"live, and endeavour to do good, this trial ought to be a new era in your life, despise the wrongs that have been done to you, and forget them."*

I can do all but the last, and memory brings them before me in so many different views at different times, that every hour visits me with pangs unknown before. I wish I could have watched the departure of the last sun that was destined to shine on me, with a pious smile, and blessed

heaven for a long life, after having done much good here; but as I have become so miserable, and am so irresistibly impelled, I am not without hope that I am permitted to lay down a burden which I have not been granted the power to support, whatever may have been the will.
I have never, to the last, been favoured with any reason by Miss Gibson for her breach of promise.
I do not know what the ladies think in these matters: perhaps they conceive it a sufficient reason if they imagine the have got a better match. That point I shall not dispute, but Miss Gibson knows herself, that she often said of her own accord, that she was satisfied I would be
a good husband. These were amongst the last words she said to me, on the Sunday on which our engagements were renewed. She never at any time hinted at an objection; on the contrary, she paid me compliments of which I was utterly undeserving. In the letter she asks to be free of her engagement, she even says she prefers no other to me. However, the minds of women have puzzled men of experience, they are beyond my reach. I admit, that previous to this, I had formed a very high opinion of Miss Gibson, and was therefore the less prepared to bear any trial that might be inflicted on me by her. That, however, and all my other trials are now at an end.

After every exertion, and finding that my fate was inevitable, it is astonishing how well I have become reconciled to it.
I have (not without emotion, but free from despair) taken my last view of various places which at one time were highly interesting to me, and I have seen many acquaintances and friends whom I know I shall never
see again.
I have had longer time for preparation than most men. Although I could not, without being noticed, relinquish altogether my ordinary
pursuits, or show publicly any visible alteration in my conduct, I have scarcely for a second of time forgotten the awful situation in which I stand. It can render me no service to cant to man, that I never could have done at any time, under any circumstance, and I will not do so yet. It is not the pretending to be good, &c., &c., &c., and making a noise about it, that will avail; but it is the being really good, &c., &c., &c., in silence, that will do so.

I will make no pretensions, there is no necessity for doing so, it is enough to be known here (perhaps too much) that I have latterly at least done my best, and I know by whom I will be judged.
At a time like this, hypocrisy itself throws off its mask.

This brings to my mind that it was a condition betwixt Miss Gibson and me, and often expressed, that I should, after our union, attend the church, at least once every Sunday.
This I had not the least objection to, it was reasonable, and would have been necessary under the circumstances, but I might now have some reasons to inquire, what she intended I should learn there, not certainly to break sacred ties, promise, engagements, or oaths, or, as Shakespeare has it :-

"Make marriage vows as false as dicer's oaths."

This, however, I never could have done, that did not go often to church. Miss Gibson will recollect that she used to tell me I was a good practical Christian, and too honest, and not cautious enough in acting to please myself, without following the general example of others. This was saying more in my favour than I deserved. I have no doubt she is now ready to retract. My sufferings ought to have made me better in every respect, and I sincerely hope they have done so. As I am not granted the power to resist, I am, better prepared just now than I would have been at an after period.
When one full of bodily health, not far gone in years, easy in his circumstances, and, previous to this calamity, of a very happy disposition, can thus reconcile
himself, it is astonishing that others, oppressed with age, poverty, disease, and all the other ills of life, should cling so unreasonably to existence.
Indeed, I may say, for one in my situation, and considering
the extent of my ambition, I was perfectly independent in my worldly circumstances. This is sufficient to show that a fortune, under other circumstances, was itself no object to me.
I had at one time resolved to travel, with the view of endeavouring to forget my injuries and leave my sufferings behind.
This I found could be of no avail, all places are now alike to me.

Existence could not have been supported anywhere, and, from my absence of mind, and consequent indifference to comfort, &c., I could not have lived apart from my own relations.

The scene is now near closing. I feel not the common repugnance to death so much spoken about, if it had only been an honourable one. I had been happy.

Often, on the afternoons of Saturday, when a mere child, I have visited alone the solitary place where my bones were to rest, even at that time, with a kind of melancholy pleasure, and then I am sure there was not a living being of more buoyant spirits, or fuller of life and glee, and frolic and fun of every description. The people in that neighbourhood speak of this to the present moment. I wish to sleep peacefully in this spot.

I wish

"life's fitful fever o'er."

I admit I cast

"many a longing, lingering look behind."

When I do so, what do I see?

One who, for a length of time (certainly myself nothing loath, but the very reverse) has unceasingly urged my entering into the most sacred and important of all engagements, which, after being entered into repeatedly in the most solemn manner, she herself wished to dissolve, and instantly formed another, without the least feeling towards me or delicacy towards herself and sex.

A dying man may surely be allowed to state what he believes or rather knows to be true. I merely meant to excuse myself, but if occasional gleams of resentment dart from my dark and clouded mind, I can not help it.

I will soon be of another mood. I write from the instant impulse of the moment, without forethought or premeditation.

I do so to unburden myself, and as a satisfaction to my relatives and friends. They know I will state nothing but facts, and my reasoning, even if wrong, will be viewed by them with indulgence. Is there any thing, therefore, in what I see, to induce me to court any longer acquaintance with the world.

If Miss Gibson could only have waited a short time, a very short time, it would have been a consolation to me.

I told her, in that event, I would be insensible to any thing she might do. Nobody can know her better than I do, and I know she is too susceptible, of too loving a temperament to have admitted of any such delay upon so insignificant a plea.

> *" Heaven and Earth!*
> *Must I remember, how she would hang on him,*
> *As if increase of appetite had grown*
> *By what it fed on! Yet within a month,*
> *Let me not think. Frailty, thy name is Woman."*

Not a month, not a week, perhaps not a day after Miss Gibson sent me the two letters asking forgiveness, making excuses for hurting my feelings, and demanding, with the utmost urgency, my intentions towards her, which I stated with all kindness.

I believe she was admitting the attentions of another, or did so a very short time after, without stating the circumstances to me; dates will speak for themselves.

All this can now make no difference to me; nothing can do so. But let any person not destitute of pride and feeling, place himself in my situation, and say how he would have felt, or what might have been his fate under such feeling.

All this, too, immediately after Miss Gibson had come in possession of a fortune, which she often spoke to me in anticipation of. For more than a year previous to this, I had not met the least interruption; there had been no rival-ship whatever, and although there had, from what
had passed, and was passing betwixt us, I could have apprehended nothing. And notwithstanding of a complaint of absence, there were not, during the year, I am certain, twenty days (with the exception of a short time I was from home), that I did not either see Miss Gibson, at

Stone of Morphie, Montrose, Kinnaber, or some other place, or hear from her verbally or by letter.

As matters now stand, it can make no difference; still I had reason to expect that Miss Gibson would have spared my feelings as much as possible.

I thought her own feelings might have dictated this to her. There certainly was something strange in her parading the streets with another, in the open manner in which she has been in the habit of doing, since the receipt of my last letter.

Taking the whole of this matter in view, I believe few have been treated in the way I have been, and I do think full justice can not be done to me, without publishing the whole. I can not now convince myself, that such conduct does not deserve a full disclosure. This is my conviction at the present moment, but I leave it to others, who are better able to judge. No other occurrence could have so unmanned me. From my interference for others, I have seen ruin staring me in the face, and only latterly averted, by fortunate circumstances, that could not have been anticipated; and it scarcely gave me a moment's uneasiness.

Perpetual imprisonment, with all the squalor carceris, and torture itself, would not have reduced me to my present state. Under all this,
the spirit and the mind would have remained unsubdued. When these are deeply wounded, all is over.

When the heart is sickened to the core, there is no remedy. What a difference there is in the fates and fortunes of different men. I envy none their good fortune or happiness, but at this moment, I envy some whom others pity.

I wish it could have been my fate to die like Marshall Ney, and yet many thought he was cruelly treated.

What a glorious doom, compared to mine, to get a few brave fellows to shower their bullets through the heart, particularly in his case, when they would only obey his own orders. None will obey me, and I am constrained, God forgive me, to do what, till lately, could not have a place in my mind. I have spent a summer very different from what I was wont, it is passed with all its pains. Autumn has followed, and I shall fall before the leaves.

Of a truth I have

"fallen into the sear, into the yellow leaf."

The variegated fields that used to delight me, now pall upon my sight, and the changing foliage affords me no delight. I have no refuge but in the silent and peaceful grave.

That I would have obtained damages in a court of law, there can be no doubt. Whatever I may have said, however, perhaps by way of threat or otherwise, under my sufferings, I never could have resorted to such a measure.

I would

" sooner have coined my heart's blood "

than raised cash by such means (indeed any body would have been most welcome to my blood, that would have saved me from spilling it with my own hands).

When I spoke of seeking redress, it was on the idea that I could by no other means expose conduct, which I thought, and still think, most reprehensible. At no time did I ever think of pocketing a farthing. No one will blame me for this.

What everybody seems so anxious to grasp at, has, for a considerable time past at least, been a matter of entire and total indifference to me.

Whatever riches it might have been my lot to be possessed of in other circumstances, I never could have been induced to live extravagantly; such a mode would not have been to my taste.

I can say what few can; I believe I never asked a favour in my life, that is, for myself or relations.

When this matter came to be spoken about, I was astonished on overhearing people say

" there is no doubt but he will get ample damages,"

just as if this could have healed my wounded feelings, or cure the heart-ache.

It was a gross, a sordid, and vulgar idea; an idea that I spurn with all my heart and soul. Had I even died a beggar (which, God be praised is not the case), and left those depending on me beggars, I am sure they would sooner have solicited alms from the cold hand of charity, than accepted of recompense or favour from those who had deprived them of their protector. I do not wish to punish Miss Gibson, or the individual she has preferred to me.

No, no. I have inflicted all the punishment on myself. Had I been prone to revenge, or wished to return evil for evil (as many in my situation would), I might have taken vengeance. I had only to do what I have done. I had only to die at any rate. A man who is reduced to the dreadful alternative that I have been reduced to, would not fear any kind of death or mortal suffering.

Were it not for the dreadful act itself, however, I might almost say that I die innocent, whatever previous offences I may have committed, for I have not a wish to hurt a human being, not even those who have reduced me to my present condition.

Mr Gibson seems to think that I ought to be pleased, if I can form a connection with another.

Such an idea could never enter my mind. Men, I suspect, are more true to their attachments than women.

This I did not previously think. Situated as I was, and having others to care for, I was not particularly desirous of changing my mode of life, till Miss Gibson persuaded me to do so. She knows this to be the case, and that what I mentioned to her in my letter of the 9th May, and it the Statement of Facts, forwarded to her father, on this point, is far within the mark and short of the truth. This, as may be supposed, was done from delicacy.

She knows at whose instigation the first letter was sent to Pitcaithly, although certainly that could not be gathered from the letter itself. She knows how I stood aloof, after receiving her answer to it, and how she immediately afterwards did so much to explain it away. After a connection was formed, I could not think of breaking it; particularly so long and peculiar a connection as ours had been. There is nothing I can less excuse Miss Gibson for, than for pretending, in her letter seeking

back her promise, that there had only been one given, and upon one occasion, and when she speaks of not having been allowed time.
This, however, she does entirely away in her letter of the 9th May. The fact is, and Miss Gibson knows it, that (besides the different engagements and vows, which had previously passed betwixt us, which are stated in my letter of the 8th May, and admitted by hers of the 9th), on the Thursday immediately preceding the Sunday so often mentioned, she asked me particularly to attend her in the garden. The time, I by some means mistook; and she told me afterwards, it was for the purpose of renewing our vows.

It certainly was wrong, after all this, to pretend that she was taken by surprise, or that she stood in need of time to consider of a matter which had been so often discussed. There was a want of candour in it, that struck me particularly at the time; but I had enough to upbraid Miss Gibson with at the time, to take very particular notice of all these matters. What passed betwixt us on the Sunday was mere matter of course, and I would have looked upon our engagements every whit as strong, although I had not seen Miss Gibson that day. No doubt, by that means there are some letters that would not otherwise have been in my possession, and therefore Miss Gibson may think that she might not have been legally bound.

Certainly one in her situation in life ought to hold a moral obligation as strong as a legal one. Although one letter had not passed betwixt Miss Gibson and myself, the engagements, in a moral and honourable point of view, would not have been the less binding. It would appear, from her anxiety to get possession of her letters (and, as I have said, it was by mere chance there was one in existence), that when this object should be accomplished, her mind would be at ease; that she would hold any verbal obligation as nought; that when palpable evidence was wanting, the evidence of her own breast could be concealed from all but herself and me; and that she could, without compunction, represent the whole as ideal and visionary. With submission there is more here of the lawyer than the moralist; I mean of the chicaning lawyer. And although Miss Gibson, in one of her letters, hints, that she must take care of herself, as she is writing to a *"man of the law,"* I shall leave it to the determination of any person, which of us has shown most of the lawyer in the sense I have mentioned, in the last stages of this fatal business. Instead of acting with the duplicity of which men of the law are generally accused, I have been made the dupe of one whom I believed incapable of duplicity, and perhaps the subject of mirth to herself and an individual, who, however preferable he may have become to me in her estimation, I did not at one time at least consider my superior in intellect. I will not now venture to put myself in competition with any person on this head.

Some people would comfort themselves with the assurance that all this had been ordained,

and that what must be, must. I will not dispute that point; but if it was predetermined that I should form a connection of so important a nature, I wish to God it had been with some guileless, artless lassie, whatever might have been her station, or with some *"Highland Mary"* from the harvest rig. In that event I had at least a chance of being happy. It may be said I have this still in my power. This, however, is not the case.

I had entered into a serious and solemn engagement, and I never could enter into another, nor could I live but in a state of misery, after that was broken in the circumstances it has been. There are reminiscences connected with that engagement that can never be obliterated from my memory. Miss Gibson can not have forgotten, at least ought not to forget, how we anticipated the happiness we had in prospect, and how we imagined ourselves in the possession of all the happiness and enjoyments of the state in which we were to enter, that we hoped to be blessed with pledges of our affection, and Miss Gibson spoke with pleasure of my fondness for children. Can this be forgotten? No, not by me; but it appears it can, and that in a very brief space too, by one in whom it might have been as little expected.

In an honest and proper point of view, the accession to Miss Gibson's fortune, should rather have been the means of cementing an attachment which had been formed under circumstances less auspicious, than of rending it asunder.

Supposing the accession to have been on my side, I do not need to ask myself if I would or could have withdrawn, it would have been impossible, the idea never could have had existence. I know what would

have been my feelings on the occasion. I need not express them. Miss Gibson was not so young as not to be qualified to judge and act for herself in entering into engagements, nor so old as to be
entitled to have recourse to subtleties for getting clear of these afterwards.

"Gentle Maid,
Keep your promise plight, leave age its subtleties,
And grey-haired policy, its maze of falsehood;
But be you candid as the morning sky,
E'er the high sun sucks vapours up to stain it."

   What has, perhaps, made this bear stronger on me is, that my mind has, for as long as I can remember, been strongly impressed with the peculiarly sacred nature of any engagement or understanding of the kind. Indeed, that idea, I believe, is imbibed by most of us, from our national songs and other writings, and there are few that do not hold poetical ideas of the subject. Theoretically, I had believed it impossible that such a breach could take place, and I never could have dreamed that, practically, I was myself to be made the unsuspecting and unfortunate victim, to prove the contrary. That Miss Gibson is making light of, and laughing at, the matter, I have from the best authority.
That she has also already spread it, and mentioned circumstances which had gone to the public, there is no doubt that she has shown and published my last letter, there can be no doubt.

   { Miss Helen Gibson mentioned the particulars to a lady in town. }

   Well, she has succeeded in bringing about what she wished. She is at full liberty to laugh at me. I suppose few, after all, bad as the world is, will envy her of her sport. It is not in all cases the extent of the wrong, but the reflection of by whom it is inflicted, that plants the sting.
When Caesar saw Brutus stab at him, he offered no resistance, his heart burst, and muffling up his face in his mantle, he fell at the base of Pompey's statue.

All is now over. I die in perfect good will towards every human being. If my feelings may have led me to say any thing offensive respecting Miss Gibson I am sorry for it.
She has my entire forgiveness.
If I have erred in any thing, I hope she will forgive me, and it will be wise in her to forget whatever may have passed betwixt us.
If I could have done this, I would have been happy.

There is no use in repining. I never did so before…………………………………..]*

* This is part of the last sentence, which is erased.

"Men's minds are too ready to excuse guilt in themselves."

Titus Livius

Roman historian and philosopher

(59 BC-AD 17)

Original

Poems

by

George Beattie, Esquire

The Appeal

Say, what is worse than black despair;
'Tis that sick hope too weak for flying,
That plays at fast and loose with care,
And wastes a weary life in dying.

Though promise to be a welcome guest,
Yet it may be too late a comer.
'Tis but a cuckoo voice at best,
The joy of spring, scarce heard in summer.

Then now consent this very hour;
Let the kind word of peace be spoken;
Like dew upon a wither'd flower,
Is comfort to the heart that's broken.

The heart, whose will is from above,
May yet its mortal taint discover;
For time, which cannot alter love,
Hath power to kill the hapless lover.

Farewell Sonnet

Farewell, maid, thy love has vanish'd;
 Gone off like the morning dew;
Farewell, maid, my peace is banish'd;
 Adieu! a sad, a long adieu!

Weary world, I now must leave thee;
 Sun and moon, a long farewell;
Farewell, maid, no more I'll grieve thee;
 Soon you'll hear my funeral knell.

Soon the lips that oft have kiss'd thee,
 Mouldering in the dust will lie;
And the heart that oft hath blessed thee,
 Soon must cease to heave a sigh.

Soon the tongue that still rehearses
 All thy beauty, fickle fair;
Soon the hand that writes these verses,
 Shall to kindred dust repair.

Friends that constant were, and true aye,
 Fare-you-well, my race is run;
Heartless, lorn, benighted, weary;
 Every earthly hope is gone.

Gloomy grave, you'll soon receive me;
 All my sorrows here shall close.
Here no fickle fair shall grieve me;
 Here my heart shall find repose.

John o' Arnha'

A Tale

It was in May, ae bonnie morn,
When dewie draps refresh'd the corn,
And tipt ilk stem wi' crystal bead,
That glissent o'er the spangelt mead,
Like gleam o' swords in fairy wars,
As thick and clear as Heaven's stars;
While Phoebus shot his gowden rays,
Asklent the lawn - a dazzlin' blaze;
The wind but gently kissed the trees,
To waft their balm upo' the breeze;
The bee commenced her eident tour -
Culling sweets frae ilka flow'r;
The whins in yellow bloom were clad,
And ilka bush a bridal bed;
A' Nature smil'd serene and fair;
The la'rocks chantit i' the air;
The lammies frisket o'er the lea -
Wi' music rang ilk bush and tree.

Now "sighs and vows," and kisses sweet -
The sound of lightly tripping feet -
Love's tender tale - the sweet return -
The plaints of some still doomed to mourn;
The rustic jest, and merry tale,
Came floating on the balmy gale;
For, smiling, on the road were seen
Baith lads and lasses, trig and clean;
Linkin' blythely, pair and pair,
To grace Montrose's Annual Fair! -
Montrose, "wham ne'er a town surpasses"
For Growling Guild and ruling Asses!
For pedants, with each apt specific …

To render barren brains prolific;
For poetasters who conspire
To rob Apollo of his lyre,
Although they never laid a leg
Athort his godship's trusty naig;
For preachers, writers, and physicians -
Parasites and politicians:
And all accomplished, grave and wise,
Or sae appear in their own eyes!
To wit and lair too, make pretence;
E'en sometimes "deviate into sense!"
A path right kittle, steep, and latent,
And only to a few made patent.
So, lest it might offend the Sentry,
I winna seek to force an entry;
But, leav't to bards inspir'd and holy,
And tread the open field of folly;
For certes, as the world goes,
Nonsense in rhyme's as free's in prose;
And are we not distinctly told
By 'Hudibras' in days of old,
That "those who write in rhyme still make
"The one verse for the other's sake;
"And one for sense, and one for rhyme,
"Is quite sufficient at a time."

As for your critics, ruin seize them,
I ken I canna sing to please them;
A reason guid - I dinna try -
They're but a despicable fry,
That vend their venom and their ink,
Their praise and paper, eke for clink.
Thae judges partial - self-eleckit,
Why should their sentence be respeckit;
Why should the silly squeamish fools
Think fouk will mind their measur'd rules?
They spill not ink for fame or glory,
Nor paper blacken, con amore;
'Tis Mammon aye their pens inspire,
They praise, or damn, alike for hire; ...

An', chapman like, their critic treasure,
Is bought and sold again by measure;
Some barrister new tane degrees
(Whase purse is lank for lack o' fees),
Or churchman just come frae the college,
Wi' scull weel cramm'd wi' classic knowledge,
Draw pen to laud some weary bard,
Or deal damnation by the yard:
But first they toss them up a maik,
To learn what course they ought to take:
If "tails," the critics quickly damn him,
If "heads," wi' fousome flattery cram him.
In either case they're paid their wages,
Just by the number o' their pages.

How soon are mortals led astray -
Already I am off my way;
I've left my bonnie tale, to fesh in
A wicked scandalous digression;
By bards of yore, who sang of Gods,
Clep'd underplots and episodes;
But "Muse, be kind, and dinna fash us,
"To flee awa' ayont Parnassus;"
Or fill our brains wi' lees and fiction,
Else fouk will scunner at your diction.

I sing not of an ancient Knight,
Wi' polished lance and armour bright;
Nor, as we say, wi' book bedeckit
In "iron cap and jinglin' jecket,"
High mounted on a champion steed,
Eneugh to fley poor fouk to dead -
Or modern Dux, wi' noddin' crest,
An' starnies glancin' on his breast -
Or garter wuppit round his knee
To celebrate his chivalry; -
Heroes fit for southern bardies!
Mine walks a-foot and wields his gardies;
Or, at the warst, his aiken rung,
Wi' which he never yet was dung, …

Unless by more than mortal foe -
By daemons frae the shades below,
As will be seen in proper time,
Provided I can muster rhyme.

The valiant hero of my story
Now rang'd the fair in all his glory,
A winsome strapper, trim and fettle,
Courtin' strife - to show his mettle,
An' gain him favours wi' the fair -
For dastard coofs they dinna care.
Your snools in love and cowards in war,
Frae maiden grace are banish'd far;
An' John had stak'd his life, I ween,
For favour frae a lassie's een.
Stark luve his noble heart had fir'd -
To deeds o' pith his soul aspir'd;
Tho' these in distant climes he'd shown,
'Twas meet to act them in his own.

Now thrice he wav'd his hat in air;
Thrice dar'd the bravest i' the fair;
The 'Horner' also wav'd his bonnet,
But wish'd, belyve, he hadna done it;
For scarcely had he counted sax,
Before a double round o' whacks
Were shower'd upon his banes like hail,
Right, left, and centre, crack pell-mell -
Sair to bide, and terrible to tell.
The hardest head could ne'er resist
The fury of his pond'rous fist;
He hit him on the ribs sic dirds,
They rair'd and roove like rotten girds;
His carcase too, for a' the warl',
Was like a butt or porter barrel.
Now John gaed round him like a cooper,
An' show'd himself a smart tub hooper;
Wi' mony a snell an' vengefu' paik,
He gar'd his sides an' midriff ake;
Upon his head-piece neist he hammert, …

Until the 'Horner' reel'd and stammart,
He cried out "Mercy! plaque upon it!"
Up gaed his heels - aff flew his bonnet,
An' raise to sic a fearfu' height,
It soon was lost to mortal sight.
Some said, that witnessed the transaction,
'Twas cleekit by the moon's attraction,
Or nabbit by the fairy legions,
To whirl them through the airy regions.

Sonnet

But far it gaed, or far it flew,
The feint ane either cared or knew.
Yet strange to tell, tho' very true,
Again it never cross'd his brow,
Nor ever kyth'd to mortal view.
Some said they heard it cry "adieu,"
As thro', the air, sic clear and blue,
It skimm'd as quick as ony dow.
An' weel I wat, to gie't its due,
It was baith sleekit an' spleet new,
Of as guid stuff as ever grew
Upo' the back o' ram or ewe,
Or ever fendit rain or dew;
Weel twisted out o' haimert woo -
Weel ca'd thegither and waukit too -
Weel dy'd and litit through and through;
The rim was red - the crown was blue!
But now it's gane? Eheu! Eheu!!

And here maun end my dowie sonnet
Upo' the 'Horner's' guid braid bonnet;
Weel wordy o' mair lofty strains,
For happin' sic a head o' brains,
Still prone on earth the vanquish'd lay,
View'd by the rabble with dismay;
Now groaning, startit frae the ground,
And swore he'd have another round.
No sooner was this socht than granted, …

The victor vow'd 'twas what he wanted.
Each took his ground - the ring was form'd;
Wi' pain the 'Horner' rav'd an' storm'd;
His roofless pow, and gaucy face,
Show'd marks of ravage and disgrace;
Which added horrer to his mein -
A gruguous wight he was, I ween.

The victor squar'd his manly figure,
An' gar'd his gardies whizz wi' vigour;
They rent the air in every quarter,
He said, "My lad, ye've caught a Tartar;"
Syne, wi' a most tremendous whup,
Again he turned the 'Horner' up,
Till first his head and neist his feet,
In turn cam' crack against the street;
Just like a squirrel in a cage,
Or mountebank upon a stage;
Wi' heels ower head, and head ower heels,
Ower barrows, benches, stands, and creels;
The mulls and cutties flew like drift,
The vera stour raise to the lift;
The lasses, wi' amazement skirl'd,
As ower an' ower an' ower he whirl'd
Like whirlegig, or wheel a-spinnin',
The spaiks were like to lift their linen.

The fair was now in dire commotion,
Raging like the roaring ocean:
Like hail the sweeeties strew'd the street.
"Come, hain your siller, pick an' eat,"
Was sounded through the busy crowd,
A signal eithly understood.

Rob M'Intosh, a Highland piper,
Wha thought the crap could ne'er be riper,
Wi' twa three gangrel ballad singers,
Began to ply their restless fingers.
"O hooly there, ma bonnie bairns,"
Quo' John, "Haud aff your theivin' irons," ...

He shook their doublets and their wallets,
An' gar'd his cudgel claw their pallets;
They threw their fangs, and flew for shelter,
Content wi' paiks, to 'scape a halter.
Now wild huzzas, baith lang an' loud,
Were yammert by the gapin' crowd:
They cried, "O had he been alive
In seventeen hundred forty-five,
When Charlie Stewart, the vile Pretender,
Made moyen to be our Faith's Defender;
And marched his legions down our streets,
Withouten brichen, sheen, or beets,
He'd gar'd them flee like chaff and stubble,
And spar'd the English troops the trouble
O' stickin' baignets i' the throats -
O' hunger-bitten Highland Scots.
He loes his King and country weel,
And sends Reformers to the Deil,
Still as he swills the foamin' porter,
He wishes each a full head shorter."

But Muse, I charge thee, hurry on,
An' let us frae the fair begone;
A bolder theme maun swell our lay,
A dreadful night succeeds this day,
As will be seen in proper time,
Provided I can muster rhyme!

The busy day drew to a close:
As soon as John had tane his dose
O' whisky punch, and nappy ale,
Had smok'd his pipe, and told his tale,
He judg'd it far his wisest scheme
To streek his houghs and scamper hame.
He scorn'd to soak 'mang weirdless fellows
Wi' menseless bazils in an alehouse;
Enough he deem'd as good's a feast;
That excess made the man a beast.
The lawin' paid, an a' thing snod,
He soon was skelpin' on the road; ...

Quick past the Port and Dummie's Wynd,
The fleetest soon he left behind;
Neist by the Loch and Rotten-raw,
An' up the Loan for Arnha' -
His native spot, his peacefu' hame,
The place from whence he took his name,
Now render'd famous by his fame.

An' now the weary westlin' sun
Had kiss'd the tap o' Catterthun;
His hinmost blink shone on the knowes,
The lazy mist crap in the hows;
The wind was lown, creation still,
The plover wail'd upon the hill;
The cottage reek rase to the sky;
The bat in silence flicker'd by,
And moth and beetle, foes to light,
Commenced their drousy twilight flight;
The ploughmen, now their labour o'er,
Enjoy'd the balmy gloamin' hour,
Right wazie wax'd and fou o' fun,
They whisselt down the setting sun;
Some slyly slipt to meet their joes,
As they came tripping frae Montrose.
Ye pauky louns! hale be your hearts,
Weel ken ye how to play your parts;
For oft that gloamin', ere she wist,
Full mony a bonnie lass was kisst,
An' ran's as if chas'd by bogles eerie,
But soon was clasp'd by her ain dearie;
Right blythe to find they were mista'en,
They gae their kisses back again;
Shame fa' the saint wad ca't a crime,
Or deem't unmeet for prose or rhyme. ...

Now gradual shades of gloamin' grey
Crap gently o'er the partin' day;
The air was sweet - kind heav'n anew
Refresh'd the earth wi' pearly dew;
A balmy, soothing, silent shower,
That cheer'd ilk herb and fainting flower,
Frae morning scowdert i' the blaze
Of Phoebus' ever darting rays.
The hum of stragglers frae the fair
Cam' floating on the peacefu' air;
The robin chantit, frae his spray,
A requiem to departed day,
In notes sae waesome, wild, and sweet,
They gar'd a lightlied lover greet,
The blackbird whisselt deep and mellow;
A hollow voice cried - "John Finella!"
Now straight the hero turned him round
To see from whence the eldrich sound;
When right a-head, an ancient dame
Kyth'd eerie through the twilight beam,
Upon a crummock staff she leant her;
Fast John cam' leeshin' up ahint her;
Her coatties past the knees were kiltit,
In eldrich notes she croon'd and liltit.

The Witche's Song

"O why sud my auld heart grow sair ...

To hear the lasses crumpin' fair;
They'll hae their day, as I had mine;
Like me they'll think on auld langsyne;
For I've haen sweethearts o' my ain,
An' to be dautit I was fain:
They roos'd my glossy jet black hair,
But now my pow's baith lyart an' bare;
They prais'd my alabaster skin,
Alas! now wrinkelt, derf, and din;
They said my pawky een were bonnie,
My mow as sweet as heather honey,
But now my een are blear'd and blin',
My mow conceal'd 'tween nose and chin;
Full eighty winters thick hae spread
Their cranreughs o'er my palsied head,
Out ower my crummock laigh I bend,
I'm wearin' to my journey's end;
I'm borne down wi' grief and care -
The load of life I scarce can bear.
A wither'd trunk, a leafless tree,
Is a' that now remains of me;
The days are gane that I hae seen,
Now I maun hirple hame my lane,
Wilyart, waesome, will, and weary,
O what cou'd mak' my auld heart cheerie!
But wae betide them that wauken my wraith,
I rede them beware o' trouble an' skaith;
For tho' I'm baith cripple an' hafflins blind,
They'll rin right fast when they leave me behind."

"Guid ev'nin' to ye, teethless granny,"
Quo' John, "ye're creepin' unco canny;
Ye're surely's auld's the deevil's mither -
Come, streek your houghs, we'el gang thegither,
For nane dare pass and leave auld wives,
Unless they're weary o' their lives:
Yea! how came ye, my winsome dame,
To ken Finella was my name;
Unless, in compact wi' 'auld Nick',
Ye're come to play me some foul trick; ...

An' troth I scarce believe ye're sterlin',
For vow ye are an ugly carlin'."

Wi' hollow voice, and accent cramp,
She stammert out - "You bloody scamp!
Your deeds, before this time to-morrow,
Shall cost ye muckle dool an' sorrow;
And mony sad sights shall ye see,
Before in sleep ye close an e'e;
Your worthless carcase whilk ye brag on,
I winna leave a rotten rag on,
But strip ye straight frae head to heel,
Ye vaig! like skinnin' of an eel.
For auld's I am, I can do wonders -
If I but wag my stick it thunders,
Lightens, rains, hails, or snows,

Or ony weather you'll suppose:
A buckie I to sea can rig out,
And of an egg-shell make a frigate;
Nay, in a thimble skim the flood,
Provided it be made of wood;
Without a curpin, bit, or saddle,
Upon a broom-stick ride astraddle,
With which I cut the viewless wind,
An' a' thing earthly leave behind,
Wi' warlocks whirl at barley-brack:
Right round the warl', as round a stack:
Play hide and seek ahint the moon,
An' list her dowie tenant croon;
Or mount up to the welkin's harns,
An' play bo-peep amang the starns!
Quicker than hail, by whirlwind driven,
I skim the milky way of heaven,
Or scud whare northern steamers play,
Yet tread this earth ere break of day."

Thrice wi' her teethless chafts she mumpit,
While nose and chin on ither thumpit.
Thrice she wav'd her skinny hand, …

And thrice invok'd the infernal band;
Thrice backwards round about she totter'd,
While to hersel' this leed she mutter'd:
Frae the east - frae the wast,
Thunder roar, lightnin' blast;
Frae the south - frae the north,
Pour wind and water forth:
Will-o-wisps! wirrycows!
Warlocks wi' your lyart pows,
At three quarters after ten,
Hover round auld Martin's Den.
Elspet, Mauzie, ho! ye hags,
Stride-legs o'er your broom-stick nags!
When the night grows rough and mirk,
Canter round auld Logie Kirk,
When ye hear the Kelpie howl,
Hie ye to the Ponage-pool;
There ye'll see the Deil himsel'
Leadin' on the 'hounds o' Hell'.
Over mountain, muir, and dale,
Ghaists and spectres, wan and pale -
Riding on the roarin' storm,
Dance in dread array before 'm;
The shadows rise! quick! and quicker!!
The tempest brews thick! and thicker!! ...

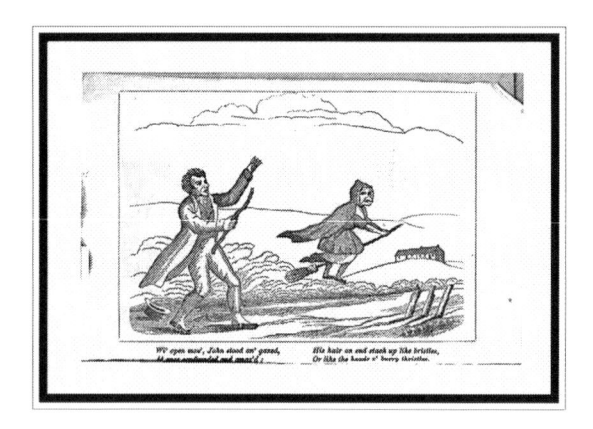

Now its time for me to bicker,
For oh! the charm is firm and sicker."
Wi' that her joints began to swacken,
Awa' she scour'd like ony maukin;
Ower dykes and ditches swift she frisket,
Through bogs and mires she lap an' whiskit;
Sae featly did she wing her flight,
In a twinklin' she was out o' sight.
Wi' open mou', John stood an' gaz'd,
At once confounded and amaz'd;
His hair on end stack up like bristles,
Or like the beard o' burry thristles;
An' aye as on the road he stoitit,
His knees on ane anither knoitit.

Frail man, alack! but seenil thinks,
While round him fortune's sunshine blinks,
(And having reach'd that point of fame,
Securing him "a deathless name"),
That ere ae fleeting hour gae past,
He may be streekit i' the blast;
Or lair'd, by spunkies i' the mire,
To dree the Water-kelpie's ire;
Hae a' his honours frae him torn,

And of his maughts, like Samson, shorn;
The agent too, mayhap the same,
Aye, sure in gender, not in name,
Which here is deem'd by much too long
Either to be said or sung.
A sudden gloom o'erspread the air,
Ilk creature seem'd oppress'd wi' fear;
The harmless bird crap to its nest,
And beasts o' prey retired to rest:
Black murky clouds began to muster;
And Boreas to rave and bluster; ...
The lightnin' twinkl'd i' the air
As yet wi' faint and feeble glare;
At distance too, the thunder grummelt, ...

An' throu' the welkin growl'd and rummelt,
The wind sough'd mournfu' throu' the trees,
Unearthly sounds swell'd i' the breeze;
Eftsoons the lightning's languid gleam
Blaz'd forth in sheets of livid flame,
And objects, shrouded deep in nicht,
Burst naked on the wond'ring sicht;
On Loan-way path each whalebone post
Were instant seen, and soon were lost;
And straucht again the groanin' trees
Kyth'd fetchin' wi' the balfu' breeze;
The thunder rair'd wi' furious thuds,
An' blatter'd throu' the low'rin' clouds,
Still clear an' clearer ilka flash,
Yet near an' nearer ilka crash;
The lightnin', thunder, wind, and rain,
Flash'd and roar'd and dash'd amain;
And O, how black the troubl'd air,
In absence of the lightnin's glare.
John crap alang. Toward the richt
He thocht he spied a cottage licht,
And steer'd his course in that direction,
Aneath its roof to seek protection;

But weary fa' the faithless licht,
It quickly vanish'd frae his sicht,
And left him in an eerie swither
Glampin' round, he kendna whither;
Again the fleeting taper glanc'd,
Again towards it John advanc'd;
It flar'd and flicker'd i' the wind,
Sometimes before, sometimes behind;
From richt to left - from left to richt,
It scatter'd a bewildrin' licht,
An' in a wink the glimm'rin' ray
Flash'd on his sicht, then died away;
Aye Willy-an-the-Wisp was there
Shedding forth his nichtly glare,
An' rousin' keen his fatal fire,
To wyle him to the weary mire. …

John row'd ower dykes, and lair'd in ditches,
Mutterin' malisons on witches.
Neist ower the plain, and down a hill,
He heard the clackin' of a mill;
Again the spunkies wav'rin' licht
Discovert to his wildert sicht
In boiling wraith, the North-Esk stream
Thuddin' onward, white wi' feam,
He heard a voice, wi' muckle dool,
Croonin' in the Ponage Pool,
And this it said, or seem'd to say -
"Ah, willawins! alack for aye,
O sair's my back, an' sair my banes
Leadin' the Laird o' Marphie's stanes;
The Laird o' Marphie canna thrive
As lang's the Kelpie is alive."
The thunder growl'd in lower tone,
As if to let the voice get on.
"God help ye! be ye freend or fae,"

Quo' John, "its wrang to use ye sae;
To me your griefs ye needna tell,
For waes my heart, I'm waur mysel;"
When, by the lightnin's glare, he saw
A sight surpassing nature's law -
A stalwart monster, huge in size,
Did straucht frae out the river rise,
Behind, a dragon's tail he wore,
Twa bullock's horns stack out before;
His legs were horn wi' joints o' steel,
His body like the crocodile.
On smellin' John, he gie'd a scoil,
Then plung'd and gar'd the water boil;
Anon he stood upon the shore,
And did for vengeance loudly roar. …

> A stalwart monster, keen in eise,
> His legs were horn wi' joints o' steel,
> Did straight frae out the river rise;
> His body like the crocodile.

Now John his painfu' silence broke,
And thus in daring accent spoke;
"Stand aff, ye fiend, and dread my wraith,
Or soon I'll steek your een in death:
Not you nor a' the hounds o' hell
Can my undaunted courage quell."
When waving straight his club on high,
That whisselt as it cut the sky -
"See ye, Sir, that gnarell'd aik,
Wi' which if I but gie ae straik
Athort the shanks or ower the head,
I'd dye the North-Esk river red,
And make at once the azure flood;
One purple stream of Kelpie's blood;
To show how easily I'll drub ye,
See, there I've flung away my club, ye,
For wi' my ain twa neives I'll smack ye
Tho' a' the deils in hell should back ye;
Sae, therefore, if you wish to thrive,
Be stepping ! - show your havins ! - dive!!

"Yelta billie," quo' the Kelpie,
"I carena for your threats - God help ye!
Gae bluster somewhere else, for here
Ye maunna think to domineer;
If I but grip you by the collar,
I'll gar you gape, and glower, and gollar,
An' thratch an' thraw for want of breath - ...

Ae squeeze o' that wad be your death;"
When, shakin' fierce his horny paw,
He gae a wild and loud gaffa:
Raised sic a rutherair and clatter,
The red brae tummelt i' the water;
The brig across the North Esk river
Did echo back the sound and shiver.
Had Mary Brig been then, I reckon,
That brig had frae its centre shaken.

"It is but richt your wraith to settle,"
Quo' John, "that you should know my mettle.
I'm weel ken'd here an' far awa -
My name is John o' Arnha'!
I slew three hunder Dublin bouchers,
For whilk I'm fit to show you vouchers;
I gar'd the pows flee aff their bodies,
Like nippin' heads frae carl doddies.
I've been through Hollan', Spain, and France,
And at Vienna learn'd to dance;
I tript it neat in silks an' satin,
An' to the damsels jabbert Latin;
This lingo here but few can speak it
Better than a pig could squeak it;
But gin ye only understand it,
Ye'll hear how nicely I mowband it;
Rummilforgan bardinarus -
Hoo nig fig gnippiti gnarus -
Drumhargelbargum skipperatis -"
The Kelpie scronnocht "Punctum satis! -
Your crack-jaw words of half an ell,
That rumble like a witch's spell,
Are nae the leed of ony tongue,
That ever in a head was hung,
Sin lingo was confused at Babel;
They mind me of a Turkey's gabble."
Quo' John, "They're Latin, but by jingo,
Ye'se get the rest in haimert lingo;
Sic' themes were never made to suit …

Your dozen'd lugs, ye duxy brute:
An' you that aye 'mang water buller,
How can you be a classic scholar!
In Africa I've preached to pagans,
At Coromandel danc'd wi' dragons;
On India's plains I've ruled mullatoes;
At Etna's flames, I've roas'n 'tatoes;
I've seen it spew its liquid lava
Ower a' Jerusalem and Java,
And rain, in hellish showers, its danders
On Holland, Poland, France, and Flanders;
I in its wame heard Vulcan ruddy
Upon his triple tempert studdy -
A limpin' spaviet bruikit wicht,
Wi' oily hide - a perfect fricht;
He swat and yarkit wi' his hammer,
The sparks flew frae his steel like glamour;
Twa black, outlandish gruesome fellows,
Were puffin' at his smiddy bellows;
Upo' the richt a mighty stove
For forgin' thunderbolts to Jove -
This nicht they're whizzin' through the sky,
Sae better to you mind your eye."
Said Kelpie, "That I'll take my chance on,
But faith, I sadly dread ye're scancin';
I mark him for a smeerless dolt,
Wha'd jouk t' eschew a thunderbolt;
Let rain descend and tempests roar,
I'll meet you on this dreary shore;
Though lightning blaze and thunder rattle,
I'm here prepared to give you battle;
I charge you braggart to prepare
For deeds of might - not words of air."

"I ne'er," quo' John, "like some, grow vain,
Or fecht my battles o'er again;
I only dinna wish to cheat ye,
To raise your wrath and syne defeat ye;
It's meet, before the battle rage,
You ken the foe ye've to engage. ...

I scorn a' leears and their lees;
I've been on islands made o' cheese:
Cross'd lakes o' bladdo milk and whay,
As braid and deep as Forth and Tay.
Frae Catterthun to Copenhagen
I rade upon a fiery dragon.
(Right through the air like 'Sancha Pancha',
And brave 'Don Quixote de la Mancha'),
Ten mile o' tail hung at his rump,
Compar'd to some 'twas but a stump.
Upon the sedgy banks of Nile
I've tiltit wi' the crocodile;
Wi' unicorns and alligators,
Fell tygers, elephants, and satyrs.
Like Hercules, the wale o' men,
I've dar'd the lion in his den:
When vengeance throu' my peepers glowr'd,
The stately monarch fawn'd and cowr'd,
An' creepin', lickit at my feet,
Like ony collie on the street.
Upo' the coast of Labrador
I've heard five hunder kelpies roar -
Five thousand faith! - the deil ane fewer,
And each ten times as big as you are;
I offer'd battle to them a' -
The cowards youl'd and ran awa'."
(The kelpie "grinn'd an eldric laugh;"
An' rubb'd his hooves upo' the haugh);
Quo' John, "ye needna scrape and nicker;
I'm neither fey nor waur o' licker;
I tell the truth - and hark ye sirrah,
I slew upon 'Del Feuga Terra',
A Giant, in height twal ell some inches,
An' sax between the oxter kinches;
Lang fresh he lay preserv'd 'mang snaw,
And frosty winds that there aye blaw;
But vultures pick'd his big banes bare,
And lined their nests wi' blood-stain'd hair;
Compar'd to him ye're but a dwarf,
The wind o's neives had gar'd you swarf - ...

This very day too, i' the market,
Five hunder sturdy hides I yarkit;
Between the shore and Kittlenakit,
There's few but I baith pran'd and paikit,
Spar'd neither man nor mither's son -
Yea, claw'd the back o' 'Horner John'!
Sae clean and snell the cracks I gaed 'm,
The heels flew ower the ugly head o'm;
And tho' ye be the water-kelpie,
I'll wad my whittle I sall skelp ye."

When castin's coat, he spat in's looves,
And bade the Kelpie use his hooves;
In dour conflict the parties clos'd,
Head to head - hands to hooves oppos'd;
Teugh was the tulzie, and for lang
Success in equal balance hang.
The Kelpie tried wi' John to grapple,
But Arn caught him by the thrapple,
And gar'd his carcase sweep the stanners,
Whilk made a noise like corn fanners;
He puff'd an' blew like ony whale -
He scourged the water wi' his tail,
An' threush on John as wi' a flail.
John pran'd him down among the mud,
And bade him lash his ain heart's blood,
That ran in torrents frae his side,
And chang'd the colour o' the tide.

The fiend, forjeskit, tried to 'scape,
Throu' frequent changin' o' his shape;
In various forms he did appear;
Sometimes a horse, sometimes a deer -
A wren - a hawk - a goose - a fox -
A tender lamb, or pondrous ox -
A ravenous wolf - a tim'rous hare -
A savage lion, or growling bear;
Then straight began to dive and frisk
Throu' and throu' the troubled Esk;
Row heels-o'er-head upo' the banks, ...

Wi' mony sic unseemly pranks,
An' nicker, bark, squeak, grunt, and gabble,
As he'd taen out's degrees at Babel:
But a' his airts could not avail him,
In every shape did John assail him;
And to ilk bellow, roust, and roar,
He lustily cried out, encore!
Till echo, for ten miles around,
Did to the horrid scoil resound.

Now terror siez'd the Kelpie's soul,
An' for assistance he did yowl!
At's call anon haill legions drive
Like swarms o' bees frae out a hive;
Like midgies after summer shower,
(Frail tenants of a fleeting hour);
Or like the locusts sent on Pharaoh,
Enough the stoutest heart to harrow.
A thousand phantoms skimm'd the breeze,
"As thick as mites in rotten cheese;"
Not harmless spirits, boding luck,
Like Robin, Mustard-seed, or Puck;
Or Brownies, aye discreet and civil;
But a' intent on working evil.

In wild array, the warlock men
Held orgies in Saint Martin's Den;
Deep i' the glack, and round the well -
Their mystic rites I canna tell;
None form'd of flesh, e'er dar'd to scan
The secrets of their dark divan.
Towards the west, auld Logie Kirk
Threw livid gleams athort the mirk;
The boards o' coffins fed the flames
(New houkit by the weirden dames),
Whilk, dipt in sulphur gae them licht
To hatch their spells by magic's sleicht;
They blaz'd and crackelt i' the blast,
And round a ghastly glimmering cast; …

The last remains of human clay,
That in the grave's dark chambers lay,
Were turn'd up to the pale blue licht;
The smell was loathsome - dire the sicht;
The skulls, and banes, and boards in cairns,
Lay scatter'd round amo' the ferns,
The hags, wi' mony a "horrid stave,"
Gaed whiskin' round ilk herriet grave.
The corbies scraight - the owlets scream'd,
A gusty cawdron boil'd and feam'd,
In which the beldames, eident, threw
Ingredients hideous to the view;
An' ay's they steer'd them wi' a theevil,
They mummelt "crowdy for the deevil."
And for a theevil they did use
A sturdy stump o' knotty spruce.
Wi' whilk a son came crash, O vow,
Outower his father's bare auld pow!
An' still the faithfu' bark retains,
The sacrilegious sinfu' stains,
Of lappert blood and human brains.

The thunder roar'd - the sweepin' blast,
Their reekit riven rags, blew past,
An' show'd their parchment thro' the glim,
Reistit, squalid, swarth, and grim;
The skin hang down in shrivell'd flaps,
Like spleuchans o'er their teethless chaps;
Throu' skinny lips their blasted breath
Mix'd wi' the wind and smelt of death.
A waesum, wild, wanliesum sicht,
Enough to quench the fires of nicht,
And blanch the lightning's livid licht.
Nae "winsome wench" was there, I ween,
Like 'Cutty Sark', to cheer the scene,
But blackest horror reign'd profound,
And threw its veil o'er all around.

Wi' breathless terror, and with awe,
John spied what cow'd him warst ava'; …

*The dame wha ga'e him sic a fricht,
An' frae the Loan-head took her flicht;
The hag that vow'd to work his ruin,
And set the hurricane a brewin':*

*"Elspet, Mauzie, fatal sisters,
Of the thread o' life the twisters" -
She cried "come quickly, let us brew
Frae hemlock, hellebore, and yew:
And by the cauldron's paley leam
We'll do the deed without a name;
Let each fling in her darge of death,
To 'nick the thread and choke the breath.'
But are ye sure he hasna pass't."*

ELSPET

I smell the braggart i' the blast.

MAUZIE

Then, sisters, here's a bishop's gizzard -

ELSPET

The tongue of Michael Scott the wizard.

GRIZZEL

*Three yauldrin's eggs, wi' devil's blood;
Five draps in each, ere since the flood.*

MAUZIE

*Three brander't bats, weel stew'd and slic'd,
Wi' stour o' dead men's een weel spic'd.*

ELSPET

Twa howlet's een - a corbie's maw; - …

The gullet of a hoodie craw.

MAUZIE

Scum the cauldron - feed the fuel -
Come, steer about the smervy gruel.

ELSPET

The liver of an unspean'd kitten -

MAUZIE

The thumb o' Faustus' doddy mitten.

GRIZZEL

The kaim and bells of cock that crew
Ere morning night's black curtain drew.

ELSPET

The dying drops by Voltaire sweaten.

GRIZZEL

The gagger lip o' Card'nal Beaton.

MAUZIE

From wand of Sidrophel a sprig -
Three curls of Justice Jeffries' wig -
Wi' nine draps of his black heart's gore,
Extracted frae the very core. ...

GRIZZEL

Weel done, Mauzie, that's a spell ...

Wad conjure a' the deils in hell;
Pour the heart's blood, drop and drop;
See how it flares upo' the top!

Three an' three, an' three, make nine, -
Steer about the hellish brine."

They scum'd the cauldron, fed the fuel -
They steer'd and pree'd the smervy gruel.
The mair they steer'd, the mair they pree'd,
The mair increas'd their hellish speed.
They flang and lap, an' lap and flang -
Fleyt and yammert, grat and sang -
Flew ower and ower the dreary biggin',
An' raid stride-legs upo' the riggin'.
O mercy! what a shamefu' sicht -
The bats and howlets scream'd wi' fricht;
Wi' mony wild, unearthly cry
They skirr'd alang the blazin' sky.

Wicked hags, abhorr'd and shameless,
Your ither pranks shall here be nameless;
For vow! your cantrips to hae seen
Had petrified a priest to stane;
An' flesh wad creep to hear it utter'd,
The sinfu' jargon that ye mutter'd.
Ay, legs wad totter - knees wad bend -
Blood leave the cheek - hair stand on end -
Cauld sweat distil - the bleach'd lip quiver;
The haill machine wad shake and shiver;
Een wildly stare, and stout hearts fail,
To hear sae strange sae wild a tale.

The vagrant dead, a gloomy host,
Now march'd frae Pluto's "dreary coast,"
And onward scour'd, in waefu' train -
The shades of those wham John had slain.
Three hundred fleeting forms, and more,
A' grim in death and soil'd wi' gore;
Goblins whinnert thro' the air …

Wi' chowlin' chafts and burnin' hair;
Gruesome fiends, black, gruff, and grim,
Weel charg'd wi' brunstane to the brim;
Daemons, dragons, spectres dire,

Spewin' reek, an' riftin' fire;
An' grisly ghaists, and "devils damn'd,"
Wi' liquid fire and sulphur cramm'd,
Flew to the spot, and full in view
Danc'd round poor John th' infernal crew.

New murder'd corses skimm'd the heath,
Wat wi' the cauld dew-draps o' death;
They glided past like snaw or sleet,
There faces pale's their win'in' sheet;
Some glowr'd and thratch'd, in deadly thraws,
Wi' death-fix'd een and open jaws;
Syne glampit at the vacant air,
An' vanish'd wi' the lightning's glare.

Now grimly kyth'd amang the crew
"The master-fiend that Milton drew."
He dought appear in ony shape,
Down frae a Titan to an ape,
Or, as his whimsies might prevail,
Up frae an emmet to a whale;
Or less, or bigger far than either,
Or in nae shape ava thegither;
That night, albeit, wi' solemn air,
He filled the Judge's sacred chair;
To mete out justice to his lieges,
His gravity was most prodigious;
Wi' specks on nose, and three-tail'd wig,
The wary fiend loom'd bluff and big;
Dark lurid clouds around him hung,
And vengeance hurtl'd on his tongue;
His wig, wi' sulphur powder'd well,
In ringlets o'er his shoulders fell,
Upon a robe of sable hue,
Made frae the stuff that never grew- …

That ne'er was spun by mortal hand, -
The produce of another land!
The forkit lightning form'd his chair!
His bench, a murky cloud of air;
Condens'd in form, it stood before 'm:
Chief justice of th' infernal Quorum.
Swith wi' ae glance the motley crew
Were rang'd within his eagle view.
Alack-a-day! waesucks for John!
His mergh an' mettle now are gone;
Courage, vigour, might, and glory,
Are fleeting all, and transitory;
Naething steady here is found-
The very earth itsel' flees round,
Just like a tap, or whirliegiggin',
That fouk can scarcely keep its riggin',
But are in danger, O Gude guide us!
Of being toss'd on Georgium Sidus!
Forc'd to a comet's tail to cling,
Or whirl round on Saturn's ring.

Nae man can be a man for ever,
The hour is come and John maun shiver,
And shake like willow wi' the wind,
Or Quaker after having sinn'd;
For wha cou'd fecht wi' forms o' air,
Or ware their flesh on banes sae bare?
An' weel kend he, it was nae joke

To tig wi' fiends that vomit smoke;
Or yet wi' wirrycows to mingle,
That brunstane beish, or bock up ingle.
He stood aghast, in waefu' case,
Wi' duntin' heart and ruefu' face;
Tho' still he strove his fears to hide,
He thocht upon his ain fire-side;
How neighbour Tam, secure frae harms,
Lay sound asleep in Elspa's arms,
While he was daidlet like a wonder,
Drench'd wi' rain, and deav'd wi' thunder; …

And piercing wind, and lightning's sheen,
Were like to blind his lookin' een;
In danger, too, at ilka breath,
Of being "claid in his last claith;"
For sic a crew wad thocht nae sin -
To "birze his saul ayont the skin;"
Or lang before the night was done,
To douk him deep in Acheron.

Ahon! for man's uncertain state!
What waes on life's grim journey wait!
What dangers are we doom'd to brave
"Between the cradle and the grave!"

The chieftain now, wi' yell and whoop,
To order call'd his grisly troop;
"Thrice he yowl'd throu' lungs o' leather,"
To bring the ghastly bands thegither.
This done - for music loud he roar'd;"
A sullen voice growl'd - "Yes, my Lord;"
And in a wink before him stood
A figure neither flesh nor blood.
At first the mirk obscur'd its form;
It hover'd dimly through the storm,
And whisper't John, "Know, to your cost,
I am the Patagonian's ghost,
Whom you in Terra Fuego slew,
Musician to this hellish crew.
If I had only play'd my spring,
I'll gar your ribs, you rascal, ring,
As ye did mine upon Cape Horn:
Ye'se never see the light of morn."

When lo! a flash o' livid light
Unveil'd him quickly to the sight.
He tower'd aloft, just like a steeple;
Or say, like Saul aboon the people;
His een were dismal, hollow sockets,
"As empty as a poet's pockets;"
I mean a poet in days of yore, …

For now they've gowd an' gear galore;
But muses vile, their lays inspire,
When Pegasus is rode for hire!
Howe'er so sweet they spring from art,
Gowd fires the head, but chills the heart.

Sae fares it, Wattie Scott, wi' you,
Ye "piper to the bold Buccleugh,"
Ye "Screw your pipes, an' gar them skirl,"
Till siller frae our pouches birl.
Ye write baith in an' out o' season,
Three verse for rhyme to one for reason;
It's true your lines rin smooth an' clink weel;
But oh! you like the bookman's chink weel!
As soon's ye clench each flowing line,
Twa gowden guineas clink and shine:
They charm your ear, they charm your eye,
"With all a poet's ecstacy."
Heavenly music, heavenly fire,
Eneugh auld Plutus to inspire,
Or gar the Deevil streek his lyre;
E'en poesy draw from Turks and Jews,
For gowd may sometimes fee a Muse.
O shame upon your venal lyre,
It heats my vera blood to fire,
To hear your fulsome partial praise
Peal'd through "Don Rod'rick's" lofty lays!
There living heroes ride sublime
Upon the surge of flowing rhyme;
But weary fa' your tunefu' tongue,
The dead lie silent and unsung;
Wi' foreign mools deep cover'd o'er
Upon Corunna's dreary shore.
Belike they mauna grace thy page
That canna yield thee patronage.
I grudge not WELLINGTON his fame;
I grudge not BERESFORD a name;
Or "glory to the gallant GRAEME!"
But should not every honour due
Be paid the dead and living too? …

By Heaven! I swear ye're sair to blame?
That MOORE should "rest without his fame."
How could you, Scott, forget the grave
Where sleep the ashes of the brave?

But yet, Sir, glory's wreath shall bloom
Around his hallow'd, silent tomb;
And streaming eyes shall view the spot,
When "Rod'rick's Vision" is forgot.

You seek the court, and flee the lawn!
To wealth you cringe - on power you fawn!
Pour incense at the courtier's shrine:
Wi' you, the Great are aye Divine!
You dinna "sing to village churls,
But to high dames and mighty earls."
Then sing, Sir, to the rich - the great -
The proper gudgeons for your bait:
Help Southey wi' his Birth-day Odes!
Make princes angels, victors Gods;
And as you greet the royal ears,
Forget not, oh! to "rend the spheres!"
And give them honour, grace, and glory,
As I do in this humble story.
For you to fawn sae, 'tis a shame!
Indeed poor Southey's nae to blame;
For wha could Laureate be appointit
That wadna laud the Lord's anointit -
His ministers and a' their measures,
The pomp of princes and their pleasures;
That wadna gloss ilk public greivance,
And screen the hirelings of St. Stephen's;
Nay, laud a spy or ruthless jailor -
But wae betide thee, "Watty Tyler!"
Thou'st laid the Laureate on his back,
An' gard him shiver for his sack:
It's true, dear Bays, and well you know it,
Yet still you are a pretty poet;
I therefore pray thee to excuse
The havins of a hamely muse: ...

She ne'er was taught finesse or fawning,
Like 'Castlereagh' and 'Mister Canning'.

It's easy for the "best of kings"
To deal about his straps and strings,
And ony courtly cringing wight
To dub a Marquis or a Knight;
Or to create, by the same rule,
A Renegade his poet and fool!
A sordid elf, to pipe for pay;
In politics the 'Priest of Bray'!
But can he mak' an HONEST MAN? -
Ah! sorrow fa' me if he can!
So sang the Bard, now dead and gone
Poor BURNS! Apollo's dearest son!
"'Tis said, and I believe the tale,
His humblest reed could more prevail -
Had more of strength, diviner rage,
Than all that charms this laggard age."
Yet still a narrow-minded few,
A feeble, canting, creeping crew,
Conspire to blast his honest fame,
And heap reproaches on his name;
Because, alas! the Bard has shown
Far finer feelings than their own,
He wasna just a saint like Southey,
That never sinn'd nor yet was drouthy:
What tho' he lik'd a social glass-
What tho' he lo'ed a bonnie lass? -
He ne'er disgrac'd his well strung lyre,
By chaunting balderdash for hire;
Nor roos'd he ony courtly elf,
Or bow'd the knee for warld's pelf.
The mavis as she hails the morn,
The speckl'd gowd-spink on the thorn,
The lark, on dewy pinions borne,
Pour forth their lays for sic reward
As did their kindred rural bard;
Ae kindly blink o' Jeanie's e'e
O'erpaid him for his minstrelsy. ...

His tale is told, his song is sung -
Deaf is his ear, and mute his tongue;
The pigmies now may safely rail -
He canna answer for himsel';
And if he dought, wha wad hae dar'd
To tamper wi' the mighty Bard?
It wad be folly in a wren
To beard the lion in his den.
Wae worth the Bard, again I say,
That sings for guerdon or for pay.
Now, by my fay, I'm going bonny on,
I'd maist forgot the Patagonian;
Like Butler, wi' his bear and fiddle,
I've left the subject i' the middle;
But to my story now I'll fast stick;
I mauna fa' the Hudibrastick.
Well, soaring o'er the squalid host,
We left the giant's grimly ghost;
Like the oak above the underwood,
In majesty the spectre stood.
His banes were bare, and bleach'd like linen,
While ev'ry art'ry, nerve and sinnen,
Were screw'd in concert, flat and sharp,
To whistle like the AEolian harp.
Ilk tendon, taght like thairm, was lac'd;
Twa wounds, seem'd sound holes, on his breast;
And as the wind at times fell low,
Or ceas'd a hurricane to blow,
His fingers then supplied the blast,
As o'er the twanging chords they past;
And neither thunder, rain, or fire,
Could e'er untune that awsome lyre.

As soon's he rear'd him to the storm,
His shrivell'd fibres 'gan to mourn;
And frae his hollow trunk soon came out
A' the notes upo' the gamut.
First dismal sounds of deep despair
Burst hollow on the troubelt air;
Join'd by the minstrel's vocal tones - ...

Unearthly wails, and dolefu' groans;
The air was sad - the key was low -
The words were wild - the measure slow:
Anon he trill'd it, light and airy,
Sweet as the harp of ony fairy,
When lightly trip the tiny crew
O'er hillocks green, and tipple dew;
As if to show his lyric skill,
And that the tones were at his will:
But voices grummelt, "Please your honour,
We canna hear him for the thunner!"
When Sathan bellow'd, fierce with ire -
"You duxy lubber, brace your lyre!
Still higher yet! you fiend, play higher!!"

Now, swith wi' vir, he whirl'd him round,
An hideous instrument of sound!
His fleshless fingers swept the lyre
With all a minstrel's force and fire:
Oh then, indeed! the coil began,
Sic sounds ne'er reach'd the ear of man:
From right and left, before, behind,
He flang his music on the wind;
In whispers, sighs, loud yells and screams,
Such as are heard in devil's dreams;
Eldrich, eerie, uncouth strains,
That turn'd a' their heads and brains:
Till midnight hags did round him gallop,
An' gard their wither'd hurdies wallop!
Hobgobblins round an' round him whirl'd,
Auld grey-beard warlocks lap an' skirl'd,
Pou'd the hair frae ithers' pallets,
And tore, in wraith, the witches' callets!
The lightnin' flash'd - the wind blew sharper,
Louder squeel'd the fleshless harper!
O'er treble height he rais'd his lays,
The thunder growl'd a double base!
'Till swith inspir'd by his ain lyre,
He up and till't himsel' like fire-
Hurra'd, an' cheer'd, an' feez'd his chanter, …

An' lap, like Meg to Rob the Ranter!
Shook his brainless skull in passion,
And roar'd like ony bull o' Bashun.
As thro' the mazy dance he whirlt,
The vera ground beneath him dirlt.
Still loud and louder howl'd the storm -
The harper skirlt up "Tullochgorum;"
Follow'd fast by "Callum Brogie,"
"Delvin Side," and "Boat o' Logie."
Wi' vengefu' vir, and norlan' twang.
Till a' his banes and fibres rang;
An' a' the devils in a ring
Yarkit up the Highland fling;
They yell'd and whiskit round and round
And duntit wi' their paws the ground;
"The vera moudiworts were stunn'd:"
E'en Sathan seem'd to enjoy the sport;
He cried, "My hearties, that's your sort;
Come, keep it up, my jolly boys!
Nor let me interrupt your joys;
Ill wad it suit my robes and wig,
To whirl in a waltz or jig;
But be assur'd, neist haly night,
I'll skelp it up wi' a' my might:
Fandangos, 'jigs, strathspeys, and reels,'
Ay, till the fire flee frae my heels."
The Assembly echoed their applause,
And cheer'd him thrice wi' loud huzzas!
The vera ghaists play'd antic pranks,
They screight an' shook their spindle-shanks!
An' lent each other ruthless paiks
Athort the bare and merghless spaiks;
While still, at ilka thud and sough,
They cried, "weel done! - hey! - hilloa!! - whoogh!!!"

Clappit their wither'd hands an' leugh,
'Till, 'mid the din of dance and battle,
Their banes were heard for miles to rattle!
Beatin' time, expert and nimble,
Douff like drum, and snell like cymble;. ...

An' aye's they fell to crockinition,
Their wizzent timbers stour'd like sneishin;
An' flew, in duds, athort the lift,
As choakin' thick as yowden drift.
Puir John was fain to clear their range, or
Sooth his ribs had been in danger;
For mony a time, when eident loupin'
They slyly tried heels up to coup 'im;
An' fidgin' fain to try his mettle,
Did mony a lerrup at him ettle;
But Belzie bade them stand aloof,
Till of his guilt they brought some proof.

When lo! a Spectre, lank and pale,
Advanc'd to tell his waefu' tale;
Wi' mony a scar his visage frown'd,
His bosom gash'd wi' mony a wound:
His een were out, but thro' the sockets
The lightnin' play'd like Congreve rockets!
His maughtless hands on's thigh-bones clatter'd,
His fleshless jaws on ither chatter'd,
The wind sang thro' his sapless form,
Which rockit to the roarin' storm,
And issuing mony a dreary sound,
Join'd concert with the scene around.
"Grim King of brunstane, soot, and fire,"
He said "I come at your desire;
An allagrugous, gruesome spectre,
A' gor'd and bor'd, like Trojan Hector:
How slim and shrivell'd is that corpus,
That ance was plump as ony porpus;
In darkness, and on whirlwinds borne,
On me ne'er blinks the light of morn;
Nor zephyrs, blawn by breath o' day,
Can on my pallid carcase play:
My flesh, devour'd by hungry worms,
Has left my banes to dree the storms
Of wind and rain and fire 's you see -
O mercy! what will come o' me." …

He shook, convuls'd, and strove to cry-
His tears were drain'd - the source was dry;
The rain ran down his cheek-banes, clear,
Unmingl'd wi' ae briny tear;
His moisture a' was drunken up,
And bitter, bitter was his cup:
Deep frae his breast came mony a groan -
He paus'd a while, and then went on:
"Ance dear to me the morning ray -
Ance dear the radiant beams of day;
And sweet the gloamin's purple gleam
That dy'd the bosom of the stream;
But now, mair welcome to my sight
The darksome hues of dreary night,
And a' that nature's face deforms,
Dire earthquakes, famine, fire, and storms;
I carena though this globe should moulder,
An' a' creation gae to sculder!"

To whom the chief - "Your murmurs cease!
I see the hardship of your case;
But this is not the point in hand-
Come, tell me quickly, I command -
Upon your oath - if that's the man
Who circumscribed your mortal span?"
(His right hand, pointing streight to John,
Who clos'd his eyes, and heav'd a groan).
He swore - then said, "May I be scourg'd
If I am not of malice purg'd,
And eke revenge, and partial counsel,
Albeit the brute has used my sconce ill;
Wi' mony words I winna deave ye,
Mark down depones affirmative."
Syne chowl'd his chanler chafts at John,
And vanish'd wi' a' dolefu' groan.
John chowl'd again - and cried, "I scorn ye,
Ye shadow of a sly attorney;
If such as you I'd only slain,
My arm had ne'er been rais'd in vain." …

Swith, wi' a low and hollow sound,
A Figure startit throu' the ground,
And rais'd baith yird and stane upright:
O vow! it was an awsome sight.
A headless trunk, in anguish, stood,
Sair bor'd wi' wounds, and smear'd wi' blood:
Ae arm a stump - the ither bore
The gausty pallet, grim wi' gore.
He loutit him wi' due respeck,
An' toutit throu' his hummel neck:
His speech was eldrich and uncouth,
'Cause, losin's head, he'd lost his mouth:
He spake a language, rough and rude,
Yet he was eithly understood.
The Judge exclaim'd - "Enough! retire!!
And hark ye! raise a rousin' fire!!"
He flang at John the gory pow,
An' disappear'd a' in a low.

The Harper, in a mournfu' strain,
Sang how by John he had been slain;
And how he lay upon Cape Horn,
His flesh by rav'nous vultures torn;
Sang how they pick'd his banes sae bare,
And plucket frae his pow the hair
To nestle saft their savage young:
A dowie sang as e'er was sung.
An' how, without a' earthly motion,
His ghost had cross'd the Atlantic ocean,
Five thousand miles frae his cauld hame,
Swift gliding o'er the saut sea feam;
While, as he skim'd the ocean along,
He harpit to the Mermaid's song;
And he harpit high, and he harpit low,
As the air was calm, or the wind might blow;
Until his will and weary ghost
Came bump against the Scotian coast;
And soon by the breeze frae the land he smelt
It was there where his bloody murderer dwelt,
More he said 'twas bootless to tell, …

The rest was known to Nick full well.
Here the 'Justice' nodded assent,
And harping away the Minstrel went.
The Kelpie likewise gae his aith,
That John had tried to stap his breath,
An' did misguide him past resistance,
Afore he roar'd out for assistance.
Now mony a gaunt and shadowy form
Rode hideous on the roaring storm;
In grim procession, rank and file,
Their line extended mony a mile:
They pointed to their gaping wounds,
And skim'd alang wi' eerie sounds:
As each pass'd John in sad review,
The blood stream'd frae his wounds anew,
Which, plainer told than words might tell,
'Twas by his murd'rous hands they fell.
Like vision in a Prophet's dream,
The chief bestrode the North-esk stream;
Ae foot in Mearns, and ane in Angus
(Lord keep sic gentry out amang us!):
Colossus-like, he tower'd on high,
Till, wi' his wig, he brush'd the sky;
Then, loud as thunder, roar'd out "Havock!

The sound rang throu' the hill o' Garvock;
O'er Marykirk and Coble-heugh,
And down the dale wi' hollow sough;
While Craigo woods, and Martin's Den,
Re-echoed "Havock" back again:
Loud howl'd the yawning caves of nicht;
The watch-dogs yirr'd and youf'd wi' fricht;
The foxes wildly yowl'd wi' wonder,
And whing'd, and cow'rd, and left their plunder;
The timid teuchit slouch'd its crest,
And cuddled closer to its nest;
The watchfu' mate flaff'd i' the gale,
Wi' eerie screech and plaintive wail,
Now soar'd aloft, now scuff'd the ground,
And wheel'd in mony an antic round; …

The trouts div'd deeper i' the brook,
The hare, like ony aspin, shook,
And mortals quak'd on beds of fear,
As echo pierc'd the drowsy ear;
Their rest disturb'd - they wist not how,
The clammy sweat stood on the brow;
They hear'd the wind and beating rain,
An' dover't o'er asleep again.
Wi' mony a sigh and dolefu' grane,
John gaz'd stramulyert on the scene:
Dim wax'd the lustre o' his e'e,
He guess'd the wierd he had to dree;
Ilk creature's dread 'twere vain to tell,
E'en frae the benmost bores o' hell,
The damn'd rebellow'd back the yell!

Like lions prowlin' for their food,
Or tygers bath'd in human blood;
Grim furies spread their forkit fangs,
An' drove at John wi' furious bangs:
Neist witches claught him in a crack,
An' roove the duds frae afT his back;
The spunkies round his hurdies hirsel'd,
Till's vera hide was peel'd and birsel'd.
Wi' wicked glee the warlocks dous'd him.
And splash! into the river sous'd him!

Oh! never sin' he first was cradelt,
Was John sae sadly dung and daidelt.
Again they trail'd him to the shore -
For mercy he began to roar:
In turn the Kelpie cried, "Encore!
Mercy! surely! ha, ha, te hee!
Sic mercy as you show'd to me!
Sic mercy as you show'd the Bouchers -
Ow! whare's your Latin now and vouchers,
Your fiery dragons and mullatoes,
Your burning mounts and roas'n 'tatoes!

Your silks and satin, fibs, and scancin', ...

Your airy flights, and foreign dancin':
We hae ye, billie, i' the grip,
An' damn the dog that let's ye slip;
As lang's the blood runs i' your veins,
Or, while there's flesh upon your banes:
You never mair shall see your hame;
Nay, from the book of life your name,
Before the cock proclaim the morn,
Is doom'd to be eras'd and torn."

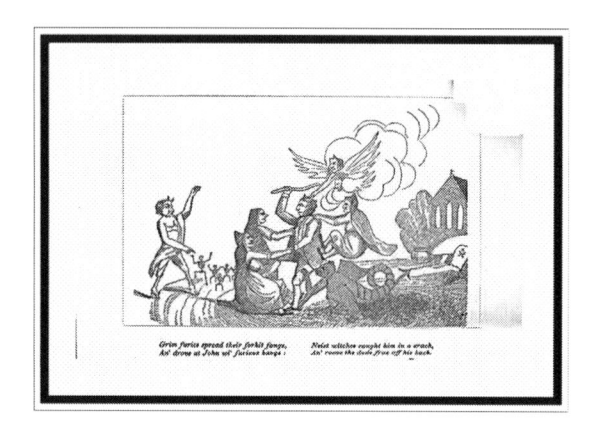

Grim furies spread their forkit fangs,   Noist witches caught him in a wrack,
An' drove at John wi' furious bangs;   An' reeve the duds frae off his back.

Now fierce each miscreated form
Career'd upon the mid-night storm,
Around their prey, wi' ghastly grin,
And stunn'd his ears wi' horrid din:
They gnash'd their teeth, and spat and snor'd;
Some squall'd like cats - some hoarsely roar'd;
The wildest howls, compar'd to theirs,
Might seem the music of the spheres.
Earth trembl'd thrice! another shake
Had clear'd the cuff o' Atlas' neck,
And launch'd this mighty Ball apace,
To range the bounds of endless space.
It cogl'd thrice, but at the last
It rested on his shoulders fast.
Still, huge in stature, stood the chief,
Like Lochnagar, or Teneriffe;
When clouds upon their summits lie, …

They seem to prop a low'ring sky:
He loudly howl'd - "Ye furies catch him,
And to the sooty regions snatch him:
Swith! do your work - flay, blast, and burn,
The hour that severs night from morn
Is on the wing and soon ye'll hear
The silver voice of Chanticleer:
Then haste before the dawn of day
Deprive us of our lawful prey
Come! clapperclaw him while ye may."
Now a' the crew prepar'd at ance
To shower a volley on his banes,
And peal'd forth sic an awsome yell -
He swarf'd wi' fear, and senseless fell
Upon the sward, wi' hollow groan,
And lay as cauld and still's a stone;
While, in their reckless random speed,
To number him among the dead,
The fiends row'd ower him where he lay,
And grappelt ither for their prey.
But, ere he met his final doom,
Aurora peep'd athwart the gloom;
The grey cock clapp'd his wings and crew -
The Harper loud a parley blew;
The morning air sang i' the blast; -
The hour of retribution's past!
And helter-skelter, swift aff flew
The Deil an' a' the infernal crew:
They scream'd - then vanish'd frae the sight,
Like empty visions o' the night.
The bleeding shadows of the slain
Fast glided to their graves again,
A' cauld and pale, as snaw-flakes driven
Athwart the dusky arch of Heaven,
When winter waves his frozen spear;
And sternly rules the "varied year;"
And wing'd, with speed, the fiendish host
Betook them to another coast;
But what that coast, or where it lay,
Is not for silly Bard to say. …

And now the thunder ceas'd to roar,
The forked lightning flash'd no more:
Rain ceas'd to fa' - the wind to breathe,
An' a' was calm and still as death
A', save the rushing o' the stream,
And past events seem'd like a dream.
No farther light the record gives,
Save that the valiant hero lives,
A pilgrim on this mortal stage,
And has attained a good old age;
That it hath been his happy lot
Five times to tie the nuptial knot:
To be the spouse of five sweet flowers
As ever blush'd in bridal bowers;
A dire reproach to every dunce

That never grac'd the altar once!
Lang may he live, unvex'd with care:
"None but the brave deserves the fair;"-
Lang may he live, baith hale and sound,
And never feight another round,
"Till Death slip sleely on, and gie the hinmost wound."

JOHN o' ARNHA'

The Murderit Mynstrell

How sweitlie shonne the morning sunne

Upon the bonnie Ha'- house o' Dun:
Siccan a bien and lovelie abode
Micht wyle the pilgrime aff his road;
But the awneris' hearte was harde as stane,
And his Ladye's was harder still, I weene.
They neur gaue amous to the poore,
And they turnit the wretchit frae thair doore,
Quhile the strainger, as he passit thair yett,
Was by the wardowre and tykkes besett.
Oh there livit there ane bonnie Maye,
Mylde and sweit as the morning raye,
Or the gloamin of ane summeris daye:
Hir haire was faire, hir eyne were blue,
And the dymples o' luve playit round hir sweit mou;
Hir waiste was sae jimp, her anckil sae sma,
Hir bosome as quhyte as the new-driven snawe
Sprent o'er the twinne mountains of sweit Caterthunne,
Beamand mylde in the rayes of a wynterie sunne,
Quhair the myde of a fute has niver bein,
And not a cloud in the lift is sein;
Quhen the wynd is slumb'ring in its cave,
And the barke is sleeping on the wave,
And the breast of the ocean is as still
As the morning mist upon Morven Hill.
Oh sair did scho rue, baith nighte and daye,
Hir hap was to be thiss Ladye's Maye.
Ae morning a Mynstrell, aged and poore,
Came harping to thiss Ha'-house doore;
His heart seimit light, thoch his hewit was bare,
And spairlie covent wi' thinne quhyte haire;
His bearde adown his bosome fell -
Streamand like snowe in a wynterie gale.
Sae sweit and blythesome was his laye,
The gowd-spinke dancit upon the spraye; …

The lint-quhite chirpit frae the busch,
And sweetlie sang the lark and the thrusch;
Quhyle dyght in grein, the fairie crew
Dancit frae the grass the morning dew,
For the daemons of nighte had taken their flighte
As soon as they saw the morning lighte,
And the ghaistis had left the drearie yewe;
Oh they trippit sae lightlie over the lea,
Thair nymble feet scant mocht ane see;
Thair doublettes were grein, as grein mocht be,
And they shonne in the sunne lyke the Spainzie flee.
And aye the Mynstrell harpit and sang,
Till his notes throu' ilka chamber rang:
Thoch decrepit, forlorne, and raggie was he,
There was merghe in his fingeris, and fyre in his e'e;
Thoch his voice it was broken, and tremmult full sore,
He sung Caledonia's battels of yore;
Hir mountains sae wylde, and her sweit smyling playns,
And the graces and luves of hir nymphs and hir swayns.
He brushit the wyre wi' mickle glee;
He lyltit his notes righte merrilie,
As giff nae dolowre michen he dree.
The Ladye of Dun scho rung hir bell -
"Quhat noyse is thiss - pray quicklie tell;
Quhat meins thiss lylting and deray?
A bonnie-lyke rippit thiss, by my fay!"
-"A Mynstrell, Madam, aged and poore,"
Quod the Damischell, "is harping at the doore:
And oh, my Ladye, I'm wae to see him,
And wishe I had onlie somethyng to gie him,
For his doublette is raggie, his hewit is bare,
And the wind sings throu' his thinne quhyte haire,
Albeit his layes be blythsome and sweit,
He hasna a bachel to cover his feit." -
"Harping at thiss tyme of the morne,
Upon my lyfe it canna be borne;
Ye menseless woman, gae tell my men
To flyng the catyffe o'er the Denn,
And let him perische i' the deip,
For raisand the Ladye o' Dun frae her sleip." ...

The Damischell lookit sae wae and sae meik,
And a pearl of pity stood cleir on ilk cheik, -
"Shall I tell him, my Ladye, to wend o'er the lea,
And he winna come back for bountith or fee;
The sillie auld carl, may peace gae wi' him,
I'm sure, dear Ladye, thiss tyme ye'll forgie him."
Her voice was sae sweit, and she bendit hir knee,
And the moisture of ruthe dimm'd hir bonnie blue e'e,
Quhilk glissent lyke the sunne throu' a cloud in June,
Or the mylder radiance of the moone,
As scho rides in the heavens all alone,
And the thinne mysts of summer sail round her throne:
Ane angell from God mocht hae kisst that sweit face,
And returnit to Heaven all pure from the embrace.
"Swythe, out of my presence! ye heard quhat I said,"
Quod the Ladye - "'Tis meit that my behests be obey'd."
The men they had dancit to the Mynstrell's laye,
But readie their Ladye's behests to obeye -
Thae fleichin, sinfu', murtherous men,
They flang the harper o'er the Denn,
And loot him perische i' the deip,
For raisand the Ladye o' Dun frae hir sleip.
He priggit for mercie - he prayit for grace,
Quhyle the tearis ran doun his aged face;
He vowit to Heiven he maint nae offence,
And beggit the men to lett him gae hence -
To hirple his waas to the cot - house doore,
And cheir with his layes the semple and poore;
For thoch his comforts here were but few,
His bosome beat to Nature trewe.
"Nae mercie here," quod the men "can be given,
But we hope, auld man, you'll meet it in Heiven;
Our Ladye's behests we are bound to obey,
Albeit we hae dancit to your roundelay;
Then stryke on your harpe the last sound of woe,
Before that you sleip in your cauld bed below!"

The Laird o' Dun had power of the law;
The Mynstrell was flung in, harpe an a':
The Mynstrell he groan'd, and his harpe it rung, …

And mute for aye was his tunefu' tongue!
A waesome syght it was to see -
Him launchit sae quick to eternitie!
Ance kythit o'er the streame his bearde sae hoare -
Syne his spirit wingit its way to gloare;
And niver mair was that Mynstrell sein;
But aye and anon, at morn and at e'en,
His harpe it sounded to the breize,
And a figure was sein to glide throu' the trees,
And groans were heard, sae loud and sae deip,
The Ladye o' Dun could niver mair sleip;
But aye the mament scho winkit an e'e,
Scho saw before hir, as plain as mocht be,
The Mynstrell wyde gapin and wreathin in paine,
And suein for mercie he couldna obtaine,
And wringin his hands in wylde despaire,
And waggin his head and his thinne quhyte haire,
Quhyle veive in her fancie wad scho see,
The ghastlie glowre of his death-set e'e;
And his clay-cauld hand wad presse hir cheike;
Oh then wad scho start frae hir bedde and shreike, -
"Haud aff that hand! oh, withdraw that e'e;
For Heiven's sake, take him away from me!

His bearde seemis smearit over wi' feame:
Oh! I wish it were, but its nae - a dreame!
For he looks sae wyldie in my face
That I wish to God he had metten wi' grace!
Lord! send to my saul the balsame of peace:
Oh, quhen shall I fynde it? Neuer - neuer!
It has fledde this bosome for euer and euer!"

The Bark

Oh, red, red was the rising sun,

And red the earth he shone upon,
And red the ocean beneath him roll'd,
And its surface was like burnish'd gold;
Yet hoarse and hollow was its roar,
As it gurlg'd against the rocky shore;
For although the wind seemed fast asleep,
It held its influence over the deep;
And those that heard a sound so hollow,
Prophesied that a storm would follow,
While evermore, as the drowsy wave
Receded from the briny cave,
Soft murmurs stole upon the ear;
Such as the pensive love to hear:
And the raven, perched upon the rock,
To each murmur joined his prophetic croak.
Yet every thing in the sea, in the air,
And on the earth, was mild, serene, and fair!
So lovely, gentle, bright, and bland,
That I thought myself in fairy land.

A little bark, with seeming glee,
Was rocking on the golden sea,
And spreading wide her snow-white sail
To catch on its breast the coy gale.
But not a breath on its bosom blew;
Albeit the saying is noways new -
Still women and wind prove oft untrue;
And which of them vex poor seamen worst,
If I can tell - may I be *****.
Now methinks I hear the landsmen cry ...

"Hear is the bathos profound - O fy!
A tarry sailor is the poet."
Say I, "that's true any lubber might know it."
Yet seamen feel as keen as others,
And why should not seamen and landsmen be brothers?

As yet this bark, with seeming glee,
Was rocking on the golden sea;
And no distinction 'twixt windward and lee.
Around her the playful sea birds lave
Their plumage in the sparkling wave;
And they sported upon the glassy sea,
Like guileless lambs, on the flowery lea:
They dived below, and they rose again,
And they seemed like speckles on the main -
Now disappearing, now returning,
Like the watery beams of an April morning;
But the sail that hung as white and as still
As the snow upon Benvoirlich Hill,
Now shook and flapped against the mast,
Precursor of the coming blast, -
Though from what point that blast might blow,
As yet the steersman did not know.

A blackened blast now blew from the sea,
And soon it was seen the land was the lea.
The bark now lay to the leeward side;
And along the surface began to glide;
Dipping her gunwale in the ocean,
She shot ahead with a rapid motion.
The breast of the sail was full, and now
The waves in wrath were dashed from the prow;
Spitting, splashing, she floundered along -
Strait in each stay, and stiff in every thong.
The hollow sound was heard no more,
But the breakers in vengeance lashed the shore,
The clouds, erewhile of a crimson dye,
Now mustered murky in the sky;

They marched in front of the morning sun, …

And his shining for that day was done.
No more the sportive sea birds lave
Their plumage in the sunny wave;
The curlew's melancholy wail
Came deep and plaintive on the gale -
A solemn sad foreboding cry:
The startled mew flew screaming by.
The breast of the ocean gleamed no more
Like a yellow lake of molten ore;
But soon it assumed a dark, dark hue -
I pity that bark and her weary crew.

The wind and the sea still louder roar;
There is no safety in seeking the shore, -
A pile of rocks, both bold and steep,
There frown majestic over the deep;
And evermore, on the topmost rock,
Is heard the raven's dismal croak.
The lovely morn - the magic light
That gilded the earth and the ocean so bright,
And painted all creation gay -
Like happiness, had passed away:
I look'd yet wistful from the strand,
But I saw no more of fairy land.

Still louder it blew; and the briny spray
Was blown like drift athwart the bay,
White and thick as the winter snow,
That scours the plain when tempests blow;
And often over the deck it flew -
In showers upon the dripping crew;
In balls the yesty foam flew past,
Borne to landward on the blast.
A sunken rock in the offing lay,
Unknown to strangers in that bay;
No buoy, nor beacon, erected there,
To guard against the fatal snare.
The labouring bark, with sudden shock,
Was impelled against that hidden rock!
It seemed that an opening in her side, …

Voracious, drank the briny tide, -
For she yawed around with a palsied motion,
Then sunk to the bottom of the ocean,
Down in the navel of the bay,
Quick as the sea-fowl after its prey.
As anxious I gazed with pity and awe,
The crew, like specks, on the surface I saw;
I sorrowed to see their woful case,
And the tears and the spray mixed on my face,
I saw them grapple with the wave,
And I saw them sink to a watery grave!
Their hour was come, and they soundly sleep
In the roomy bosom of the deep.
I either heard a distant cry,
Or the wail of the wind as it whistled by;
But which of these now matters not -
It cannot change their awful lot.
I listened again, but I heard no more,
Save the howl of the blast and the ocean's roar,
And the scream of the mew and the curlew's wail,
As they flitted past upon the gale:
Then mournfully I bore away,
And I swabbed from my cheeks the tears and the spray,
But I'll never forget what I saw that day.

Native Music

Oh, strains! for ever, ever dear;
While thus you swell your varied note,
Methinks angelic forms are near;
Aerial warblings round me float!
Now sadly sweet the numbers glide,
And pity mourns the tender woes
Of her who wept a "widowed bride,"
Where soft the classic Yarrow flows.
And now the strains, in tears they steep,
For him who leaves his native shore;
Who, doomed to cross the western deep,
Shall never see Lochaber more.
Breathe, gentle airs! and draw the tear
For her, the maid in beauty's pride,
Who mourns her absent lover dear,
By Logan's fairy-haunted side.
Symphonious sounds! whose warbled strain
Comes caroled sweet from yonder glade;
Ye bring my childhood back again -
Ye speak of days for ever fled!
Days of delight! when free to stray
Where slow the North Esk winds along,
I listened to your love-lorn lay -
I joyed to hear your Doric song.
So the poor Swiss, as pensive slow,
He journeys o'er some foreign clime,
If chance he hear these wild notes flow,
That soothed him on his hills sublime.
So with delighted ear attends;
So courts their magic melody;
Bethinks him of his home and friends,
And gives them sad, a tear - a sigh.

KETTY PERT

TUNE: *"The Boatie Rows"*

THEY ca' me auld Ketty Pert,

And my man Tammie Allen,
But ne'er did I my Tam dezert,
For a' that's 'tween us fallen.

Chorus

By zellin' mussels, vlukes, an' eels,
I win my daily breed;
At night wi' meat I vill my creels;
To beg I ne'er 'ad need.

When ance, wi' murlin by my zide,
Down to the zands I gaed;
Zurrounded was I by the tide,
Upon a mussel bed.

This prayer unto my zell I zays -
Lord, a' my zins vorgee;
I've lived by mussels a' my days,
Now 'mang them I maun dee.

When young I was baith vair and vleet;
And now, the Lord be thankit,
I can gae up throu' a' the street,
And nane gan bo' my blanket.

Oh that some honest gentlemand
Ahint wad turn free;
And as by chance come to the zands
And zee auld Ketty dee. …

God provideth, in his providence,
Vor low as weel as high:
Just when I thought I wou'd go hence,
Twa gentlemend cam by.

By this time I began to float,
And heedeously to roar;
The angels cam aff in a boat,
And reach'd me wi' an oar.

I, wi' a zair and beating heart,
The boat at last did reach;
And thus was zaved auld Ketty Pert,
And laid upon the beach!

Ketty Pert's Petition

Invocation

My blessin's on that face, ye bonny creature -

Benevolence sheens in ilka feature;
Blythe that ye seem to lean on pity's side,
In thee my present errand, freely, I'll confide.
I crave your grace, not for mysel', but for anither,
Wha fifty years sin' syne might been my mither;
To tell you a' her wants wad mak you eery,
For, oh! the tale's baith lang, and unco dreary.
The muse said mildly - "Tune thy harp,
And round the chords meet strains shall warp;
For well I know the case is such
As needs a smooth, but smarting touch."
'Tune thy harp,' quoth I: 'in troth, I coudna duid,
Though 'twere to save my dearest drap o' bluid:
I am, ye ken, to this trade young and raw yet -
I'll need to rise a wee fore I can fa' yet.'
She, smiling, took my harp, - and with her lily hand,
To real concert pitch screwed up every band;
Then, handing it to me, said, now 'tis compleat.
With a scrape and a bow, I made my retreat.
Hear, gentlefolks, an' brithers a',
Frae Fishergate to Rotten Ra';
Our sister Ketty's like to fa',
Wi' cauld an' hunger;
She, honest woman's, what we ca'
A mussel-munger.
Her purse is tuim - her house is bare;
For want o' Tam her heart is sair:
I'm sure, 'mang Christians, sic a share
She ill deserves!
Oh! I could tell you mickle mair -
Wad shak' your nerves. …

Tam was for lang as blind's a mole;
With patience Ketty did the burden thole;
But mony a silent sob and sigh there stole
Frae her auld breast;
When he slipt aff, the thing did her console,
Was - Tam's at rest.

She mussels sheel'd, an' wan her bread,
Till abler fouk took up the trade;
Now, puir auld stock, she gaes a' claed
In bits o' raggies;
Troth, little profit has she made
By fisher maggies.

When Wellington o'erthrew Bonaparte,
Illumin'd winnocks shone in ilka airt, -
Ketty deck'd her's up as clean an smart -
As ony san'le;
Tho' little light was there, it shew'd her heart,
A bawbee can'le.

Oh! strike your purses, dinna stare,
There's little doubt ye'll gather mair;
To th' puir ye surely ay can spare
Some few bit orts!
Oh! help a widow claed wi' care
O' mony sorts.

THE DREAM

" Hence, terrible shadow!
Unreal mockery, hence!"
William Shakespeare

*L*AST night I dreamed a dream of horror. Methought,

That at the hour of midnight, the bell tolled,
With slow and solemn peal; and straight, beneath
The pale cold moon, a thousand spectres moved,
In "dread array," along "the church-way-path,"
All swathed in winding-sheets as white as snow -
A ghastly crew! Methought I saw the graves
Yawn and yield up their charge; and I heard the
Coffins crack, and the deadal drapery
Rustle against their hallow sides, like the
Wings of the renovated Chrysali,
As they flutter against the ruins of
Their winter dormitory, when the voice
Of spring awakes them from their drowsy couch,
To float aloft upon the buxom air.
Although the round full moon shone bright and clear,
Yet did none of these awful phantoms cast
Their shadows on the wan and silent earth;
Nor was the passing breeze interrupted
By their presence. Some skimmed along the earth,
And others sailed aloft on the thin air;
And I observed, when they came between me
And the moon, they interrupted not her
Pale rays; for I saw her majestic orb
Distinct, round, and clear, through their indistinct
And airy forms: and although they moved
Betwixt me and the tomb-stones, yet I read
Their sculpture (deeply shaded by the bright
And piercing beams of the moon) as distinctly
As if nought, dead or living, interposed
Between my eyes and the cold monuments.

The bell ceased to toll; and when the last peal ...

*Died away on the ear; these awful forms
Congregated in various groups, and seemed
To hold converse. The sound of their voices
Was solemn and low, and they spoke the language
Of the "days of other years." In seeming
Woe, they spoke of events long gone by; and
Marvelled at the changes that had taken
Place since they left this mortal scene, to sleep
Within the dark and narrow house. Voices
Issued from the mould, where no forms were seen:
These were still more hollow and sepulchral;
They were as the sound of the cold, bleak wind,
In the dark and danky vaults of death when
It moans low and mournful, through the crannies
Of their massy doors, shattered by the hand
Of time - a serenade for owls most meet,
And such the raven loves, and hoarsely croaks
His hollow response from the blasted yew.
Often have I heard, when but a stripling,
'Twas meet to speak a troubled ghost, to give
It peace to sleep within the silent grave.
With clammy brow, and joints palsied with fear,
I said, in broken accents - "What means this
Awful congress, this wild and wan array
Of shadowy shapes, gliding here, and moaning
At the silent, solemn hour of midnight?
Have the crying sins and unwhipt crimes
Of mortals, in these latter days, reached you
Ev'n in the grave, where silence ever reigns,*

*At least as we believe? Or complain ye -
Of holy rites unpaid, - or of the crowd -
Whose careless steps those sacred haunts profane?" -
Straight a fleshless hand, cold as ice, was pressed
Upon my lips; and the spectres vanished
Like dew before the morning sun; and as
They faded on my sight, a sound was heard
Like the peal of many organs, solemn,
Loud, and sonorous; or like the awful
Voice of thunder in the sky, - or mighty …*

Tempest, roaring in a boundless forest,
Uprooting trees, razing habitations,
And sweeping the earth with desolation;
Or like the voice of millions, raised in song:
Or the dark ocean, howling in its wrath;
Or, rather, like all those together, in
One wild concert joined. Now the mighty coil
Died gradually away, till it resembled
The last murmur of the blast on the hill;
Of storms, when it lulls itself to rest; and
The echo of its wrath is faintly heard
In the valley; or the last sigh of the
AEolian harp, when the breeze, that erewhile
Kissed its trembling strings, is spent and breathless!

The next whisper was still lower; and the last
Was so faint and feeble that nothing seemed
To live between it and silence itself.
The awful stillness was more appalling
Than its dread precursor; and I awoke
In terror! But I never shall forget
What I heard and saw in that horrid dream.

Much Ado About Nothing

WHERE the Grampians rise in dread array,
An' their awful forms to the south display,
An' grimly frown, as they did of yore,
Owre the swampy plains of red Strathmore.

On the sunnie airt o' a dun hill side
Rears an ancient town, an' a town o' pride,
For gude drink fam'd, - where, tradition says,
A housekeeper winned in other days.

'Twas late on a Saturday afternoon,
In the waning o' a September moon,
When the e'ening dews were ting'd wi' frost,
The hero o' our tale for a time was lost.

The crops were safe in the farmer's yard,
An' smugglers a' for the warst prepar'd;
The waukrife gaugers lounging about,
When this maist pitifu' case fell out.

They sought him up, an' they sought him down,
An' they sought him roun' about the town;
They sought him far, an' they sought him near,
But never a word o' him could hear:

Nae marvel they were fashed an' grieved,
For they thought him tint, or else mischieved;
Nae marvel ane an' a' were vext,
For they kentna where to seek him next.

O! had ye seen his radical spouse,
Wi' her angry een, an' her dusky brows;
It was a sight to hae speaned, through life,
The warmest youth frae the thochts o' a wife! …

Her maidens saw that her grief was great,
An' humbly did in attendance wait;
An' ay they sigh'd, but naething did say,-
Yet they cuist in their minds where the loun might gae.

O! then she bade them up an' rin,
An' no come back till they brought him in;
An' ay the saut tear stood in her e'e,
An' the woman was grieved as a woman might be.

O! then the children forth she sent,
To ransack every houff they kent;
An' specially, wherever they past,
Nae to look the alehouses last.

An' hour an' something mair did glide
Sin' he was snug at his ain fireside,
An' twenty minutes were aff an' gane
Sin' his dear mate was makin' a mane.

Weil ye may guess that her heart was sair;
Weil ye may trow she had cause for care;
Blythe ye may learn that naebody leugh,
For the woman had cause to be grieved aneugh.

Lang, lang, they sought him, baith out an' in;
An' lang the bairns throu' the streets did rin,
Until they snuffed his retreat at last
In a cellar dark, but the door was fast.

There high on an anker he sat stride-ride,
Wi' a gill-stoup cronie safe at his side -
Mair-be-token wi' the gauger; a' the three
As warm an' as happy as carles might be.

There dimly they boozed by the glimmering light
Throu' the chinky wa's, but their joy was bright;
An' they quaffed awa' at the barley bree,
For the drink was guid, an' the drink was free. ...

The drink was free; an' the matron's care
Was chiefly caused by the stranger pair,
Wha, while they got it sae, wadna fash
To trouble her wi' the needfu' cash.

She wrung her hands, an' she screwed her mou',
An' she wished them onie thing but fou;
Na, na, the carlin had better sense
Than to wish them sae at her ain expense.

Some will lament, baith loud an lang,
An' make a din when little is wrang;
But she had cause for sorrow an' thought -
The rogues were getting a dram for nought!

THE GERMAN LAIRDIE

FIRST PRINTED IN THE "MONTROSE REVIEW"

TUNE: "Neil Gow's Fareweel to Whisky."

O GEORDIE Geulp is on the Sea,
The cliffs of Dover on his lee;
For shame! that Britian's King should be
A wee bit German lairdie O.

An' is it come to this, ohon!
That royal James maun flee his throne,
For sic a maughtless weary drone
As a puir bit German lairdie O.

Auld Neptune, this is what I crave -
Oh may he meet a wat'ry grave,
An' soundly sleep beneath the wave -
A droukit German lairdie O.

We swear that ne'er a foreign loun
Shall ever wear the British crown;
By Heaven! we'll put the sharger down -
The wee, wee German lairdie O.

Waesucks that sic a feckless thing
Should ever mint at being a king!
But Scotia soon will cow his wing,
An' pu' his German beardie O.

An' Scotland's sons will send him over
To his hungry hame, Hanover;
Again he'll never be a rover,
But delve in his kail-yardie O.

An' he'll sup kail and guid kail-brose,
He'll clite his shoon an' darn his hose, …

An' lead a life of sweet repose -
The cantie German lairdie O.

Till death, wi' his wanchauncie dart,
Shall spit him through the hollow heart;
Wi' life itsel' he syne maun part,
To rot in some kirk-yardie O.

On Mr Kinloch of Kinloch
LEAVING HIS NATIVE COUNTRY

"YE poor auld man, why grieve sae sair,
   Whase locks are waving barely?
What means the sigh, the starting tear?
   What gars you weep sae sairly?
Has cauld misfortune's with'ring hand
   Hung o'er thy grey head sairly?
Or hae you lost in foreign land
   Your ain kind-hearted Charlie?"

It's no misfortune's bitter blast
   That blaws baith late and early;
It's no my son - he's safe at last -
   That gars me grieve sae sairly:
But it's for 'honest Geordie' gane,
   My heart for him is burning -
An exile frae his native hame,
   He's barr'd frae a' returning.

Poor Scotia mourn'd when he took leave;
   She saw his tears come sairly,
She hung her head and sair did grieve -
   She minded on Prince Charlie.
He wept not for his ain sad fate,
   Tho' he was prest unfairly;
He saw his country's bitter state -
   'Twas that that wrung him sairly.

"Adieu, my native hills, adieu!"
   He said, in silent sorrow;
"The bonny sun I winna view
   Rise o'er your tops to-morrow." ...

A silent gloom the hills o'erhung,
The heather dowie waving,
The birds a lamentation sung,
As he "farewell" was raving.

My country bleeds - my country faints!
But nane, nane will relieve her;
Those that should soften her complaints
Most cruelly deceive her.
Her sons, wha a' her waes regret,
They daurna try to save her;
Her day is gane! her sun is set!
And freedom's fled for ever!"

A Fragment

*L*ET everything in the creation,
  Igo and ago,
Be keepit in its proper station;
  Iram, coram, dago;

Meaning man, or beast, or thing,
  Igo and ago,
Priest or prophet, prince or King.
  Iram, coram, dago.

Let politicians rave and rant,
  Igo and ago,
And rich old misers roar for want;
  Iram, coram, dago.

Let lawyers keenly watch each handle;
  Igo and ago;
Let tabbies deal out tea and scandal;
  Iram, coram, dago;

Let blackguard gamesters cheat and quarrel;
  Igo and ago;
Let drunkards bouse and drain the barrel;
  Iram, coram, dago;

Let honest men declare the trouth;
  Igo and ago;
Gi'e hempies in a halter scouth;
  Iram, coram, dago;

Let kings sit mighty on their thrones,
  Igo and ago,
While their bedesmen beg for scones;
  Iram, coram, dago; …

Let taylors keep upon dry land;
Igo and ago,
Let rabbits burrow in the sand;
Iram, coram, dago;

Let navies float upon the tide,
Igo and ago,
And witches upon broomsticks ride;
Iram, coram, dago;

Let dolphins tumble i' the sea,
Igo and ago;
And lampkins bleat upo' the lea;
Iram, coram, dago;

Let loathsome toads squat in a syre,
Igo and ago,
And salamanders live in fire;
Iram, coram, dago;

Let dandies put on proper airs;
Igo and ago;
And let the clergy mind their prayers -
Iram, coram, dago -

Leave aff their fawnin' and their fleechin',
Igo and ago,
And mind their Bibles and their preachin'!
Iram, coram, dago.

Jamie West

Among your group of public men

Take Jamie West of Ferryden,
The king of a' the fisher crew -
A fisher and a pilot too:
Sometimes sober - often mellow;
Still he was a pushing fellow;
Industrious as the busy bee,
He drew his riches from the sea:
For mony vessel from afar
He, skaithless, brought across the Bar,
When waves were rolling mountains high,
And tempests howling in the sky:
And moored them safely at the quay,
Where they lay snug as ships could be.
And mony Mary, Jean, and Janet,
He steered between the Leads, and Annet,
Down the river to the ocean,
With pleasant breeze and gentle motion;
And then the breeze that he liked best
Was his namesake breeze, from the lovely west;
For it filled their sails, and made them glide
Upon the bosom of the tide,
Some south, some north, some o'er the sea,
Like fillies frisking on the lea.
Nor did he search with less devotion
The dark recesses of the ocean, -
With hook and line and tempting bait,
Alluring to their awful fate
Cod, ling, and turbot, plaice and skate;
Which straight were carried to Monross,
And whilom vended at the Cross,
But now they've found a mart more meet
Than just the centre of the street.
Still Jamie West increased his store,
For he had goods and gear galore: …

Besides a leal and loving wife,
The pride and comfort of his life;
With health and walth of buirdly weans,
Baith strapping lads and sturdy queans!
And, still as fortune on him smiled,
A house was reared for every child;
A clock in each to watch old time,
And cheer the inmates with its chime.
Still Jamie ran his busy race,
In health, in happiness, and peace,
Till drink - the curse of human life,
The source of sorrow and of strive -
At times, its wicked pranks began
To work upon his inner man!
For oft he moistified his skin
In jolly Ruixton's little inn,
And other houffs - I need not tell -
The very counterparts of hell:
And then he dealt abuse and blows
Promiscuously 'mang friends and foes.
His vengeance knew no bounds or rule;
No man was spared - not e'en Slag Coul!
Poor ill - less creature! 'twas a sin
To het him for the constant grin
That mantled aye upon his face:
There was no laughing in the case,
Tho' Jamie thought - ('twas all mistake)
Poor Slag was smiling at his neck:
And woe betide them, man or brat,
That dared to say "Your thrapple's fat."
Then words would pass we dare not name -
Dark epithets of sin and shame,
And vengeful threats and foul reproach,
In neither English, Erse, nor Scotch,
But in some strange outlandish speech,
Transposing evermore the "h";
For sooth these people deem it better
To throw aside this useless letter;
Except in that especial case
Where others never give it place. …

But here the mischief is not ended;
Assaulted fame must be defended;
And reparation made for blows,
Discoloured eyes and bloody nose,
With other wrongs; likewise the payment
Of broken glass and riven raiment;
And eke the worst of all disasters,
The doctors' fees and doctors' plasters.
But, last ava, and warst ava,
The gudgeons too maun gae tae law;
And steps are ta'en, by Lawyer Pillage,
To ruin and herry half the village.

GEORGE BEATTIE'S SIGNATURE

An Original

Essay

by

George Beattie, Esquire

It is confidently reported that Mr Walter Scott has sold copyright for Two Guineas per line.
John Milton sold 'Paradise Lost' consisting of 10,575 lines, for £15, being at the same rate of about a 'plack', or third of a penny sterling, per line; so that by the standard of the present day, one line of namby pamby is worth 1480 lines of Milton's 'Paradise Lost'. In other words, that seven lines of Mr Scott's poetry is worth the whole of that poem. Ergo, Mr Scott is 1480 times a better poet than Milton ever was; and that old blind gentleman, when in life, had 1480 times less influence at the court of Apollo and the Muses than Mr Scott now has, "O tempora, O mores".
I wonder what Addison, Pope and Johnson would have said to this.
Change of times or taste can do nothing towards reconciling such a prodigious and overwhelming difference.
I am aware that I am the insignificant 'Daw' in the fable, pecking at the feathers of the 'Bird of Paradise'; but we have a proverb that says, "a two-penny cat may laugh at the king".
It is universally admitted that Mr Scott is a great poet; and that, in general, he is completely exempted from the vanity, envy and egotism of the 'lake' vermin: so much the more that he should have forgotten the much lamented Sir John Moore, who fell for his country, at the scene of a poem in which the bard has been most lavish of his panegyrics.
He could not have forgotten !
It must have proceeded from some cause less justifiable than a slip of the memory.
He may have pleased some of his political and party-friends and patrons at the time; but although he should sing away his soul in song, he never can atone to the world for his most inhuman, and unpoetical insensibility, to the fate, and the fame of his illustrious countryman.
   As the Laureate Crown is worn for life, it is absolutely necessary that the wearer should, in principle, be a renegade, and in politics a "Vicar of Bray".
The choice of the bard to presently fills the office was, on that score, therefore, highly judicious; for should a whig monarch ascend the throne, or should his royal highness, the Prince Regent be induced to change his ministers, this lyric thunderer will be most ready 'again' to change his politics, to dismiss his old, and invoke a new, Muse.
The "Second Lay of the Laureate" will then issue from the press, proclaiming, in "numbers sweet", how the author, (when balmy sleep had sealed his eyes, and steeped them in the bland and opiate dews of oblivion, at a moment when his sacred and holy

temples, instead of laurel were crowned with poppies), had been visited in a dream by the Editor of 'The Courier' (a renegade like himself, and, if possible, a greater fool), and the Editor of 'The Quarterly Review', in the semblance of 'angels of light', when in fact they were 'fiends of darkness'. That these arch-imposters, with the music of Heaven on their tongues, and Hell in their hearts, prevailed on him to abandon every honest and virtuous principle, and, 'Faustus - like', to sell his soul to Satan, who, for a time, had exercised dominion over it, but that his body had pathless retained its former shape and hue on 'Terra Firma'.

That soon after his teeming brain had been delivered of that divine and far-famed poem "Watt Tyler", he had only spoken, written, and sung by the inspiration of the 'Evil One', who was a red-hot ' Tory'! and, therefore, that he could not, in justice, be held accountable for the doctrines promulgated through such diabolical agency.

In fine, that he had been in a state of infernal enchantment.

That the direful spell broke with a crash that "rent the spheres", at the very instant the 'Whigs' came into power.

And oh! how that moment would be blessed and hailed by the Laureate, as a new era in his life.

Oh! astonishing! lamentably astonishing! that he should have so long wallowed in error, and groped in the darkness. But now, refulgence, irradiating and shedding a ray of glory around his honoured head, and tinging the green bays with streaks of burnished gold, like the leaves in autumn; it behoved him instantly, not only to retract, but to make ample and suitable atonement for his former errors, preparatory to obtaining remission of his political sins, and absolution for his shameless apostacy.

His first performances would be "The Carmen Triumphale of the Whigs, the friends of liberty and mankind, over the recreant Tories, the enemies of freedom and tyrants of the world".

"The Resurrection of the Habeas Corpus, the palladium of British Liberty, the birth-right of every Englishman, and the best security of the British constitution"… an Ode. "The Liberty of the Press, the safeguard of the state"… an Ode.

Then a laboured and flowery 'panegyric' on William Smith, Esquire, M.P. for Norwich; and a most virulent satire on the virtuous Lord Castlereagh, wherein the truly dignified, consistent, and clean-fingered Mr Canning, when some, in their ire, term "the King of Jobbers" and "The Arch-apostate",

will be made honourable mention of, accompanied by a right witty parody on "The Pilot that Weather'd the Storm" : in which the bard will raise such a well-brewed tempest of foam and froth , for the purpose of wrecking the pilot, that he will run the risk of being wrecked himself with a hurricane of his own raising.

He will next beg "ample room, and verge enough" in the pages of the 'Edinburgh Review', to write down the 'London Quarterly' ; and, in the columns os the 'Morning

Chronicle', to send to perdition that infernal pander of ministers, and their minions, the 'London Courier'.

The appearance of these exquisite performances will be duly advertised, with a solemn and prophetic warning to all his majesty's liege subjects to make out their last wills, and prepare absolutely to die and perish, from sheer admiration of his powers, assuring them, on his "minstrel faith", that he receives no 'pension' from government, and that those he intends to charm, with ecstasy, out of existence ought not to forget him in their last bequests.

Whether he has, or has not, a pension, I neither know nor care; but of this I am convinced… if a person, who, at one time, possessed some share of the better feelings of the heart, and was unfeignedly touched with the miseries of his unfortunate fellow creatures; but who, afterwards, from motives not less obvious than dishonourable, unblushingly apostatises, and

> " Sees stern oppression's iron grasp,
> And mad ambition's gory hand,
> Sending, like blood-hounds, from the slip,
> Woe, waste, and murder, o'er the land ";

Not merely with callous indifference, but with open and insulting exultation.

If such a person, who, in his better moments, defended the liberties of mankind, becomes renegade, , and, with all his heart, strength, soul, and mind, urges their oppressors to the adoption of every unconstitutional measure… spies, dungeons, tortures, gibbets, and racks… for crushing these liberties… he ought to be 'pensioned'… with a halter; and it is to be hoped he has yet sufficient virtue left to direct him in the proper use of it.

Notwithstanding his disgusting cant and slang about his own superior sanctity, an the vain-glorious display of his many, many virtues and accomplishments… he ought to know that the feet of honest men would rise instinctively to kick such an affected, self-sufficient, and venal 'weathercock', as he is… deserving neither the name of a poet nor a man.

His self-complacency and egotism are beyond all parallel.

The most disordered maniac who imagines himself emperor of the world, and believes that what "he wills is fate"… or who, like the astronomer 'Rasselas', is satisfied that the weight of regulating the solar system lies on his shoulders… could not be capable of playing more "fantastic tricks", or entertaining a more unwarranted and ridiculously overcharged idea of himself and his concerns.

In his view of the matter, none have written or sung, or ever will write or sing, like his dear self.

Nature and Apollo, with all the Muses in their train, have combined in endowing him "with the largest dower that Heaven indulges a child on earth".
He is to live in ages past; and those to come, he modestly tells us, are to crown him with their "sure rewards":

> *" That green wreath which decks the bard when dead,*
>   *That laureate garland crowns my living head ".*

The 'Edinburgh Review' has put these pretensions of the laureate in a proper point of view, and, by most apt quotations from his poems, has sufficiently exhibited his consummate vanity.
A reader of the review of his "Lay of the Laureate", &c., in that work, might suppose that the reviewer had been at more than ordinary pains in culling the egotistical passages, for the purpose of making the poor bard ridiculous
This, however, is by no means the case: it is a fair specimen of the performance.
On turning to the poem itself, it will be found that the author, by his own showing, is not only exempted from all the infirmities that "flesh is heir to", but that the angels in Paradise cannot bear a comparison with him.
After the preceding quotation, immediately follows…

> *" Then when the sacred sisters for their own*
>   *Baptised thee in the springs of Helicon,*
> *They promised for thee that thou should'st 'eschew'*
>   *All low desires… 'all empty vanities';*
> *That thou should'st still, to 'truth' and 'freedom' true,*
>   *The applause or censure of the herd despise;*
>   *And, in obedience to their impulse given,*
> *Walk in the light of nature and of heaven ".*

This over-tops all that has been quoted in the 'Edinburgh Review', and another critic quaintly observes upon it… "if Mr Southey's god-mother (the muses) 'did promise' for him that he should 'eschew all empty vanities', their god-son has lived in the constant violation of their promise, ever since he arrived at that questionable period, his years of discretion".

> *" O wad some pow'r the giftie gie us*
>   *To see ourself as ithers see us,*
>   *It wad frae mony a blunder free us,*
>   *And foolish notion ".*

Poor Southey flatters himself that all his well-merited and multifarious castigations have been inflicted from sheer envy of his high situation and talents.
If he could see "himsel' as ithers see him", he would find that he never was farther mistaken in his life.
Although we have "seers" in this quarter that have pretensions to the "second sight", yet, I never heard of any of them that had discovered wherein this gentleman's talents lay; and it is believed that this is a puzzle that will remain unriddled till the end of time.
We can not exactly know with what degree of veneration, respect, and wonder, the 'laureate crown' may viewed by the English; but Mr Southey may be assured that the sturdy sons of Caledonia look upon it, in its true light, as a mere bauble, that could only be worn, or respected, by a fool.
As for the laureate himself, they care as little for him, and less, than for any old blind piper that plays from door to door for his daily bread.
The description of the silly, tinsel, mummery and parade of a birth-day at court, is read by them with far less interest, and is less regarded… than the homely and honest festivities of one of their own penny weddings.
A strathspey on the Highland bagpipe, or one of Burns' songs, they consider worth all the trash of birth-day odes that have been written or chanted for centuries past; at the same time, they are far from being deficient in the essentials of loyalty.
   Mr Southey imagines that all the bards are dying from envy, because he has carried off the laurel crown; but if he could see his office "as ithers see it", he would be convinced that, with the exception of the other two partners of the 'Lake Company', Messrs Coleridge and Wordsworth… there is not a bard in Britain would have accepted of a retainer fee for the annual prostitution of his muse: not that any person grudges his 'salary' and his 'sack'; or, as we say in Scotland, his "wage and his sap"; they are not equivalent to the fetters which he has voluntarily doomed himself to wear.
It is well known that on the death of Colly Cibber, in 1757, Bard Gray had the honour of refusing the office of poet laureate, to which he was induced by the disgrace brought upon it through the inability of those who had previously filled it.
Then, who in the name of wonder would accept of it after Southey… perhaps some 'government spy'; and, in this era of retrenchment, it is probable these two offices may be conjoined.
There is not the least doubt but Messrs Castles, Oliver, and Richmond, would write birth-day odes vert prettily.
Who can read some of the early, pathetic, and simple pieces of Mr Southey, where he uniformly defends and protects the poor and unprotected against the tyranny of their powerful oppressors, and contrast these with his latter productions, without the most painful emotions.
That he should now join the heartless ruffians of the press in his abuse of the lower

orders of society, who, from the pressures of the times, without any fault of their own, have been forced

*"to beg their bread,
And steep their hard earn'd bit in bitter tears":*

And to assist his courtly patrons in culling terms of the deepest obloquy and reproach, to lavish on that unfortunate class of the community… such as, "the swinish multitude", "base ragamuffins", and other disgraceful epithets, which he would not dare to apply to the horses and dogs of these noble patrons… are circumstances to be lamented, but which, thank God, can very seldom happen in the nature of things. Such a direful and disgraceful violation of every good and virtuous principle can only take place when this globe shall carry on its surface another human being capable of humbling and degrading himself as Mr Southey has done.

Mr Southey, either from vanity, flatters himself, or, with a view of cloaking his venality, wishes to flatter the public into the belief that he has changed his principles and political opinions, from encrease of knowledge and maturity of wisdom. If, however, he possessed this "giftie", which Burns laments the want of, he would find the 'ratio' assigned erroneous in the extreme.

For it appears most palpable to every person, except himself, that every moment he lives adds a stone to his cairn of folly, and that his vanity encreases in due proportion with his imbecility.

The poor man speaks pompously of his grey and reverend locks, shaded by his laurel crown. He looks on his August person, and chuckles with the self-complacency of an Adonis inspecting himself at his mirror.

He speaks of his venal, abandoned, and prostituted Muse, as if he were still a vestal virgin. He flatters himself that his fame will last while the sun gives light to read his poems, and that he will live for ever.

As 'Colly Cibber', after death, lives in the 'Dunciad', so will Mr Southey in the 'Edinburgh Review'… "a bloated mass of insolence, absurdity, and self-conceit". His picture will be viewed with wonder in that work when his poems are forgotten: even his prose lubrications in the 'Quarterly Review' will not furnish him a twig to grasp at in sinking ignobly to the shades of oblivion.

A person may honestly change his opinions; but that man must be seized with inexpressible horror, on reviewing his past life, who can condemn others in such strong terms, merely for holding the opinions which he once did himself. Well may the words of the able reviewer of Coleridge's "Biographia Literaria", in 'Blackwood's Edinburgh Magazine', be applied to the laureate.

"He seems to believe that every tongue is wagging in his praise… that every ear is open to imbibe the oracular breathings of his inspiration".

"No sound is so sweet to him as that of his own voice; the ground is hallowed on which his footsteps tread; and there seems to him something more than human in his very shadow".

"Opinions that seem to tally with his own wild ravings, are holy and inspired; and, unless agreeable to his creed, the wisdom of ages is folly".

His admiration of nature, or of man… I had almost said, his religious feelings towards his God… are all narrowed, weakened, and corrupted and poisoned by inveterate and diseased egotism, and, instead of his mind reflecting the beauty and glory of nature, he seems to consider the mighty universe itself as nothing better than a mirror, in which, with a grinning and idiot self-complacency, he may contemplate the physiognomy of Robert Southey, Esq., poet laureate".

"So deplorable an delusion as this has only been equalled by that of Johanna Southcote, who mistook a complaint in the bowels for the Divine 'afflatus; and believed herself about to give birth to the Regenerator of the World, when sick unto death of an incurable and loathsome disease".

So like as these 'Lakers' unto each other, that the description applies most aptly to all the three… Messrs Southey, Wordsworth, and Coleridge.

On reading the poetry of the one, a person feels a certain indescribable sensation, as if eating an egg without salt… of the other as if drinking whey… and of the last, as if taking a dose of magnesia.

In short, this 'Lake' poetry is what the English language can not express…
a farrago of 'merghless, foizonless, farrachless' nonsense…

" To my gueed auld proverb confeerin',
Neither gueed fish, nor flesh, nor yer sa't herrin".

Now, when this long note is drawing to a close, I could not, if asked, state distinctly for what purpose it has been written.

Vanity is not a deadly sin, but when connected with apostacy, intolerance, and the naseous qualities, it renders the possessor, at the very least, an object of derision and contempt.

From the tone and tenor of the note, I am aware it may be supposed that the writer, forsooth, thinks 'himself a bit of a poet'.

This he denies in the most explicit terms. He knows well he has no more pretensions to the title of a 'Poet' than he has to that of the 'Pope of Rome'; and he has no intention of becoming candidate for either of the offices; but he will not relinquish a privilege, common to all, and successfully exercised by many of his majesty's liege subjects, viz., that of writing and publishing nonsense, in such quantities, in such shape, and in such a manner, as he shall think proper… in prose, in verse, or in neither; in English, in Scotch, or in no language at all: and even, in this age of intolerance, it is presumed no person will have the hardihood to claim exclusive right to the exercise of this privilege, unless Mr Southey, in the zenith and madness of his ambition and vain-glory, shall take it into his venerable head that his laureate crown is equivalent to a patent, conferring on him the power to quash all competition in an art, in the prosecution of which he has been so eminently successful!

Epilogue

In the Old Nether Churchyard of St Cyrus on the very spot where George Beattie's existence was terminated in this world, a monument was erected on Wednesday the 29th of September in 1824, with the following inscription from the pen of his close friend (a first cousin to the Ayrshire poet, Robert Burns), James Burness, Esquire :-

TO THE MEMORY
OF
GEORGE BEATTIE
Writer in Montrose,
Who died 29th September 1823, in the thirty-eighth year of his age.
THIS MONUMENT WAS ERECTED
BY THE FRIENDS
WHO LOVED HIM IN LIFE AND LAMENTED
HIM IN DEATH.

IN HIS DISPOSITION
HE WAS
JUST, CHARITABLE AND BENEVOLENT;
IN HIS PRINCIPLES,
FIRM AND INDEPENDENT;
IN HIS GENIUS,
FORCIBLE AND PATHETIC
AND
IN HIS MANNERS,
PLAIN AND SOCIAL.
HIS VIRTUES ARE DEEPLY ENGRAVED
in the hearts of those who know him and
his Literary Productions will be admired
while taste for original humour and vigorous expression remain.

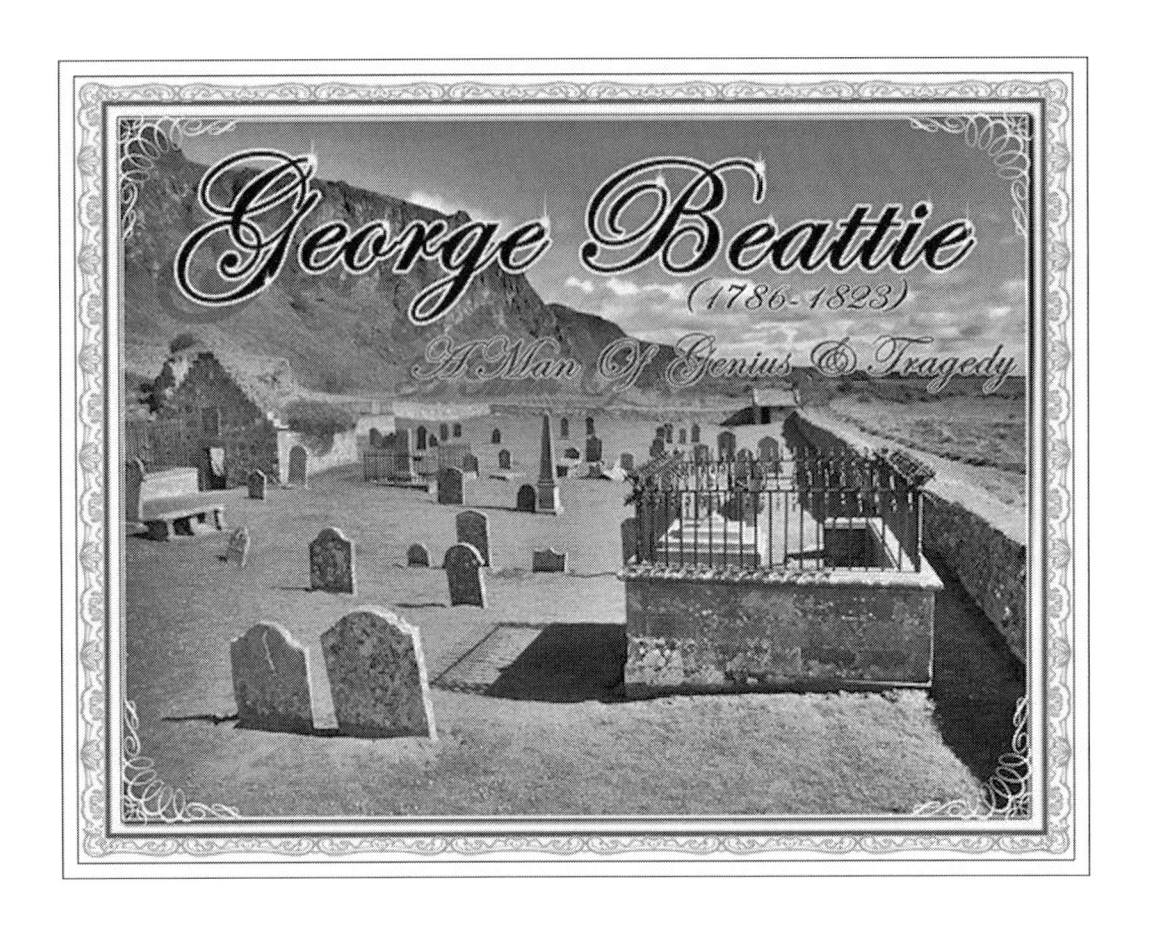

George Beattie
(1786-1823)
A Man Of Genius & Tragedy

The Love we share is timeless;
With no goodbyes to say.
All hands which part upon this earth,
Will touch… another day.

~ Barry Dominic Graham

In Memoriam

WHERE GEORGE BEATTIE SLEEPS

Down where the trailing mist-cloud weeps,

And ever moans the restless sea
By the lone graveyard mournfully,
Beneath the cliffs George Beattie sleeps.

Here, where alone the curlew screams,
Or circling daw gives harsher note:
Sole living things about the spot;
He sleeps the sleep that knows not dreams.

Surely no fitter resting place
Exists for him whose spirit, wrung
By cruellest wrong, was madly stung
To break the tie of human race.

O potent charm for human woes,
Soul-soothing death, thou seemed so fair
To him, who, racked with wild despair,
Sought peace with thee, and deep repose!

O sorely-tried, we blame thee not;
Thy faults were more of blood than will,
Thy thoughts were thoughts of those who fill
With good the high or lowly lot. …

Still, in this thought I find relief,
That hadst thou known the firmer faith
From which the future draws its breath,
Thou might'st have triumphed o'er thy grief.

But this at least we must concede:
No specious formalist wert thou,
Observer of unholy vow,
Or blind slave of a narrow creed.

The hand that serves a brother's needs,
The generous heart, the tender ear,
The starting sympathetic tear
Were thine, the soul of all the creeds.

And while I hold not all is best,
I feel, I trust that there are still
Great compensations for all ill
In God's eternal rest.

Sleep on, of silence now a part;
No voice of love or friendship born
Can yield again to thee the scorn
Of broken vow or severed heart.

No lust of gold can interpose,
No cruel relentless art can vex,
No shallow mind can e'er perplex
The silence of thy deep repose.

The murmur breaks along the shore,
From dawn to eve the shadows creep,
The changing seasons ceaseless sweep,
But thou dost rest for ever more …

And haunted by thy memory,
These scenes the senses so benumb,
That sky and sea and cliffs become
Incorporate, and a part of thee.

O lonely place beside the sea!
O tombs so hoary and so grey!
O memory of a vanished day,
I would I were at rest with thee!

~ A.H.

Dundee, 9th September 1874.

"Goodnight sweet Prince…"

...and so it goes

MISS GIBSON'S GRAVE
(The 'SMART' Family Plot)

… until the final tear.

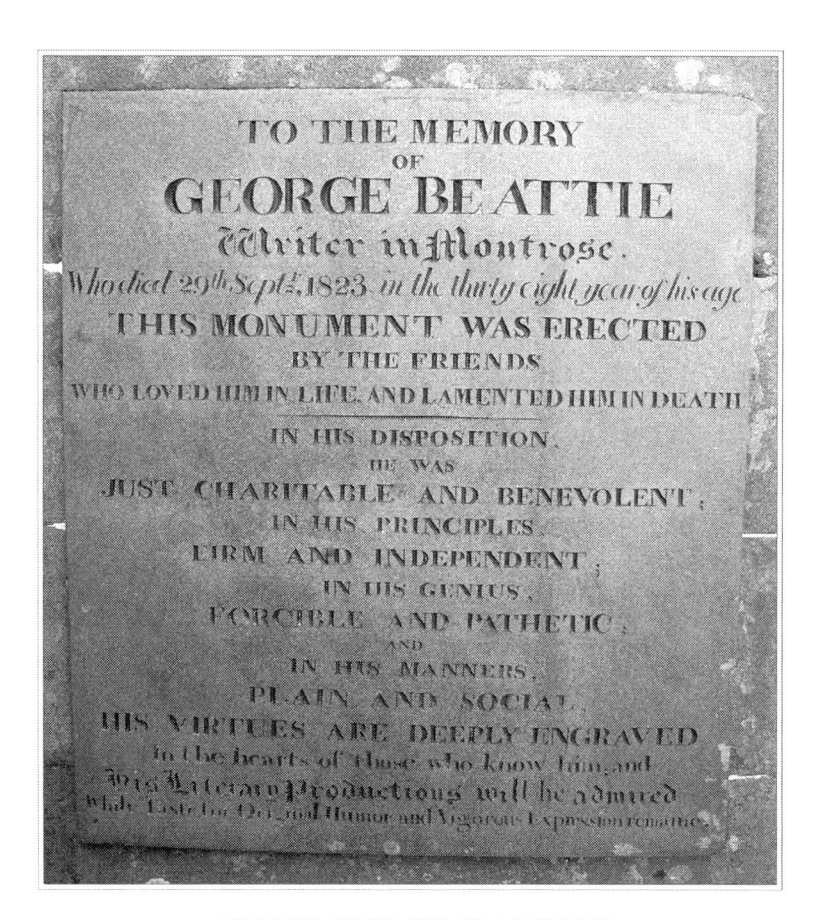

GEORGE BEATTIE'S HEADSTONE

SHADES

Like the palest shades of evening,

We are fading with the light;
As the sun serenely settles,
Yielding gently to the night.

Like the whispered breath of Angels
On a sky of winter grey;
Our Essence, in a breeze Divine,
To Heaven, drifts away.

In realms of pastel radiance;
A song but dreamt before;
We dwell in timeless rhapsody,
Where light shall fade no more.

~ Barry Dominic Graham

SCHOOL-BOY WORK in 1798 by
GEORGE BEATTIE, St CYRUS,
Author of JOHN O' ARNHA' and other
Poems.

(Used with the kind permission and courtesy of the Montrose Museum)

THE GEORGE BEATTIE PROJECT

Dundee Courier
2013

THE GEORGE BEATTIE PROJECT
AT HENRY HOGG BOOKSELLERS
Montrose, Scotland

Montrose Review
2014

Arbroath man uncovers story of tragic poet

By Nikki Mitchell
nikki.mitchell@jnscotland.co.uk
@ACP_Nikki

An Arbroath man has come to the end of a labour of love to highlight the work of an Angus poet forgotten for nearly 200 years.

Barry Graham and his associate John Molloy from Glasgow are in the process of launching a book on the life of Montrose and St Cyrus poet George Beattie on the 190th anniversary of his suicide.

The book 'George Beattie: A Poet Lost In Time' will hit the virtual shelves later this month as an e-book on Amazon.

Barry said: "I can only hope that the efforts of John and I on our labour of love mission, which have been extensive to say the least, will be extremely welcome.

"The mission is not only to revive the story of someone who was regarded at the time, in a Montrose Review memorial in 1823, as one of the most admired of any Montrose residents ever."

He continued: "As his memory and legacy has all but been forgotten, we are striving towards at least a Montrose plaque to be dedicated to him, as currently nothing exists of this nature anywhere."

Beattie was born in 1786 near St Cyrus and at the age of 13 his family moved to Montrose. He studied law in Edinburgh and returned to Montrose as a writer and attorney.

In 1815, he contributed a poem, 'John o' Arnha', to the *Montrose Review*, which bore a resemblance to Robert Burns' 'Tam o' Shanter'. It satirised a town officer, John Findlay, who boasted about extraordinary places he had visited. Beattie had several other poems published in the *Review*. The poet met a young girl, oddly named William Gibson, in 1821, and soon the two were engaged. Miss Gibson, however, called off the engagement after receiving a small fortune from a wealthy uncle. She then became engaged to a wealthy corn merchant. Inconsolable, Beattie shot himself with a pistol beside his sister Mary's grave in a St Cyrus churchyard at the age of 38.

TRAGEDY UNCOVERED: John Molloy (left) and Barry Graham who researched and published the book on poet George Beattie outside the Arbroath Signal Tower Museum where they gave a talk on their work recently.

THE GEORGE BEATTIE PROJECT
2ND PRESENTATION

Montrose Review
2014

Baptist women entertained

•• The Women's Group of Montrose Baptist Church and guests were entertained by a talk given by Barry Graham and John Molloy on their recent publication 'Maelstrom'. This book takes the story of George Beattie, the well known local lawyer and poet, a stage further from 'A Poet Lost in Time'.

•• Further research has raised more questions than answers about this man's ill-fated romance and tragic death.

•• Dan Mcmullen, a young musician, has put some of George's poems to music and, accompanying himself on the guitar, he sang four of them.

•• The meeting was well attended and copies of the book, now available at Hogg, newsagent, were sold.

•• Pictured are, from left, John Molloy, Barry Graham and Dan Mcmullen.

THE GEORGE BEATTIE PROJECT
3RD PRESENTATION

Montrose Review
2014

A GBP BOOK LAUNCH PRESENTATION

John Molloy, Barry Dominic Graham and Dan McMullen
2014

THE COURIER & ADVERTISER
WEDNESDAY, SEPTEMBER 30, 2015

POET GEORGE BEATTIE

Barry Graham, Daniel McMullen and John Molloy, who paid tribute to poet George Beattie at the St Cyrus National Nature Reserve. Picture: Andy Thompson Photography.

Musical tribute paid to forgotten poet

Work of George Beattie celebrated at nature reserve as campaign goes on

STEWART ALEXANDER

A musical tribute has been paid to a poet who ended his life in a Mearns churchyard.

George Beattie died from a self-inflicted pistol wound in the Nether Kirkyard near St Cyrus on September 29 1823, aged 38.

Largely forgotten in the 190 years since his death, researchers have fought to elevate Beattie's name to the national literary canon.

And an event was held at St Cyrus National Nature Reserve to celebrate his work, at which Daniel McMullen interpreted Beattie's work into song.

The event was organised by the George Beattie Project, led by Barry Graham and John Molloy, and included a guided walk by reserve staff.

Mr Graham and Mr Molloy released a biography in 2013 entitled George Beattie: A Poet Lost in Time, and have campaigned for a permanent memorial.

Mr Graham said: "As his memory and legacy has all but been forgotten, we are striving towards at least a Montrose plaque to be dedicated to him.

"There is nothing which currently exists of this nature anywhere."

Reserve assistant Kim Ross said: "We walked from the reserve up to the Nether Kirkyard. From there you get a 180-degree view of the reserve.

"As well as the lovely music, I also gave a talk on what makes the reserve so special."

Beattie was born the second of five children in 1786 near the foot of the Hill of Morphie in the parish of St Cyrus.

> We are striving towards at least a Montrose plaque to be dedicated to him

Name was 'held in kindly remembrance'

The single largest edition of Beattie's poems, which contained a large amount of background detail, was collated under the pseudonym AS Mt Cyrus.

The Dundee Courier of July 6 1863 carried a review of the book, which was published in Edinburgh by WP Nimmo and in Montrose by George Walker.

Though ... forty years have passed away since the poor heart-broken minstrel descended to the grave, his name is still held in kindly remembrance on the east coast of Scotland, and especially in the counties of Angus and the Mearns.

In that district (between the Moray and the Tay) there are few households, especially amongst the working classes, in which a copy of John o' Arnha may not be found, it was said.

The editorial content of that edition was not as well received as Beattie's writing. A dismissive review appeared in the Spectator magazine of August 22.

George Beattie's grave.

THE GEORGE BEATTIE PROJECT
4TH PRESENTATION

Dundee Courier
2015

" But if thou wilt be constant then,
And faithful of thy word,
I'll make thee glorious by my pen
And famous by my sword:
I'll serve thee in such noble ways
Was never heard before;
I'll crown and deck thee all with bays
And love thee evermore."

James Graham
5th Earl and 1st Marquis of Montrose,
Earl of Kincardine,
Lord Lieutenant and Captain-General of Scotland
1612 ~ 1650

HOW THIS HEADSTONE **SHOULD** HAVE READ

Bibliography

i. George Beattie, (ed) John o'Arnha: A Tale. To which is added The Murderit Mynstrell and other poems, Alexander Burnett, 1883.

ii. Andrew (Alexander) Smith, (ed) George Beattie of Montrose: a poet, a humourist and a man of genius, W. P. Nimmo, 1863 (Public Domain).

iii. Duncan Fraser, (ed) Portrait of a Parish, Standard Press Montrose, 1979.

iv. Montrose Basin Heritage Society, (ed) Vikings to Victorians, 2012.

v. William Ruxton Fraser, (ed) St Mary's of Old Montrose, 1896.

vi. James Gray Low, (ed) Closes of Montrose, John Balfour & Co., 1938.

vii. David Mitchell, (ed) History of Montrose, George Walker, 1866.

viii. James Bowick, (ed) Montrose Characters: Past and Present, David Davidson, 1880.

ix. The Montrose Review, (ed) October, 1823.

Acknowledgements

We gratefully acknowledge the help and guidance of

all those who assisted our endeavours;
but particularly the following :

Helen F. and Hannah H. M. Graham;
Dennis A. Graham, Jonathan C. J. Graham and the Kearney Family;
Alison Lindsay and the staff of the National Archives of Scotland;
Christine Sharp and the staff of the Montrose & Stonehaven Libraries;
Antony, Deborah, Simon, James and Jim Short;
Robert McHardy, Angela Murphy and Lesley Hood;
Jamie and Sonya Stuart;
Therese Alampo and the staff of the St Cyrus National Nature Reserve;
The staff of the Arbroath Signal Tower Museum;
Aileen Taylor and the staff of the Montrose Museum;
Pam Sangster, John Duff and the staff of Angus Council;
Robert W. O'Hara, Sarah Minney, W. D. Johnston and W. J. Melvin;
Rev. Colin Dempster and Rev. Dr Ian Mclean;
The staff of the Angus Archives;
The staff of the Dundee University Archives;
The staff of the National Archives, Kew;
Rachel Lang and the staff of the Legacies of British Slave-ownership Project;
Richard Watt, Kim Cessford and the staff of the Dundee Courier;
Nikki Mitchell and the staff of the Montrose Review;
Stan Mackie, Brian Stormont and the staff of the Arbroath Herald ~
(Our back cover photograph has been used with kind permission
and courtesy of the 'Arbroath Herald');
Daniel McMullen, Elaina Rose Kelly and Holden Hunter;
Eric Graham, Joe Bowman, Derek Ball and David Patrick;
Irene Birse and Ronald Petrie;
John Bell and Pearl Murray;
Henry Hogg Booksellers of Montrose;
The village of St Cyrus and The Royal Burgh of Montrose

Mission Statement

THE MISSION OF **THE GEORGE BEATTIE PROJECT** IS TO:

- ENDEAVOUR TO RESTORE THE MEMORY AND LITERARY LEGACY OF GEORGE BEATTIE TO THEIR RIGHTFUL PLACE IN SCOTTISH HISTORY.
- ENDEAVOUR TO SET THE RECORD STRAIGHT BY REVEALING THE MISINFORMATION, DISINFORMATION AND DECEITS OF THE PAST WHICH WE HAVE DISCOVERED IN THE TRADITIONALLY ACCEPTED STORY OF GEORGE BEATTIE.
- ENDEAVOUR TO ATTAIN MORAL AND SOCIAL JUSTICE ON ALL POSSIBLE LEVELS AS WE SINCERELY BELIEVE THAT THE INITIAL SUPPRESSION OF TRUTH AND THE SUBSEQUENT SYSTEMATIC OBLITERATION OF THE MEMORY AND LITERARY LEGACY OF GEORGE BEATTIE HAS BEEN AND REMAINS TO BE A TRUE MORAL AND SOCIAL INJUSTICE PERPETRATED AGAINST POSTERITY AND THE SCOTTISH PEOPLE BY CERTAIN SOCIALLY POWERFUL INDIVIDUALS ATTEMPTING TO SHIELD THEMSELVES FROM THE DESERVED CONSEQUENCES OF THEIR IMMORAL ACTIONS AND CORRUPT AGENDA.
- ENDEAVOUR TO ATTAIN AN APPROPRIATE AND PERMANENT PUBLIC MEMORIAL TO THE MEMORY AND LITERARY LEGACY OF GEORGE BEATTIE.

"That plots were laid by others to oust me and secure Miss Gibson's fortune, I know well from the inquiries that were made at myself from a certain quarter. Those who interfered were far too many for me."

~ George Beattie (1823)

About the Authors

Barry Dominic Graham

*W*as born in a convent hospital on a Cree Nation Reservation in Manitoba, Canada.

He is of Scots/Irish ancestry.

He grew up in Glasgow, Scotland where he attended St Brendan's Primary School, Yoker; Corpus Christi Primary School, Knightswood; and St Thomas Aquinas Secondary School, Jordanhill (as did some notable others, such as the actor, James McAvoy; singer, Justin Osuji and soccer player, Tosh McKinlay).

Over the years he has lived in Canada in several British Columbian locations, namely Hope, Abbotsford, and Kelowna, as well as Prince Albert in Saskatchewan.

His son, Jonathan, lives and works in British Columbia, Canada.

Barry now resides in Montrose, with his wife Helen and daughter Hannah.

He has a long-standing relationship with the St Cyrus area and possesses a profound passion for the story of George Beattie.

He is dedicated to the task of reintroducing and restoring the true story, memory and literary legacy of this forgotten Scottish treasure to their rightful place in history.

BARRY DOMINIC & HELEN FRANCES GRAHAM
ST CYRUS

cclxxx

John Molloy

*W*as born in Glasgow and has lived in London as well as his current home town of Glasgow, where he now resides.

He is of Scots/Irish ancestry.

He grew up in Glasgow, Scotland where he attended St Ninian's Primary School, Knightswood and St Thomas Aquinas Secondary School, Jordanhill (as did some notable others, such as the actor, James McAvoy; singer, Justin Osuji and soccer player, Tosh McKinlay).

He travelled the world extensively during his career with the Royal Navy.

Being adopted from an early age, John believes that his research skills were gained through his personal search for his natural birth parents.

His son, Shaun, lives and works in Scotland.

John also has a long-standing relationship with the St Cyrus area and possesses an equal passion for the story of George Beattie.

He is also dedicated to the task of reintroducing and restoring the true story, memory and literary legacy of this forgotten Scottish treasure to their rightful place in history.

JOHN & BARRY

"And now here is my secret, a very simple secret:
it is only with the heart that one can see rightly;
what is essential is invisible to the eye."
~ Le Petit Prince ~

Antoine Marie Jean-Baptiste Roger, comte de Saint Exupéry

French writer

1900 ~ 1944

Our Future Motion Picture Project :

Blood Beyond the Rose

The George Beattie Story

Previous Publications :

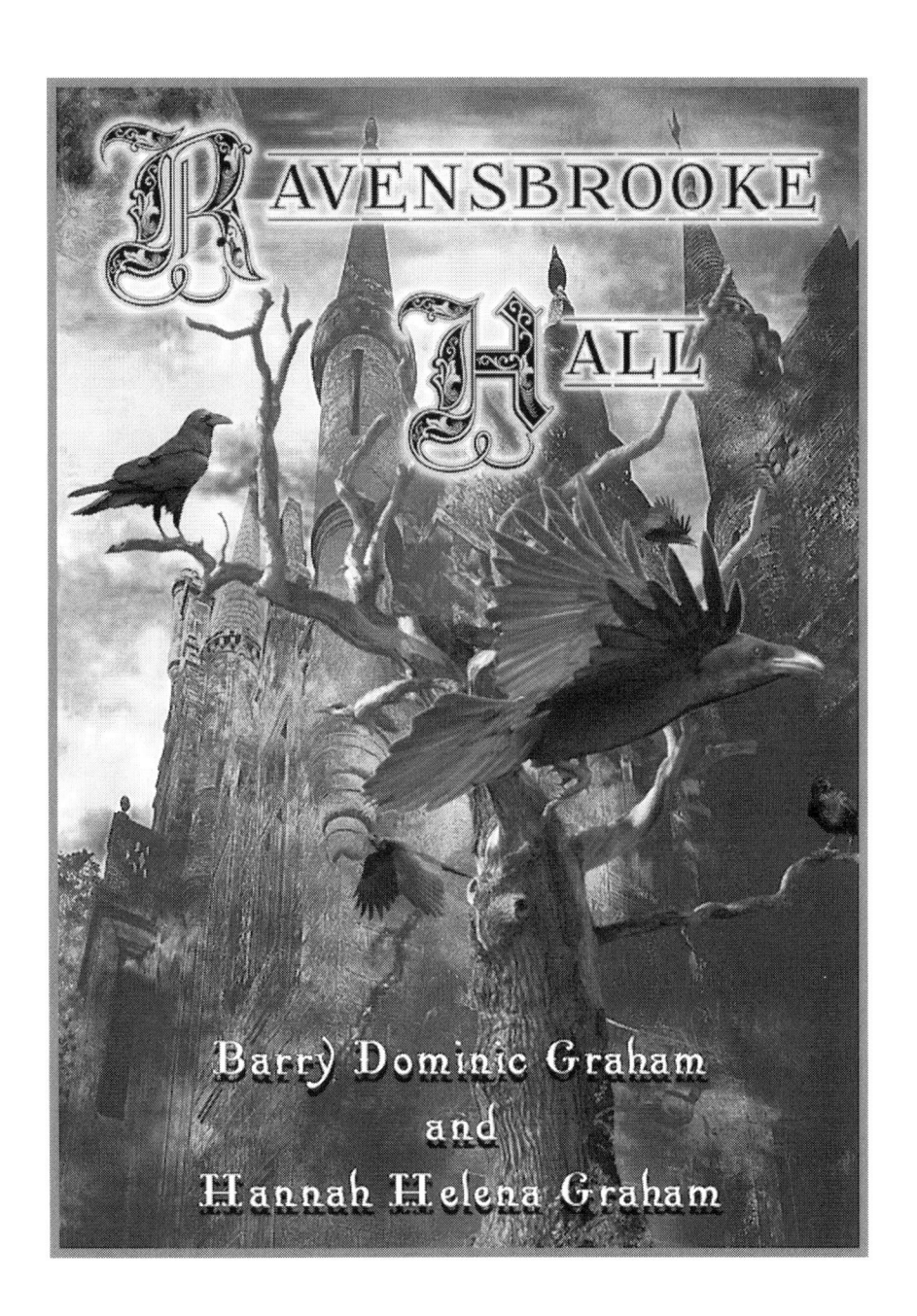

RAVENSBROOKE HALL

Barry Dominic Graham
and
Hannah Helena Graham

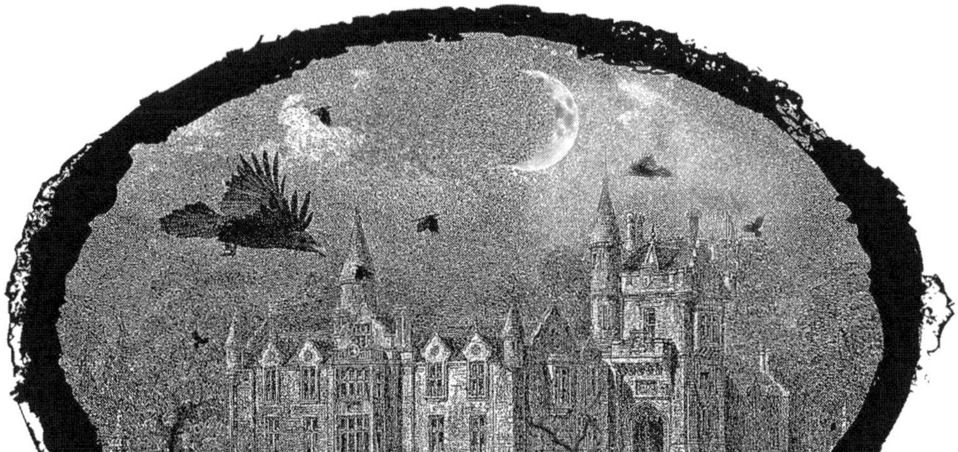

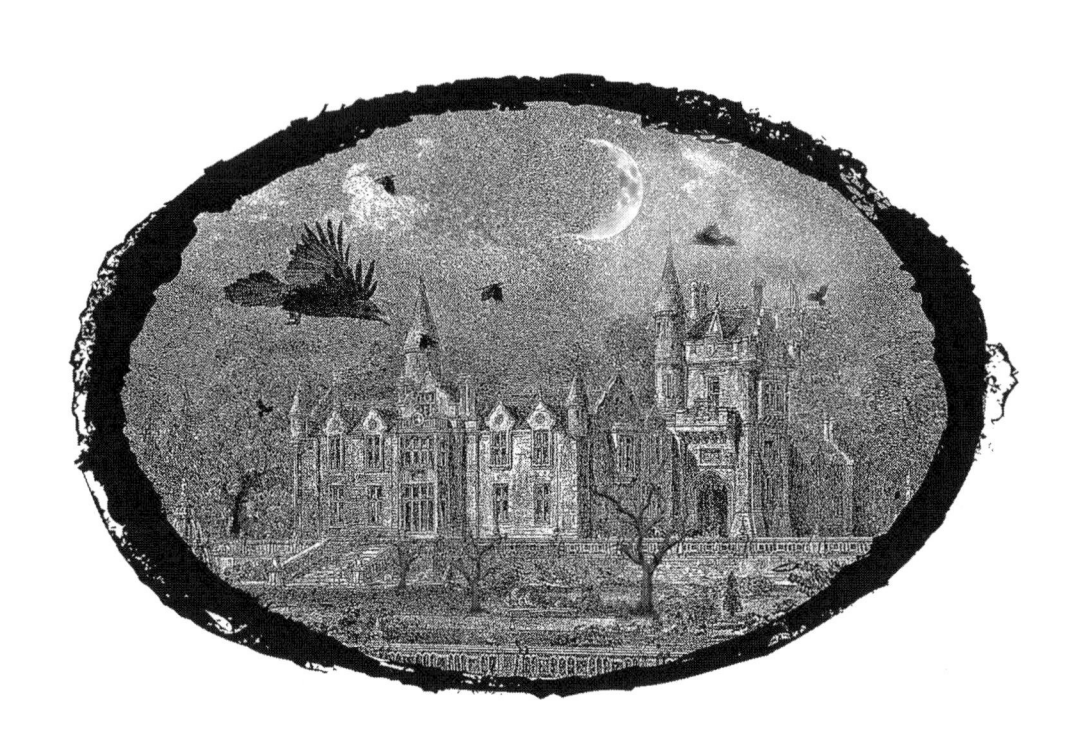

Lest the Triumph A Memoir Barry Dominic Graham	**GEORGE BEATTIE** of St Cyrus A Poet Lost in Time Barry Dominic Graham and John Molloy
Mackraw THE GEORGE BEATTIE CONSPIRACY Barry Dominic Graham & John Molloy	**GEORGE BEATTIE** of St Cyrus A Poet Lost in Time

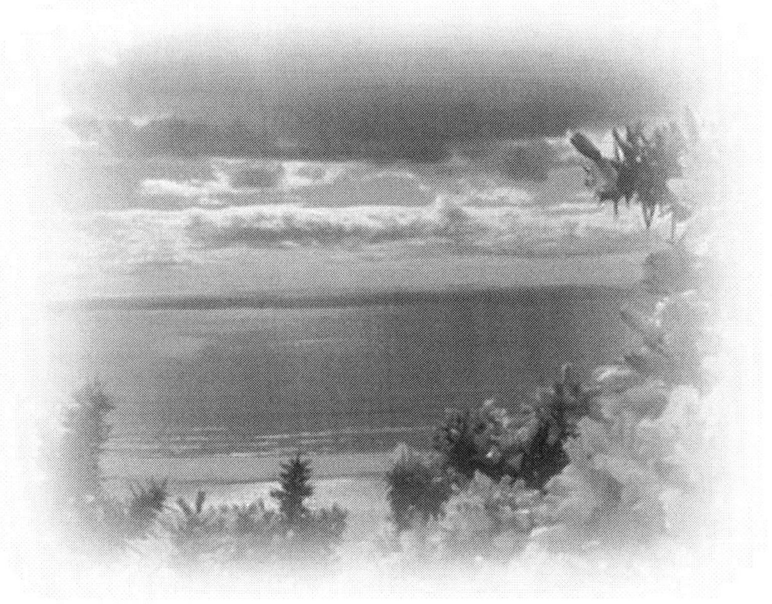

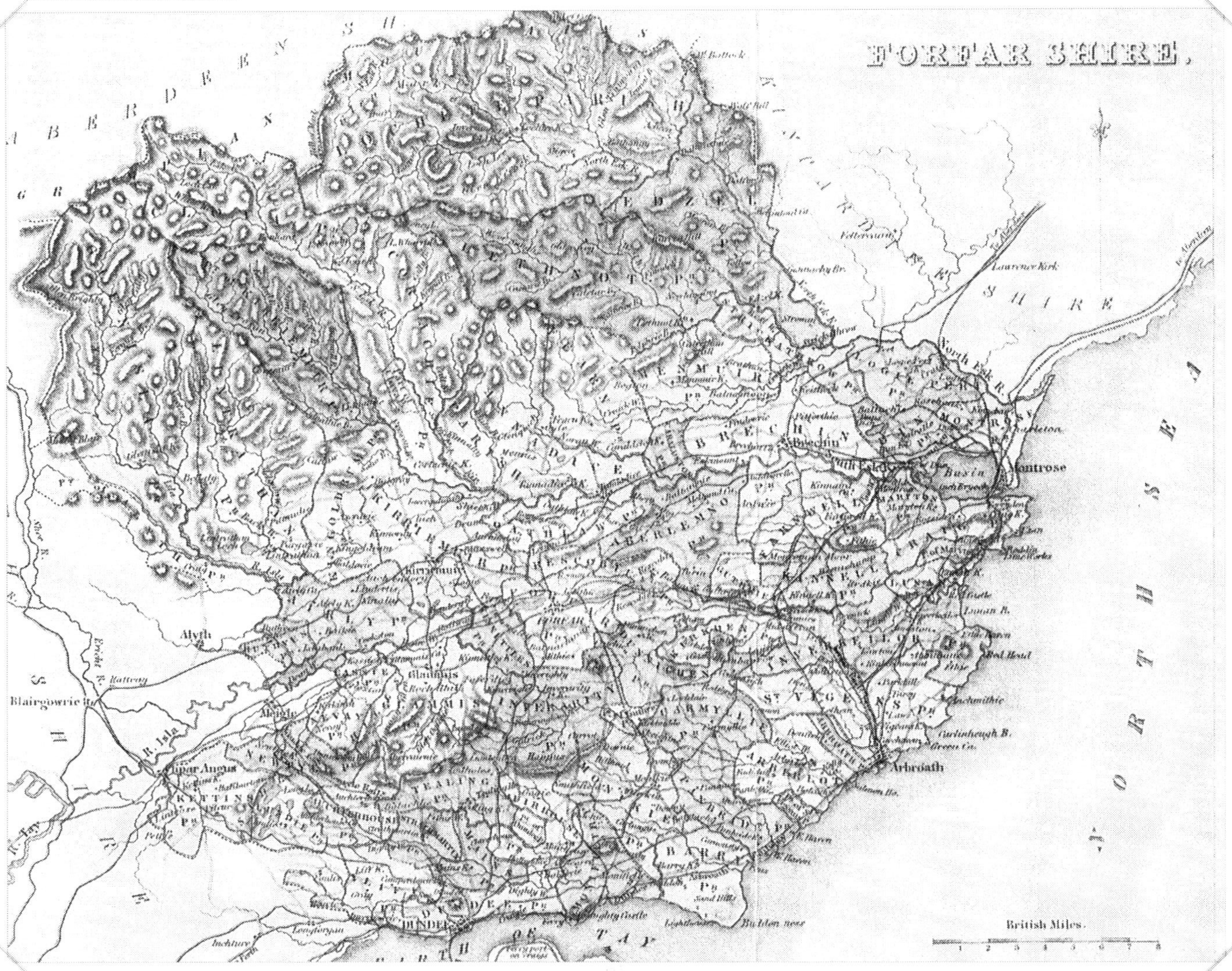

FORFAR SHIRE.
ABERDEEN SH.
KINCARDINE SHIRE
NORTH SEA
Montrose
Arbroath
Dundee
Alyth
Blairgowrie
Cupar Angus
Glammis
Brechin
Laurence Kirk
Red Head
Lunan B.
FIRTH OF TAY
British Miles.

Echt
Kincardine O'Neil
Banchory
Durris
Tilquhillie
Strachan
Findon
Portlethen
Skateraw
Muchals
Garron Point &
STONEHAVEN
Fetteresso
Dunnottar cas.
Castle R.
Fordon
Glenbervie
Cratown
Kinneff
Whistleberry
Castle
Arbuthnot
Laurencekirk
Bervy
Gourdon
Johnshaven
Fettercairn
St. Cyrus

THE GEORGE BEATTIE PROJECT
www.thegeorgebeattieproject.co.uk

A Personal Note from co-author, John Molloy:

Whilst meandering through the Auld Kirkyard one lovely evening five years ago, my closest friend, cousin and confidant turned to me and said "What do you make of this grave?"
My first instinct was, is it so different from the rest of the interments, but on closer inspection of the monument and in particular the wording on the tombstone, I realised that this was something different if not odd about this structure in front of me. In the first instance, the fine wording on the tomb relating to the deceased, was bereft of any mention of his family, that's what first I found of interest.
Why would the family not be mentioned or be deliberately left out?
In light of this my natural inquisitive self sprung into action.
Later that night after some discussion, and suitably imbibed with a good malt (is there a bad one you may ask, but I do not care for the peaty drams, but I digress horribly) .
The next day, (after breakfast and a couple of paracetamol!) we set about our task with great intent, like two battlefield commanders.
The strategy was simple.
I would carry out the remaining research into our subject, as I already had a fairly good understanding of family research brought about by being an adopted child.
I cannot speak for all adopted children, but that deep desire to trace your birth family was certainly burning within.
I had to go through a fairly rigorous regime to finally trace my ancestors, so with this fact in place, I was nominated the chief researcher. We also agreed that our findings would have to be published.
It has to be said at this point that Barry has all the literary tools in the box to realise this.
He has written poems, composed songs, and contributed many articles on his chosen history, so it was looking like the perfect team.
At this juncture I do not feel the need to bore you with the finer details of the
(still ongoing) research. The three periodicals already written, seven public presentations, an active web page and musical scores, stand testament to the work and endeavour that has gone into this project. I can sincerely say that being part of this endeavour has been one of the most rewarding and satisfying experiences of my life. I feel honoured to be part of a project that, to my mind, creates history.

It is with a deep sense of gratitude that I would like to thank Barry and Helen Graham and Daniel McMullen for their encouragement, love and understanding.
Finally, I would like to thank from my soul the main protagonist in this whole undertaking, none other than the late great George Beattie, Esquire, of St Cyrus.
His legacy has finally been re-instated back into the annals of posterity. I feel humbled by the fact that I was part of a team that has achieved this task.

In loving memory of the author, William F McHardy, 1849-1926, who passed away aged 77 on 16th December 1926. Your "Bonnie Montrose" will live on for everyone to enjoy.

Bonnie Montrose
Poems and Songs By W.F M'Hardy

Take a little piece of Montrose home with you...

WILLIAM F McHARDY'S BOOK
BONNIE MONTROSE
BACK TO PRINT AFTER 115 YEARS.

Bob McHardy, the author's great great grandson came up with this idea initially as a gift idea for his Dad, Robert McHardy Snr's 70th Birthday on 21st September 2014.

He was also conscious the original book, that was handed down, and is signed by the author's grandson William F McHardy, had seen better days – there was a real possibility that the book itself – and it's stories and history – could be lost. "History is important to us – and my Dad is a man for telling us stories of his time in the beautiful town of Montrose where he would spend every holiday as a boy."

In loving memory of the author, William F McHardy, 1849-1926, who passed away aged 77 on 16th December 1926. Your "Bonnie Montrose" will live on for everyone to enjoy.

Bonnie Montrose
Poems and Songs By W.F M'Hardy
Copyright © 2016 Fraser Web Design

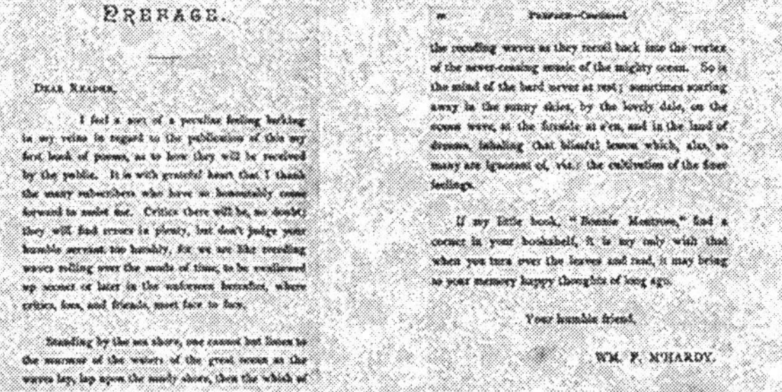

PREFACE.

DEAR READER,

I feel a sort of a peculiar feeling lurking in my veins in regard to the publication of this my first book of poems, as to how they will be received by the public. It is with grateful heart that I thank the many subscribers who have so honourably come forward to assist me. Critics there will be, no doubt; they will find errors in plenty, but don't judge your humble servant too harshly, for we are like receding waves rolling over the sands of time, to be swallowed up sooner or later in the unforseen hereafter, where critics, foes, and friends, meet face to face.

Standing by the sea shore, one cannot but listen to the murmur of the waters of the great ocean as the waves lap, lap upon the sandy shore, then the whish of

PREFACE—Continued.

the receding waves as they recoil back into the vortex of the never-ceasing music of the mighty ocean. So is the mind of the bard never at rest; sometimes soaring away in the sunny skies, by the lovely dale, on the ocean wave, at the fireside at e'en, and in the land of dreams, inhaling that blissful lesson which, alas, so many are ignorant of, viz.: the cultivation of the finer feelings.

If my little book, "Bonnie Montrose," find a corner in your bookshelf, it is my only wish that when you turn over the leaves and read, it may bring to your memory happy thoughts of long ago.

Your humble friend,

WM. F. M'HARDY.

Cover and preface from the original Bonnie Montrose

Find Us On

In bringing back this book, and a little slice of history, I wanted to also help some charities which are close to our hearts.

Every sale supports Cancer Research UK, British Heart Foundation, and Diabetes UK through Tesco's Charity Partnership, in addition to local businesses and organisations in Montrose.

Designed and printed by Derek Addison Printshop, 149 High Street, Montrose, DD10 8QN, Tel-01674 672888 Email: derek.addison@btconnect.com

THE ART
OF
JAMIE STUART

Ecclesgreig Castle

St Cyrus

The Art of Jamie Stuart

St Cyrus and Beyond

Compiled and Edited
by
Barry Dominic Graham

ABOUT JAMIE

Jamie Stuart is an artist, composer, musician and carpenter.
He is a graduate of Aberdeen College.
His interests include outdoor pursuits such as caving, canyoning, kayaking, canoeing, ice & rock climbing, mountaineering, expeditions and pioneering new routes.
He currently resides in the beautiful north-east Scottish coastal village of St Cyrus with his wife, Sonya and children, Ruadhan, Cadhla Leigh and Breigha-Mae.

" Lest the triumph "

NOTES